# Thank You (Falettinme Be Mice Elf Agin)

# Thank You (Falettinme Be Mice Elf Agin)

## A Memoir

# SLY STONE

### WITH BEN GREENMAN

**Created in collaboration with Arlene Hirschkowitz**

## AUWA BOOKS

MCD | FARRAR, STRAUS AND GIROUX | NEW YORK

AUWA Books
MCD / Farrar, Straus and Giroux
120 Broadway, New York 10271

Library of Congress Cataloging-in-Publication Data
Names: Stone, Sly, author. | Greenman, Ben, author. | Questlove, writer of foreword. |
   Hirschkowitz, Arlene.
Title: Thank you (falettinme be mice elf agin) : a memoir / Sly Stone, with Ben
   Greenman ; created in collaboration with Arlene Hirschkowitz ; foreword by
   Ahmir Khalib Thompson.
Description: First edition. | New York : AUWA Books / MCD / Farrar, Straus and
   Giroux, 2023. | Includes index. |
Identifiers: LCCN 2023015269 | ISBN 9780374606978 (hardcover)
Subjects: LCSH: Stone, Sly. | Singers—United States—Biography. | Funk
   musicians—United States—Biography. | Rock musicians—United States—
   Biography. | Sly & the Family Stone (Musical group) | LCGFT: Autobiographies.
Classification: LCC ML420.S8715 A3 2023 | DDC 782.42166092 [B]—
   dc23/eng/20230406
LC record available at https://lccn.loc.gov/2023015269

Designed by Abby Kagan

www.auwabooks.com • www.mcdbooks.com • www.fsgbooks.com
Follow us on Twitter, Facebook, and Instagram at @mcdbooks

1   3   5   7   9   10   8   6   4   2

Frontispiece: Photograph by Richard Avedon, © The Richard Avedon Foundation;
photographed April 16, 1973

To my kids—

Sylvester Jr., Phunne, and Nove

# Contents

# Foreword
## by Questlove

The very first sound that I remember hearing in life was Sly and the Family Stone. I wish I could say that it was a pleasant memory, but many of my earliest and sharpest memories are of traumas—and because music was playing in my house constantly, those traumas were fused to songs. In this case, it was late in 1972. I was almost two. I was upstairs in the bathroom and my sister and mother were washing my humongous Afro. I didn't yet know the rules of hair grooming—don't move around too much, don't open your eyes—so I was unprepared when my Afro hit a can of Ajax cleanser and the can of cleanser hit the bathtub edge and sent powder into the air. The cloud of bleach went into my eyes. It was the most painful thing I had ever experienced. It felt like my eyes were being gouged out. I screamed uncontrollably and ran down to the living room. The next thing I remember was my mother; my sister, Donn; and my aunt Karen pinning me to the floor, wrestler style, while my dad tried to get my eyes open to flush them out. I screamed uncontrollably, tried to get out of their grasp, and the whole time Sly and the Family Stone's "Just Like a Baby," a track from the *There's a Riot Goin' On* album, was playing in the background. I was tattooed in my memory by that bassline as it went from D to C to D to C.

That was my first encounter. After that, of course, I came into contact with the other songs, with "Everyday People" and "Family Affair" and "Thank You (Falettinme Be Mice Elf Agin)" and "Everybody Is a Star" and "Hot Fun in the Summertime" and the rest. And I started to be aware of the man, Sly Stone himself. I'd catch him on a talk show or a variety show, sometimes looking a little out of it but always in the thick of it, too. He had a way of talking, moving from playful to earnest at will. He had a look, belts and hats and jewelry. Everybody was a star, as he said (and sang), but he was a special case, cooler than everything around him by a factor of infinity.

Now let's skip ahead by a decade. Now it's the eighties. I'm older. Music had changed, and the way it changed me had changed also. I became a Prince obsessive, later on a Native Tongues disciple. Eventually I went on to start a band myself, which meant that the idea of idols changed, and other bands and artists became colleagues and competitors.

At that point, Sly wasn't at the center of the culture anymore, at least not in the same way. He had just one album in the eighties, his last official album, and other than that he mostly kept out of the spotlight: He'd surface on a song here and there, mostly paired with artists who he had inspired. But he stayed with me. It was more than just the Rushmore principle. It was that his work had so many ideas in it, ideas that were still relevant long after he stopped releasing music.

And soon enough, I went back in time. That's how it always

works—the songs you know are strings that pull you back into album tracks, outtakes, live performances. And so I went back from the biggest hits into his records, into the cluttered but brilliantly ambitious debut record, *A Whole New Thing*; the sustained party vibe of the second record, *Dance to the Music*; and the third record, *Life*, in some ways my favorite, a wellspring of ideas, including ideas for breakbeats. *Stand!*, the fourth album, the one that featured prominently at Woodstock, was a counterculture monument, almost too huge to get close to, and then there were the records that followed. I loved the complex rhythms and insightful songs of *Fresh*, especially the first side. Of all the records, I returned to *There's a Riot Goin' On* more carefully. It wasn't just that childhood memory. The cover art was a redesigned American flag, but the package also included a photo collage, and that collage had a picture of a woman who looked like my grandmother, who had died. It frightened me and every time that record got to the top of the pile, about to be listened to, I moved it back to the bottom. Then De La Soul sampled "Poet," also from *There's a Riot Goin' On*, for the song "Description," on their debut, and I finally got around to it. The record was deep and dark, tricky, knotty and moving, and when it got to "Just Like a Baby," and specifically to that bassline, the pain of my Ajax eyes came back in full.

Revisiting the trauma wasn't fun, but the rest of the process was—going back through all the music, trying to unravel its mysteries, realizing that for every insight I reached there were a thousand more I might never reach. And it was a process that went on for years. In fact, Sly and the Family Stone were a key part of my first film as a director, which was a re-creation of, and commentary on, an amazing concert event in Harlem in the summer of 1969. Sly and his band electrified Woodstock, of course, but they were also a vital part of the Harlem Cultural Festival a few weeks earlier. In the movie I made, *Summer of Soul*, I wanted to think about what Black music was back then, how many different faces and paces it had, how the larger culture may have thought of it as one thing when it was in fact a kaleidoscope of many things. The concert, and the movie, had many performances that popped, from Nina Simone to Stevie Wonder to B.B. King. Sly and the Family Stone not only popped but rocked and funked and hamboned and damn near jumped through the screen, across time. They were pure energy.

But the story of Sly Stone isn't complete without talking about where that energy went. That's part of the mystery and the history. After a certain point in the midseventies, the original Family Stone had disbanded and the new versions of the band that Sly put together didn't reach the same height. Some of the issue was Sly himself: his relationship to drugs, which seemed like a symptom of his relationship to his own mind and talent, and the financial, legal, and spiritual problems that were both cause and effect.

In a way this isn't an uncommon story. Some stars maintain their status. Others burn out. Black stars have a particularly rough road in America, one filled with unimaginable pressures, internalized trauma, and survivor's guilt. I have started a second movie that tries to think about these questions through the prism of Sly's life, how he processed the promise and the pressure. I don't want to say too much about it here. It'll be along soon enough.

This book came to me right at the beginning of my career as a publisher. I could hardly believe my fortune. I knew that Ben Greenman, also my cowriter, had been talking to Sly's camp for years about working on something, and that the project didn't really get off the ground until Sly was clean and his manager, Arlene Hirschkowitz, could help make it a reality.

This book is a life story, which means it's a story of a life told from a position of age, which also means that it's told with all the things that age brings: perspective and jokes and a memory that works off and on but also knows that working on and off is often just another form of wisdom. It's filled with more twists and turns than anyone can imagine, ascents and descents and every kind of outsized event. Sly has lived a hundred lives, and they are all here. There is plenty, too, that is not here. There is no real interest in settling scores or revisiting certain kinds of emotional injuries. And some of the musical questions that I would have loved to talk about with the thirty-year-old Sly, or the forty-year-old Sly, seem harder for him to recapture, mountains in the mist.

Sly inspires complicated thoughts in me, and even more complicated feelings. He makes me feel nostalgia and admiration, makes me feel young and old, makes me feel happiness and sadness and vitality and weariness and luv and haight and more. And yet, when it comes to this book, my thoughts and feelings are also simple. I never thought the day would come when I would hold it in my hands. It is the result of years of work by others that are in turn the result of decades of joy and toil in the life of Sly himself. I am so happy to play a part in bringing it into the world.

—Questlove
Publisher, AUWA Books

# Thank You (Falettinme Be Mice Elf Agin)

*

## Prelude: Sly, Say Hi

Today is Thursday. Good day to get started. Sly, say hi.
    *Hi.*
I have some questions, not too many.
    *No.*
We don't have to do them all.
    *We don't have to do them at all.*
You're not ready to talk right now?
    *Is that pointing at me?*
The phone is, yes. It has a camera.
    *Why?*
Why does it have a camera?
    *Why is it pointing at me?*
So we can film you when you talk.
    *Turn it around.*
You mean turn it off?
    *Turn it around. [Sly points at camera.]*

Okay, here. You hold the camera. It's not showing you now. It's looking the other way but it's still recording audio. Is that better?

*[Camera nods.]*

So are you ready to talk?

*About?*

About the past.

*[Camera shakes its head.]*

What do you feel like talking about? What don't you feel like talking about?

*Not anything. Not everything. Not yet.*

Okay, so we'll come back. All right. We're going to come back.

*

## Prologue: If I Want Me to Stay

**I** **decided to get clean on the fourth visit.**

The first time, I was feeling bad at home, faint and weak, having trouble breathing, so I called Arlene, who was my girl-friend back in the eighties and is now my friend and manager. I called her and she called the ambulance. I was in and out of the hospital before anyone could get comfortable with the idea of me being there. I only wanted to get home and keep doing what I was doing, which included drugs. If anyone said anything to stop me, I didn't hear it.

The second time, the doctor said, "If you go home and smoke again, you could die." I heard him but I didn't believe him. I went home and smoked again.

The third time was a terrible scene. I was exhausted that time and weakened, and the hospital wanted to keep me longer so I could get some rest and some tests. I wanted out. I wanted home. Arlene may not have agreed, but she understood that I had made up my mind. To be let go I had to sign a release saying that I took full responsibility. When they let me go, I didn't even get a wheel-chair. I got on my feet, barely. I got into the hall, barely. I started to walk, barely. That corridor went on farther than I could imagine. I had to walk like I was learning, one foot in front of the other, then sit to rest, then the other foot in front of the first one, then sit to rest. It took more than an hour to make it from the room to the car.

The fourth time came just two weeks later. That time, I not only listened to the doctor but believed him. I realized that I needed to clean up. I concentrated on getting strong so that I could get clean. My kids visited me at the hospital. My grand-kids visited me. As the stay wound down, I even had Arlene call Medicare and fight for me to stay a few more days. Finally, we had to go. But I left with purpose.

I went home. Arlene cleared the house of things (lighters, pipes), of people (dealers, users). There was even an Uber driver who had been staying with me, and he got put out too. Arlene hired caretakers instead and made sure that either she or my daughter Phunne stuck close to oversee the situation, make sure drugs didn't creep back into the picture. If it had been visit one, two, or three, who knows what would have happened? But it was visit four and I knew what needed to happen. People say that when you kick, you take it one day at a time. I didn't. I just decided that I would quit and I did. It wasn't that I didn't like the drugs. I liked them. If it hadn't been a choice between them and life, I might still be doing them. But it was and I'm not.

I'm here much of the time these days, at my house in Los Angeles. It's smaller than some of the places I've lived in and bigger than others. But it does the job. It's a house and a home. Hanging on the wall are gold and platinum records and posters from old concerts. There's one where Sly and the Family Stone was supported by Spirit and Southwind at Winterland in 1969. There's another where Sly and the Family Stone was supported by Gladys Knight and the Pips and Rare Earth at Madison Square Garden in 1970. You wouldn't be confused about who lives here.

The year after I got clean, it was Christmas in America during the pandemic, and my family came over to see me. It was the first time it had happened in this house, and everything was louder and brighter immediately. Much of the time was spent decorating: the strings of lights over the windows, a snowflake star for the top of the tree that sent colored dots spinning on the ceiling. A red stocking with a big "S" on it hung halfway up the tree. The smallest kids opened presents and also gave them—Arlene opened up a gift from the kids, a blanket, and they smiled up at her, different kinds of lights.

In the middle of it all, I turned on the TV to boxing. I like watching boxing. If I come across a classic fight, the channel's staying there until it's over by knockout or decision. This one was the Fight of the Century, Muhammad Ali against Joe Frazier, also at the Garden. Ali went the distance but took his first loss. That fight was in 1971. Ten years later, I did a song with Funkadelic on the *Electric Spanking of War Babies* album. It was called "Funk Gets Stronger (Killer Millimeter Longer Version)," and there was a verse that ran through a range of boxers, from Sonny Liston to Ali (before he was Ali, when he was Cassius Clay) to Floyd Patterson ("Floyd's still pattin', trying to stop the day") to Smokin' Joe Frazier before coming back around to Ali ("The champ was still jokin'—you know what made him strong?").

Ali was my friend. I'd see him now and then. We were together once on *The Mike Douglas Show* in the summer of 1974. By then, he had beaten Frazier in a rematch and was planning for the Rumble in the Jungle in Zaire that fall, where he hoped to take the heavyweight belt back from George Foreman. He was training for Foreman. But most of the punches he threw on Mike Douglas were at social injustice. Everywhere you looked, people were keeping people down. Black people suffered the most. And what was I doing but clowning and laughing? I made a case that what I was doing was entertainment, and that entertainment was an important part of the solution. It lifted spirits. It lightened minds. And I didn't think that it was simply a matter of color. There's a lyric from an early song of mine: "Don't hate the black, don't hate the white / If you get bit, just hate the bite." I didn't quote it to Ali but it was always in my mind and my manner. Kindness needed to radiate from every person toward every person, or it would reach no one. I tried to generate a glow of goodwill. Ali glowered back at me. I sometimes watch those old talk-show appearances. *The Mike Douglas Show* with Ali is a special one for its honesty. If you stop the show at a certain moment, you can see the tension in the frame. Or else you can move beyond that moment and watch us enjoy our friendship, express love for each other and respect for each other's ideas. Exactly where you enter a story helps decide what that story might mean. I remember trying to get Ali's attention. "Muhammad!" I said, maybe too sharply, because he flinched a little. He's gone now. I'm still here, moved beyond that moment, still joking, no longer smoking.

Back in 1971, in a song called "Time," I wrote about how time moved and grew. You can speed up time or slow it down but you can't stop it. You can try to see through time but it thickens. "Are you dense?" I once asked a reporter. Time is.

I think back through it all, through the parts of time I still hold and the parts that have slipped away. I can still hear a note bouncing out of an electric piano in 1966. I can still see the hem of a dress rising in 1970. I can still feel the lights on my face as I walked onstage in 1972. Other memories are harder to grasp. An afternoon at an airport in a city. I know that I once knew the name of the woman at the counter, because I said it to her in a way that made her laugh. But it's gone. I'm not even sure of the city: St. Louis?

Today I thought of a Bible verse I haven't thought of in years, and it came to me completely, without a piece missing. John 3:1: "Now there was a man of the Pharisees named Nicodemus, a ruler of the Jews. He came to Jesus at night and said, 'Rabbi, we know that you are a teacher who has come from God. For no one could perform the signs you are doing if God were not with him.'"

Why that verse? Can't remember. Maybe it'll come to me tomorrow, maybe the day after. There's no hurry. I am taking my time. Have you taken yours? The sun comes up, goes down, comes up again. I'm not trying to stop the day. I know what makes me strong.

**PART ONE**

# A Whole New Thing

# 1

## Family Affair
### (1943–1955)

**Life is a record. But where do you drop the needle? You can** put it down near the beginning, where a young boy in Northern California starts to discover how much music moves him. You can put it down a little later, when he assembles a band, or a little later than that, when the band appears onstage, first in front of small crowds in clubs, then in front of larger crowds, including one of the largest in history. Those are good tracks.

Or you can play the flip side of this bright and stirring story: the young boy, now a young man, facing the harsh light of fame; the young man, now a star, making his way through a house crowded with drugs and guns; the star, now letting his light be crowded out by those drugs and guns.

Or is it better to start right at the start? Find the lead-in groove. That's the outer edge of the record before the first song. Put the needle down there. You may hear some static. Pay close attention to it. It's giving you a chance to get ready.

✻ ✻ ✻

In the story before my story, there's Denton, Texas, a small city in a big state, north of Dallas and Fort Worth. In the 1920s, F. L. Haynes, Fred to those who knew him, went to Denton to set up the St. Andrew Church of God in Christ. The Church of God in Christ was a Pentecostal denomination with roots in Tennessee, only a few decades old at that point but gaining steam.

Fred's family included two girls named Alpha and Omega. In Fred's church, Alpha met a man named K.C. Stewart. Alpha and K.C. married in 1933 and brought a daughter, Loretta, into the world the following year. For a while that was the family, the three of them. Then, on March 15, 1943, a fourth face appeared. That was Sylvester Stewart. That was me.

The street where we lived in Denton is barely a memory for me. A cemetery was to the east. What was to the west? We all were, soon enough. A little while after I was born, we moved out to California. Denton went into the past and the future went into Vallejo, a city about thirty miles northeast of San Francisco on San Pablo Bay.

For a minute in the 1850s, Vallejo had been the state capital before Sacramento took over. Vallejo was a port, which meant that people were always coming in and out. They weren't just getting off ships and getting on them. They were also building them. There was a naval shipyard on Mare Island that needed workers, and that grew the town. When we arrived from Texas, Vallejo was in the middle of a boom.

Boom! There we were. Our first Vallejo address was 125 Denio Street. Back then it was just a few kids—me, Loretta, and the next sister down the line, Rose. My father, K.C., who we called Big Daddy, had a cleaning business. My mother kept the house. I never met grandparents on either side, never got any of that spoiling. When I was four, a little brother arrived, Frederick Jerome, who we called Freddie. He bunked in my room, at the bottom of my bed. New faces needed new spaces. My dad put up another house behind 125 Denio, at 127, and we moved there. And a few years after that, a fifth child, another girl, showed up—that was Vaetta, who we called Vet.

There were seven of us, and the eighth member of the family was music. Even before children, my parents played. My father played washboard, guitar, violin, fiddle, harmonica. My mother played keyboards and guitar. Music was as much a part of our home as the walls or the floor. The piano was as prominent as the kitchen table. All of us sang from as early as I can remember, and the first songs we learned were gospel songs by Mahalia Jackson, Brother Joe May, the Soul Stirrers, the Swan Silvertones. We built our future in heaven. We dug a little deeper. We put our trust in Him.

We sang at home and then we sang in church. We all sang together but sometimes one of us would get a solo. I was put in front of the congregation to perform when I was only five or six. My mother said that I really came alive in front of a crowd. More than that: If they didn't respond I would cry. Once, I was up there, singing, feeding off the audience, hearing their shouts and applause, when pieces of the crowd broke off and women started running down the aisle, holding on to their hats, still shouting. Now I see that they were feeling the spirit in the song calling them toward the stage. Back then, I thought they were coming to grab me. I turned around, jumped off the table, and started running for my life.

I stopped running. I came back for the music. From the time I was very small I could tell that I was deeper into it than most because I was so often with an instrument. It might have been drumsticks first, and then I was out on the street with my mother and saw a man playing guitar. I asked her for one. She sent my father out the next day with instructions not to return empty-handed.

Learning was looking. There was a guy in the church who played guitar. What he did with it was amazing, six strings and an infinity of things. I watched him like a hawk. He wasn't a mentor. I don't even know if I spoke to him. I just saw what he did and tried to figure out how to do the same and more. Guitar stayed with me, but I was always looking to whatever was next, taking up the bass, picking out songs on the piano. I felt incomplete without an instrument, or maybe it's more to the point to say that I only felt complete with one. When I went out into the world, I was surprised to see people who weren't carrying instruments. I wasn't sure what they did instead.

✳ ✳ ✳

I was up under the bridge with a friend of mine. We were small, six or seven, looking at clouds in the sky, at fog lower down, at reflections of light on the water. We spied on people, made up stories about them. Vallejo was all around us, which was cool with me.

In my neighborhood, we didn't know about other neighborhoods, not yet. If you got along with your parents, you were good. I got along with mine by listening. Big Daddy was big on justice. He gave me some advice early on, in his Texas accent. "Ah tayl yew," he said. "If ah ketch yew maken any kyna prob-um, ahm gonh wayh yew out. Donh evuh be stahrtinn a fight. But if somebody messiss wich yew, get a brick and make for sho' you leave them quiverin' or still." That advice stuck with me, then and forever. Don't fight. But if you see an injustice, don't stop fighting back.

I remember dodgeball with other kids. I remember Halloween. My family didn't really do costumes, but I would put a little black mask over my eyes so I could fool people and get candy. We had a contest to see who could get the most candy, and I used to win. A shopping bag was needed to hold it all.

I built roller coasters in the yard, tracks of boards nailed together. The first one was small. Freddie and I worked on that together. You could skate on it. Later I built another one that was big enough for soapbox derby cars. I did most of that one, though my father's friend Brother Wilson helped out.

By the time I was eleven or twelve my older sister, Loretta, was already grown, and since I was second in line I was put in charge of the other kids. Big Daddy's cleaning business handled some of the big buildings downtown. He would work every day. As he went out the door, he would point at the other kids and say, "Do a song with them." I smiled and told him I would.

One day, he had another request. He gave me a shotgun and strict orders to use it if a certain neighbor chased his wife into our house. She was allowed to come in but he could not follow. I didn't understand that they were drinkers and fought often. I just thought they were crazy. When I felt the weight of the weapon in my hand I cried.

When I was old enough to not be too young anymore, I went with Big Daddy on weekends to work. One of the buildings he cleaned was the Higgins Building, all five floors. I made money, but only from cleaning. If I found a coin on the floor, even a nickel, Big Daddy would make me leave it for the people in the office. It wasn't ours to take.

My mother was my best friend. How can you describe a mother? She loved me. She made me feel safe. She put the idea in my head that I could do anything and worked to keep it there. She ran the house, including the kitchen. We ate collard greens, chicken with gravy, fried chicken, cornbread. We raised chickens for a while there too.

We kept singing and playing together as a family, to the point where we got noticed and then named: the Stewart Four. We even cut a single, one side with "On the Battlefield" (which might have been the song I was singing on the table), the other with "Walking in Jesus's Name." The record was released by the Church of God in Christ, the Northern California Sunday School Dept. *Vocal with Inst. Acc.*, the label said.

The fifties was a parade of names. Truman, Eisenhower, Stevenson, Warren. That was politics, which belonged to the world beyond the town. Brando, Monroe, Taylor, Dean. That was the movies, which sometimes came to town. The radio brought more of the outside world into the house, and when we got a television, I watched everything I could. My eyes stuck most to the cowboy programs. I liked *The Range Rider*, with Jock Mahoney, tall as a tree. I liked Roy Rogers and Gene Autry. My favorite was Lash LaRue. There was no one cooler. He wore all black and used a whip. What for? To keep himself from shooting a motherfucker.

School marked time, mostly. I was smart, which teachers liked to tell me, usually because they were about to tell me that I should apply myself more. But I couldn't pay attention. Lessons didn't reach me because they didn't challenge me. I was too smart for what was being sent my way but not smart enough to understand how to use it. Activities and competitions were more fun. One year, I had a role in a school play. I was Don Pepe, a guitar player, an easy part. Another year, during the class spelling bee, I was half-watching the teacher at the blackboard and agreeing— black, bored—when another boy went up to write down the names of the contestants. He spelled my name wrong: "Sly-vester." Everyone started laughing but I took a closer look. Sly: Not bad. The correct order of letters may be better, but a reversal isn't always worse.

# 2
## ✳

## Sing a Simple Song
### (1955–1963)

**W**hat do you want to be when you're grown?" Adults like to ask kids that question. The adult in this case was the pastor of the church. I was the kid.

"The bishop," I said. That was the top man in the Church of God in Christ. The pastor started to smile. The other people in the room laughed. I was serious. It seemed like the highest job for the highest cause. Why wouldn't you aim for that?

That was my aim at twelve or thirteen. A year or two after that, I started to feel a pull from another direction. Some people called it R&B. Others said rock and roll. These singers—Little Richard, Clyde McPhatter—came out of the church, too, but went elsewhere. Sam Cook replaced R. H. Harris in the Soul Stirrers, stayed for a few years, then left to make pop records (and popped an "e" on the end of his name to mark the change).

These from-the-church singers were something. They kept what was holy and added in what was earthy, and the combination landed on me hard. I wanted to sing like them, control the stage like them. Jackie Wilson was especially amazing, pure electricity up there at the microphone, twirling around. He had an effect on the crowd and then some—he'd be falling offstage and shit, knocking the bitches out with his energy.

Ray Charles was one of the biggest names in music at that point, and the baddest. I dug the way he played. When he sat at the piano, he rocked his head from side to side. Stevie Wonder did something like that later and I know it wasn't because he saw Ray doing it. I understood it as more than just a style. It was a way of showing that the spirit had gotten into you and stayed there. Even when I started to move away from the religion I was given—I wasn't exactly God-fearing, didn't see the point in being afraid of Him or anyone else—I believed in the spirit. It worked for Ray. He was so sincere in his songs, no matter what he was singing.

You learn music in stages before you learn it on stages. I started to play other people's songs and soon enough I started to realize that I was playing my own. I would be learning something by Ray or Sam or Jackie, or Larry Williams or Bobby "Blue" Bland or Big Joe Turner, and suddenly I would realize that I had left it behind and was making something new. Sometimes it was just music. Sometimes words came along with it.

Music held people together. It held me to my brother Freddie. We would play guitar and bass and trade off. It held me to my friend John Turk, who could really play, with skill and showmanship both—trumpet with one hand and piano with the other. I mostly did one instrument at a time. I would see a poster for a talent show nailed up to a telephone pole: piano competition, guitar competition. If it required an instrument I already played, I would learn a song. If it required an instrument I didn't already play, I would learn the instrument. If I managed to win, I could make a few dollars. I managed, more than once.

The other groups didn't like to lose, and some of them liked it even less when they lost to a black group. Vallejo was diverse: white, black, Hispanic, Filipino. But diverse didn't mean fair. There was only one day when black people could swim in the public pool. That was Saturday. I remember going one day when everybody was white. I don't recall anyone saying anything to me, and if they had I wouldn't have listened. I could never get into that way of thinking. The water's the same for everyone.

**✳ ✳ ✳**

*In the midst of old Vallejo / Stands the school we love . . .*

Now it was the late fifties, and I was off to Vallejo High on Nebraska Street. In some ways it was just more of the same, classes I couldn't completely care about, teachers who told me that I should care.

But high school had some new attractions. Football was a big deal because of Dick Bass, who had been a star running back for the high school a few years before. In 1954, the Apaches—that was our mascot back then—went undefeated, averaging fifty-four points a game. Easy to remember. By the time I got to high school, Dick Bass had moved on to the Los Angeles Rams, but the Apaches were still tearing up the turf at Corbus Field. I also liked watching track. I was quick myself, but I didn't go out for teams. I didn't have the mentality for it. It wouldn't have made sense to Lash LaRue, and it didn't make sense to me either.

Just because I wasn't for teams doesn't mean that I was a loner. I got close to a black kid named Raymond Stith. I looked up to him. He dressed cool and acted the same. He was tough. He would knock a motherfucker *out*. Once he was arguing with another kid and a gym teacher made them fight it out in a ring with gloves on.

I ran with a group of guys called the Cherrybusters. People have said it was a gang but that's not a word that really applies.

We had parties. We had jackets. We didn't have a leader, but I might have been followed a little because I had a car, a cherry Chevy. Cherry wasn't the color. It was the condition. That's the first car I remember having. It even had a nickname, Booty Green, because it was light green with a green trunk of a darker shade. Booty Green and I got around town.

The car had a passenger seat, of course, and when I was sixteen or so I got a passenger, Marilyn Bethel, my first serious girlfriend. She was a pretty black girl, good smile, good grades. Marilyn didn't hang with a group, didn't try out for this crowd or that one, and that was important to me, as was the fact that my parents met her and liked her. I gave her a ride to school, and drove her home, too.

Chuck Gebhardt, who was my age, and his younger brother, Vern, lived on the other side of town. Their father was a gym teacher—the same one, in fact, who had made Raymond Stith put on gloves. The Gebhardts had a friend named Frank Arellano, and the three of them knew two girls, a blonde named Charlene Imhoff and a brunette named Maria Boldway, who went by Ria. They had a singing group that practiced around school and at people's houses, in basements and garages. Another kid had been with them and then they were without him, and they were looking for a replacement. They were looking at me.

I was all for it. John Turk and I were in a student organization called the Youth Problems Committee. Ria Boldway may have been also. It was formed "in order to better relations among students," which I guess meant finding common ground among black and white and Japanese and Mexican and Filipino. I believed in that. But I wasn't sure I believed in meeting in a room to get it done. A singing group made more sense.

What was the difference between a singing group and a group singing? A name. This group had a name. A few, in fact. For a time it was the Viscounts (that didn't work on account of there was another Viscounts that turned up somewhere else), then the Vicounts (which stuck for a little while even though it looked like there was a letter missing), then the Biscaynes (that was the name of a Chevy sedan, full-size, four pillars). If you look hard enough, you can still find most of those names someplace: a high school yearbook, a single pressing, a newspaper ad. But the name that lasted the longest was the Viscaynes, with a "V" like Vallejo.

History talks about the Viscaynes like it was a major achievement in integration, but I didn't see it that way. To me, it was a white group with one black guy (though Frank was Filipino). Chuck and I would play basketball sometimes. And I played with Ria Boldway, too. Not basketball: We flirted and then I saw her one time, sneaked it. Maybe a second time or a third, too. But we kept it quiet. Partly it was because her father didn't like us dating, which was partly because of color. Partly it was because a relationship could shake up a group and we wanted to make it before anything could shake it.

From the start, I took the lead on the music side. I had experience singing and playing, which sharpened my ear for arrangements. The Viscaynes practiced until we got good and then practiced more until we got better. We sang around town, auditoriums, fairgrounds, hotels, military bases. Parents drove us to gigs. Sometimes we stayed overnight. Sometimes we even got paid.

At that time, *American Bandstand* was a national sensation. Every city had its own version. San Francisco's was *Dance Party* on KPIX, Channel 5. A local actor named Dick Stewart (no relation) hosted. Kids danced, boys in jackets and ties, girls in dresses, as the camera got in close. Any record that could get feet moving got played: Santo and Johnny's "Sleep Walk," Johnny

Zorro's "Road Hog," Chubby Checker's "The Twist" and "Let's Twist Again," Joey Dee and the Starlighters' "Peppermint Twist." Lots of Johnnys, lots of twists.

*Dance Party* also sponsored talent shows in the area. We won enough in a row that we made it to an on-air showcase, and we did well enough there that we got a record deal. We recorded in San Francisco, a space beneath the Geary Theater, where we cut some songs backed by a local group called Joe Piazza and the Continentals. We were given two, "Stop What You Are Doing" and "I Guess I'll Be." The third song, I wrote myself. The Marcels' "Blue Moon" was a hit at the time. I wrote one of my own, same moon, different color. I rhymed "love" with "above." What else?

"Yellow Moon" was an early lesson for me in how the music business worked—and how it didn't work the same for everyone. We recorded with a producer named George Motola, who had gotten known for his association with Jesse Belvin, another Texas-to-California transplant, San Antonio to L.A. in his case, who had a big hit with "Earth Angel" and then died in a car wreck after a concert in Little Rock, Arkansas. (It was the first concert down there in front of an integrated crowd, and some people weren't happy about it. After the wreck, there were clear signs that the tires of Belvin's Cadillac had been tampered with.) When "Yellow Moon" came out, I saw that the writer wasn't me, by George—it was by George instead of me. He had a company, House of Fortune, and he kept his fortunes in-house.

I remember feeling something about it, though not exactly sadness or anger. That's just how it was. I was still young, still learning, and there would be many more chances. "Yellow Moon" had a B side, "Heavenly Angel" (credited to "E. Washington/R. Page"), and we recorded a third song, a Coasters-type thing called "Uncle

Sam Needs You (My Friend)." But "Yellow Moon" was the one that rose. We made the charts, number 17 in the San Francisco area. To me it felt like number 17 in the whole world.

House of Fortune wanted to push me out as a solo artist under the name Danny Stewart, so they flew me down to Los Angeles to work with George and a guy named Vic Lucas, who was set to manage us. That was a dream and then some. They put me up on Hollywood Boulevard in the best apartments in the world, so clean and white that I was afraid to stand close to the wall for fear the dye in my hair would come off on it.

In L.A., we did some more recording, including a version of "Yellow Moon" with my vocals sped up. That was a common trick back then: it made a singer sound younger, which made it easier to sell records to girls. I also did more playing locally, guitar with a guy named Jesse James, gigging with the KPIX house band. A sax player named Jerry Martini was part of that scene—he had been part of the Continentals, too—and he and I became friends. Most people slide through your life, there and then gone: that was how it went with Dick Stewart, with George Motola, with Vic Lucas. Others stick. Jerry stuck.

My senior year, I left Vallejo for a while. My dad was the reason, though maybe I was the reason he was the reason. I was getting smart with him. I would drive off, stay out too late, refuse to listen. I wasn't the only one acting up. Freddie had a rebellious period too, got in fights, almost started a fire on the back porch, but I was the oldest boy, which meant that I caught more hell. There were regular whuppings. Once my dad threw a buffing machine brush at my head. That was too much. I had to get out of Dodge.

I went up to Sacramento to stay with my sister Loretta. While I was there, I joined a gospel choir, the Sacramento Inspirational Choir. One Saturday, I drove to visit a girl I was seeing. When I got to the neighborhood, some people came up to the car. Booty Green had that effect. "I know you," said a tall girl with short hair. "You sang in the choir."

"That I did," I said. The girl said that she could play a little and sing a little, and she invited us into her mother's house for a jam session. That was Cynthia Robinson. She was tough and she was real. She could play more than a little, and on trumpet, which wasn't a common instrument for a girl. One afternoon, we walked by some bullies who talked shit to her about the horn. I didn't like to fight but I was real interested in fighting back. I made sure to come back around later and straighten the bullies out regarding Cynthia and the respect that she was due. They bothered her less after that. When I left Sacramento to go back to Vallejo, I thought she might stick, too.

After high school, I considered business administration for a minute. I could do quick figuring. But music was what I had heard for years, in my head and my heart and my soul, and if I was going to study anything, it should be that. Vallejo Junior College, and especially David Froehlich, sealed the deal for me.

Mr. Froehlich was in his midthirties when I met him. It seemed old but now I see that I was just so young. He had been born in Oakland, had picked up piano in his teens, and had done time in every kind of group that there was—jazz bands, dance bands, wedding bands. After the war, he went to the Eastman School of Music in Rochester, New York, for a composition degree. East, man. That gave him another instrument, the bass, and a profession, which was teaching. By the time I got to Vallejo Junior College, he had been there for a while, still doing everything: big bands, small combos, even conducting Easter choir for vespers.

I always loved singing and playing, loved hearing songs. Mr. Froehlich was the first person who made me love music as a language. He could read music. He could write it. He could hear it and he could speak it. And he wasn't the kind of guy who stood up on a tower and looked down on the rest of us. He was cool, down-home, regular. I liked that about him.

What did I learn from him? Everything. We did ear training, which taught us to recognize chords, scales, intervals, and rhythms. Then we went deeper, reading Walter Piston, a composer who taught at Harvard University and wrote music-theory books like *Harmony, Counterpoint,* and *Orchestration.* Big books—*Orchestration* was almost six hundred pages—filled with big ideas. Cadences, irregular resolutions, raised supertonics.

Above all, I learned how to learn. I could get lost in the reading, but Mr. Froehlich led me out. Take Piston's explanation of counterpoint: "The art of counterpoint is the art of combining melodic lines. The contrapuntal essence, as an ingredient of inner vitality in music is, however, something deeper than a process of manipulation and combination . . . most music is to some degree contrapuntal." That was like walking through branches at night. But when Mr. Froehlich explained it, it was clear skies. I could see the melodic lines, watch them intertwine. It's wrong to say that it was like shoelaces but it's also wrong to say that it wasn't at least a little like that.

There were a dozen students in the class, but I listened like I was the only one. I stayed after to talk to Mr. Froehlich, to ask more questions. Even after he finally excused himself, I would walk slowly back to my car, trying to get everything clear and then clearer.

At night I was still stepping up on bandstands, running local groups, trying to get something of my own going. While I drove I would flip on the radio and see what music was popular, and whether I understood it differently now. I especially liked hearing where Ray Charles was going. Back in 1961, he had put out "Hit the Road Jack," one of his sharpest songs, which finished with its business in two minutes flat. Since then he had changed his style over and over again, going deeper into blues or country, moving from "Unchain My Heart" to "I Can't Stop Loving You" to "Busted."

One day I turned on the radio and heard not music but news: Special Report, Today in Dallas, Dealey Plaza, Motorcade, Half Past Noon, President Kennedy Shot, Waiting for Word from Doctors, Doctors Making Announcement, President Declared Dead. I pulled Booty Green over and cried. The news fucked me up. I drove home and thought about it, not just what had happened but what could be done. Was there anything I could say that people weren't already saying? Was there anything I could say that would help people through it? Or was it just about feeling what everyone was feeling, expressing what was in the air? I didn't write a song that day but I remember thinking that the moment was calling out for one.

# 3
*

## You Can Make It If You Try
### (1964–1966)

**W**hile I was studying with Mr. Froehlich at Vallejo Junior College, I went to Chris Borden School of Modern Radio Technique. They offered training for future on-air talent. I went in case I needed to get a job. The class lasted twelve weeks, but then it was down to just one more week, and then I had my certificate in hand.

The day I got out of class, I went to KSOL, 1450 on your AM dial. KSOL was the main R&B station in town. After operating for years as KSAN, it had changed call letters to emphasize the format.

Near the front desk, there was a guy who looked like a manager. "Excuse me," I said. I introduced myself.

"What can I do for you?" he said.

"I want a job," I said. He didn't say anything, so I went on. I told him I was better than somebody there. I didn't mean anyone in particular. I just meant that it wasn't possible that I was worse than everyone there, and that there had to be some way to make room for me.

The man didn't look sold but he didn't look mad either. I set out to show him. There was a teletype machine that spat out yellow paper with all the news across the United States. We had one of those at Chris Borden. I started reading from it like I was on the air. "You got to hire me," I said.

"You might be right about that," he said, and did.

A job meant no more school, but wasn't the point of school to get a job? I went to Mr. Froehlich and told him it would be my last semester with him. "Why are you going?" he said. He wasn't trying to make me feel bad. It was a curious question from a friend.

I made the sign of money, two fingers rubbed together. "But listen," I said. "I'll be back. And when I come back, I'm going to be in a stretch limousine filled with women." Years later, I did send a limo for him, but I forgot to fill it with women.

In my first weeks at KSOL, it was my job to pick out records. Sheets went out that listed the popular songs of the day, and next to each title was a little box. Programmers were supposed to use it as a worksheet, but I just checked off what I liked, and sometimes those records made it on the air. I got more jobs and better jobs and eventually they put me behind a microphone for real, in the 7:00-p.m.-to-midnight slot.

That was when I completed my name. Back then, when they added a new on-air voice, they usually made up a DJ name. I was already using the Sly from the blackboard, but I didn't know the rest yet. "Sly Stewart" didn't sound quite right. Someone at the station, maybe Tom Johnson, tried to pin "Sly Sloan" on me. That didn't work at all—you couldn't even get it out of your mouth right.

"Give me a few days to think of something better," I said. It didn't take that long. I went on the air and introduced myself as Sly Stone. I was cooking with a bunch of ingredients. It sounded right. I was already smoking marijuana. And there was a tension in the name. *Sly* was strategic, slick. *Stone* was solid. (Ray Charles would even have a song called "Let's Go Get Stoned," too, but that wouldn't come out for a few years yet.) Once I had my name, I started making up little rhymes around it and putting them on-air. *I'm Sly Stone of KSOL, goodness for your mind, body, and your soul.*

One of my main inspirations was a comedian, Lord Buckley, the king of hipster slang. He was gone by the time I got on the radio, passed away in 1960, but his routines lived on. My favorite was "The Nazz," which brought the story of Jesus into line with his lingo: "Well, I'm gonna put a cat on you . . . the sweetest, gonest, wailingest cat that ever stomped on this sweet swingin' sphere. And they called this here cat . . . the Nazz." I memorized the whole thing and recited pieces of it on my show. *The rolling Stone is with you to treat you right, a KSOL brother that is out of sight.*

Memorizing trained your brain but it didn't bring it fully to life. For that you needed to get into a little room and have someone tell you that you were on the air. That was a shock to the system. Dead air needed to be filled. You had to make it up as you went so that everyone else could come along with you. That's what I did at the station. I made it up even before I knew what it was. *A little bit different every night, always out of sight, from the later hours to the early brights.*

I hauled a piano into the studio and sang "Happy Birthday" to everyone listening. It must have been someone's birthday.

I gave out the temperature, always at 59 degrees, no matter what the actual weather was. I am not sure why except that it was cool.

I did other voices, including a soft-spoken but hardheaded character named Percy who would come in and contradict me or make a joke at my expense.

I read commercials and tried to turn each one into an event. During a malt liquor spot, I pretended like I was in conversation with Milt Jackson, the spokesman, even though he had pre-recorded his pitch. When the House of Music in Oakland had singles on sale, I went rapid-fire through them all—Jackie Wilson Mary Reeves Don Covay Z. Z. Hill Brenda and the Tabulations.

One day Jerry Martini, who used to come by the station and hang, said that I should sing everything I said. Why not?

At first my KSOL show played mostly R&B and soul, like the call letters said. But 1964 brought a sea change from across the sea. When the Beatles appeared on *The Ed Sullivan Show* in February 1964, they put everything in the rearview mirror. I didn't see that show, but I saw how people talked about them after that. I couldn't ignore them on the radio. I didn't want to. Whatever was in the air went on my airwaves: not just the Beatles but the Stones, Bob Dylan, Mose Allison. Some KSOL listeners didn't think a R&B station should be playing white acts. But that didn't make sense to me. Music didn't have a color. All I could see was notes, styles, and ideas.

I tried to learn from it. I loved the Beatles for their melodies and their lyrics and their tight harmonies. And Bob Dylan, well, he was only one guy, working with just voice, guitar, and harmonica. It was so little to go on, or at least that's what people thought, but they didn't hear how dead serious he was about what he was doing, even when he was joking. He pushed his mind at you through his music.

After I introduced a record, I would sit at the piano and play along with it. It was an exercise, and it strengthened me. You cover other songs in your mind and eventually you've got it covered. Sometimes I would even decide that the original act had taken the arrangement in the wrong direction, and correct course. As soon as the song ended, I was back at the microphone.

I started to get known around San Francisco because of KSOL. I had a following and a fan club, the Magnificent Stoners. In on-air promos, a female voice read out a membership offer, which included an official card and a signed photo of me. She left a blank space for the station's mailing address and I filled it in, using a high voice that didn't quite match hers: "1111 Market," I would say in that high voice, and then come back in as myself: "You're gonna have to do something about your voice, Jo. It changes right in the middle of a sentence."

Right around the same time I walked into KSOL, I ran into Tom Donahue. Tom was a leading man in the local music scene. He had started as a DJ back east, but after the payola scandal, he came west to KYA, a San Francisco AM station that was sagging in the ratings. They needed talent with experience, voices that changed the choices.

Tom's nickname was "Big Daddy," same as my father's. It applied: He was a big guy with a big voice and eventually a big beard. As soon as he got to KYA, he and another DJ named Bobby Mitchell began to promote concerts in the Bay Area. Some were at the Cow Palace. Everyone played there: Dionne Warwick, the Drifters, an orchestra conducted by Phil Spector. Sonny Bono was at one of those shows, wasn't so sunny. Tom and Bobby started their own record label, Autumn Records, to put out records of those shows and more.

Bobby Freeman was part of the more. Bobby was a local boy made good who had started in doo-wop groups like the Romancers and the Vocaleers, had a big early hit with "Do You Want to Dance," and smaller, later hits like "(I Do the) Shimmy" and "Let's Surf Again." One night onstage at the Cow Palace, he ended his set by making up some dance moves, moving his arms in circles and rainbows, shaking his hips, doing baseball steps, tennis steps. He was trying to snatch it back from Chubby Checker, who was still twisting, again and again. It seemed to me (and maybe to him) that he was swimming.

Then it was a little later, and I had met Tom Donahue and he had met me. We talked about Autumn Records and what the label needed: songs written and arranged and recorded. I had started to do a little bit of this and that: a few songs with Gloria Scott, a singer I had met back in the Stewart Four days, including one called "I Taught Him," spoken intro, backup vocals by me. I had more ideas for songs from the radio and my own mind. I told Tom I was better than somebody, and he brought me on as a staff producer. I joined Autumn without leaving KSOL. Two heads were better than one and the same was true of jobs.

One of my first jobs at Autumn was to get a hit for Bobby. He was still showing off his swimming moves around town, but other people were starting to copy him. He needed to establish ownership. I wrote a song for him, "C'mon and Swim." Quick, easy, a dance song through and through. I arranged it and brought in some musicians, including Jerry Martini, though I played lots of it myself.

This time, my name was on the record, right under the name of the song. "(Stewart-Coman)" it said. Coman was Tom Donahue. That was his real last name, just like Stewart was mine. When I had done "Yellow Moon," all of the credit had been taken away from me. Here, it was only half. A co-write with a Co-man. Tom was a good guy and a bad mother. He broke my bed once. I was renting an apartment, was going to be out of town, and told him he could use the place to be with a girl. I came back and the bed was all fucked-up. He said he didn't know exactly how it happened but he was big, maybe 300 pounds, so I got the picture.

"C'mon and Swim" was written, arranged, performed, and recorded. Now we needed to get it out and get it attention. We focused on North Beach. It was a neighborhood in San Francisco, far northeast, right across the bay from Oakland. It had gotten famous for Beat poetry (City Lights Bookstore and the Vesuvio Cafe there) and jazz (in the late fifties, you could see Miles Davis at the Jazz Workshop, Duke Ellington at Basin Street West, Carmen McRae at Sugar Hill). One of my favorite restaurants, Original Joe's, was there: I liked their spaghetti and meatballs.

Toward the middle of the sixties, Beats gone, jazz changing, North Beach started to shift over to dance clubs: El Cid, Pierre's, Tipsy's, the Galaxie. Many were clustered around Broadway, including the Condor, which featured a dancer named Carol Doda. Carol was a big blond girl who was also from Vallejo, though she was a little older than me—Dick Bass's year, I think. Carol got famous for dancing. She would dance on a piano as it was lowered from the ceiling. She did the Twist, maybe the Watusi. She did the Swim.

Carol drew a crowd. Once she came down on the piano wearing a bathing suit on the bottom and next to nothing on the top except straps, and a little later she wore nothing on top at all. That summer, there was a big show at the Cow Palace—the 1964 Republican National Convention. During the day, the question was Rockefeller or Goldwater. At night, there was no question: Conventioneers were slipping away to see Carol at the Condor.

I even dated Carol for a while. She wasn't especially pretty but she was letting freedom ring, and that counted for something. Carol wore her titties. I mean, she wore clothes but she *wore* her titties. We were together about a month but then I had to put her out. My buddies were over and they were hungry. I asked her to make some food. She looked right at me and said, "I ain't doing it for no niggers." Just like that. I don't remember exactly how I reacted, but it wasn't with a smile. I may have put a hand out. I may have tipped over a stereo cabinet. She left without her clothes and shoes. I gave them to Vet and Rose.

✳ ✳ ✳

"C'mon and Swim" didn't sink. It floated all the way up to Number 5. Not in the area, but in the country. When you have a hit like that, you have to capitalize on it quick. Bobby started touring around behind it, a thousand dollars a night. Autumn put out a record under my name, or close—for this one I was "Sly Stewart"—called "I Just Learned to Swim," with "Scat Swim" as the B side. It didn't chart, though the second swim song I wrote and produced for Bobby, "S-W-I-M," got up to 56.

I felt proud of the success of "C'mon and Swim," but also lucky. It came out as dance crazes were in their dying days. What was killing them was rock bands. The Beatles hadn't gone anywhere since the beginning of the year. They had gone everywhere. Record labels were all scrambling to have their own Beatles. Tom Donahue had seen a group at a club in San Mateo called the Beau Brummels. He signed them, had them dress in matching suits, even started a rumor that they had come from England. I produced two songs for them, "Laugh Laugh" and "Just a Little." The first went Top 20 nationally. The second went Top 10.

Autumn tried to maintain momentum. I produced a group called the Vejtables, with a female drummer, singer, and songwriter named Jan Errico. I put out some blues-rock instrumentals myself, "Buttermilk" and "Temptation Walk," credited simply to Sly. I even fronted a band for a little while—a group we had signed called the Mojo Men that had moved from Miami to the Bay Area. I wasn't a good fit with them, but I kept writing or producing on songs like "She's My Baby" and "Dance with Me." And I was always playing, practicing, setting up bands, thinking about what would come next. The actor Danny Glover, who grew up in the area, has said that he saw me rehearsing down the block from where he lived, in a friend's basement. I don't know which friend or which basement, but if someone was rehearsing, it was probably me.

Toward the end of 1965, I was at Golden State Recorders, a studio on Harrison Street where I had produced the Beau Brummels, working with a new group, the Great Society. They were named after Lyndon Johnson's plan for improving America, and they spelled their name "The Great!! Society!!" to make sure that everyone was paying attention. The band's singer was a girl named Grace. Her husband was the drummer, and his brother was the guitarist and songwriter. The three of them were named Slick. Sly and Slick.

They were recording for the Northbeach label, which was part of Autumn, and brought two songs to the studio, "Someone to Love" and "Free Advice." They couldn't get the right sound right away, which isn't uncommon. But they couldn't get it after that or after that either. There are stories that I stormed out of the studio after four hundred takes and left an engineer to finish the session. That's not true. I remember the singer coming in not quite early enough, and the band's groove falling apart during the instrumental break. I remember leaving the room and coming back, leaving the room and coming back, seeing a musician slumped on the couch with a cigarette burning down for what seemed like forever. I remember offering plenty of free advice on both songs.

Still, in the end, we got it done. The single came out and didn't do much. I forgot about it like everyone else, went back to the studio, back to the radio, back to everything else. About a year later, "Someone to Love" got reshaped as "Somebody to

Love" when the singer, Grace Slick, left the Great Society for a new group, Jefferson Airplane. No one forgot it then.

When bands needed help, I sometimes had to bring in studio players after the fact for overdubs. That may have been how I met Billy Preston. Like me and Jesse Belvin, Billy had been born in Texas (Houston) and come to California (Los Angeles) as a kid. Before he was out of his teens, he had played organ with Mahalia Jackson, been on TV with Nat "King" Cole, backed Little Richard on tour, and even put a record out on Sam Cooke's label. Billy could make more music with his organ than a whole band, and in the studio he could advance an idea better than anybody I knew—I could just hum something and he would move it right into place.

I helped Billy make a solo album, *Wildest Organ in Town!*, for Capitol. On the cover, he was grinning and playing, gap between his teeth. On the record, he was covering the Beatles, the Stones, Stax, Motown, and James Brown, along with some originals that we wrote together. One was called "Advice." Billy went hard on organ, churching it up, over lyrics about taking the crowd higher. That's what I wanted music to do, to elevate whoever heard it. I reminded myself to return to that attitude, and that altitude.

And then there was no more Autumn. Tom sold it to Warner Bros. I had some money, so I got myself a Jaguar, a XKE, and turned it purple. It wasn't the first time that had happened. I had a 1957 Thunderbird painted purple by Lou Gordon's father— Lou was a drummer on the scene who would later move into management—but the Jaguar was something else. When you took it down the street, people turned even before they saw it, and once they saw it they couldn't turn back. I also helped my parents buy a house on Urbano Drive in San Francisco, nice place, Mediterranean feel. It was theirs but I was there too, down in the basement, where I had a studio setup and a small room. That house was a headquarters for eating and hanging and playing music. You could walk up to Ocean Avenue for anything you wanted, though what I wanted wasn't up on Ocean Avenue. I wanted a band.

# 4
# ✳

## Underdog
### (1966–1967)

**E**veryone gets their hair done. I went to get mine done at a place named Huff's Fashionette at Fillmore and Geary. Back then the neighborhood was still the real Fillmore, houses, clubs and bars, lots of black faces. Within a few years, it would be a site of urban redevelopment, which meant clearing our old buildings and replacing them with new expensive ones, clearing black faces and replacing them with whiter ones. A sad story but it hadn't happened yet.

One afternoon I went into Huff's—curls in the front, waves in the back—and met a guy who worked there, Hamp Banks was his name but he went by Bubba. Bubba was trained on hair, had gone to Moler Barber College, and before that a continuation school where he had known Bobby Freeman, though I don't think that connection came up in conversation. And there was plenty of conversation: Bubba and I started talking and kept talking, not just that day but other days, too. I kept going to the shop, and Bubba started coming to the station.

I liked Bubba. He was kind of funny. He could lie real good. He got shit done. And sometimes he brought shit around. The first time he showed me coke I shook my head and told him I didn't go for that. I was smoking weed at the time but nothing more. When another guy started to bring it around too, my curiosity went up and my resistance went down.

Getting high was one thing. Moving up in the music world was another one. I made another song called "Can't She Tell" with Billy Preston. But that was released under his name, and it wasn't enough. I wanted songs of my own. The thing about ambition is that you have to work it from all angles. You cannot be certain which direction will bring connection. I played with Freddie as the Stewart Brothers. He had a thing of his own called Freddie and the Stone Souls. I had a thing of my own called the Stoners.

By then, Cynthia Robinson was back in the picture. She had come down to San Francisco to play horn with blues acts like Lowell Fulson and Jimmy McCracklin. She heard me on the radio and came to see me at the station. After that I went to see her with some of my dogs and asked her to play with me. She had a baby daughter by then, Laura. Cynthia heard my question but before she could answer she got scared of the dogs and jumped up on a chair, leaving Laura alone on the floor.

Nothing happened with the dogs, but something happened with the offer. She took it. We played at clubs, including a place called Little Bo Peep in the Excelsior. Some nights it seemed like we were heading upward. Other nights no one seemed serious and it felt like we weren't going anywhere.

Jerry Martini visited me at the radio station and started to press the issue. "Let's play together," he said. "Start a band." He convinced me. Some of the fuel was mine but Jerry was the spark. In a way it's not wrong to say that he's the one who really started off everything.

I talked to Freddie, who came on. Freddie and I were both

mostly guitar players, but we needed a keyboard so I switched over to that. I could do it, so I did. Cynthia was with us, too, and I tried to convince Rose to come along, but she had a job, because she had a daughter. That made the possibility an impossibility. I had asked before and she had tried, but things hadn't panned out and back to work she went. "I'll ask again," I told her. She said she knew I would but that the answer would be the same.

I had rhyme. I had reason. I needed rhythm. I thought about a drummer named Frosty, a bad mother, a white boy who could play, and dreamed about another drummer, Paul Distel, a genius. Freddie suggested Greg Errico, his guy, who was also the cousin of Jan from the Vejtables. Freddie liked the hell out of Greg, who was just a teenager. Hand Feet, they called Greg.

There was a local bass player named Larry Graham, Texas to California (like me and Jesse Belvin and Billy Preston). Larry was born in Beaumont near the Louisiana border. I saw him perform at a club, maybe on Divisadero, in a trio with his mother, who sang and played piano, and a drummer. It had been a family affair since Larry was fifteen or so. At first, Larry was on guitar. There was no bassist, so Larry and his mother built one between them: during his guitar solos, she provided it from the piano; during her piano solos, he supplied bass from his guitar. Larry would also work the bass pedals of an organ with his feet. Then two things disappeared. First the organ went, and Larry switched to bass. Then the drummer disappeared, and Larry had to add percussion by thumbing or thumping the strings. I don't remember how much I understood that first time, or how much he showed me. There wasn't a presentation, just a performance. But I knew that Larry was heading toward something new, and new was what was needed.

That first set of about-to-be bandmates came to the Urbano house.

Each person had something distinct.

Freddie was quick. He could hear quick and play what was needed quick. He was also funny and could be as loud as anyone. He was the most fun in the group, for me. My brother.

Cynthia stayed close to quiet in life, but she was loud on record. She was loyal in every way from the start.

Larry was sneaky. He could be quiet or loud, both in his playing and his personality. Whichever one he was being, you knew he'd be the other one soon enough.

Jerry was mischievous and quick. He would play and play tricks. He was doing cute shit, always fucking around, but not in a way that hurt anyone.

Greg could keep a beat, not just when he was playing but when he was talking.

And then there was me. What did I have? It's not for me to say.

I was going to borrow Freddie's band name, the Stone Souls, or call the band the Seventh Stone, and there were other contenders too: Sly and the Stoners, Sly Brothers and Sisters. None of them stuck. The name was up in the air.

Then at some point it landed: Sly and the Family Stone. The band had a concept—white and black together, male and female both, and women not just singing but playing instruments. That was a big deal back then and it was a big deal on purpose. Even in the basement, I knew we had something. I remember once Rose came downstairs to check us out. She stood by the doorway, her head only a little bit into the room. It was easy to see that she was digging the music we were making.

The basement was only temporary. Soon enough we were onstage, mostly at a place called Winchester Cathedral. It was in Redwood City, which is about as far south from San Francisco as Vallejo is north. The club had been a few other clubs before, Tin Pan Alley, the Premier Room, but it was bought and rethought by a guy named Rich Romanello. The story was that when Rich first went into the place in Redwood City, it felt a little like a church to him, or else there was a radio playing the New Vaudeville Band's "Winchester Cathedral," or both.

Rich and I knew each other from around. He had managed the Beau Brummels during their Autumn years. Rich was a hustler, drove a Cadillac, was all right at times. He wanted to rethink what a club could or would do. Winchester Cathedral had breakfast shows, Sunday night mass, bring-a-friend night, boogaloo contests, light shows. He was looking around for the right kind of band for the place, and he found us. We were one of the first acts there, us and a group called the Blue House Basement. Most nights we would play our set, go and get some food, come back and rehearse, and then play a late set. Whether we were rehearsing or playing, by the time we went to sleep, it was both late and early.

In those days, we'd line up across the stage: guitar, horns, drums, keyboards. We were playing mostly covers. We did "You've Lost That Lovin' Feelin'," by the Righteous Brothers. We did "Gimme Some Lovin'," by the Spencer Davis Group. We did "What'd I Say," by Ray Charles, which was sort of a double tribute in my mind, since by that point Billy Preston was playing organ with Ray.

Other people in the band had spotlight moments. Larry sang some Lou Rawls songs in his deep voice. Cynthia starred in "St. James Infirmary" because it was a horn showcase. I added in originals, including a lightning-quick medley we called "the riffs"—it was idea after idea after idea. But I arranged every song like an original to match our sound.

One night I was standing off to the side with Freddie and Jerry, laughing about something. Cynthia saw us and thought she was the something we were laughing about. She might have felt extra worried because she and Freddie had gotten together.

What did that mean for her in the band? She came to me upset and tried to quit, told me that she really admired what we were doing but didn't think she fit in. I heard her out but knew she had to stay in. "See you at rehearsal tomorrow," I said, and her worries drifted away like smoke.

Winchester Cathedral became our second home. I knew everyone there: the people who ran it, the people who worked there, and the people who came in, too. Playing there could almost feel like a private show. Rich not only owned the club but managed us at first. He brought in other acts to open for us, including the Santana Blues Band. Our late show might start at two in the morning and stop at six, and when I came offstage I would go straight to my radio job. It was nothing but fun. I never had another thought. *Look at it one time, baby, dig it for what it is.*

We worked hard from the start. We practiced hard to make perfect. I was clear about that with the group. If you were only going to get one shot—at a label signing you, at a hit record—you had to make sure that it found the bullseye.

That's what I was aiming for. The arrow was in the bow. I rehearsed the band every day, didn't matter if it was Christmas or New Year's or someone's birthday. The rehearsals went on as long as needed. Bring a lunch, Freddie used to say. That was the only way to get better and getting better was the only way to get best.

After a few months, the late weekend shows started to get a little extra shine on them. People came up from Los Angeles and sometimes even farther.

One night I looked across the crowd of regulars and saw an irregular, a face I couldn't place. Little guy, big eyes, widow's peak, wearing a sharp-ass pinstripe suit with a sharp-ass shirt. When we finished up, that face I couldn't place was at the edge of the stage. He introduced himself: David Kapralik, producer and manager who worked with Columbia Records. Tall thoughts. Talked fast. Couldn't stand still, and I saw that he also had sharp-ass shoes. Shook my hand and I saw that he also had sharp-ass cuff links.

Kapralik was out from New York to see us, had heard buzz from a promotions man named Chuck Gregory. Kapralik liked the show, the set, the sound. He had special praise for our cover of Jim and Jean's "What's That Got to Do with Me," which we redid as a soul ballad with harmonies that trailed out like a long tail.

He invited me to have breakfast the next morning. We went for pancakes, International House of. There were enough forks clinking on plates that I couldn't catch every word of what Kapralik was saying. I heard "heard." I heard "impressed." I heard "sign." Then he put a dragnet around all those words, pulled them together, and asked whether I was interested in a record deal for the group. That slowed everything down. The question sat on the table next to the pancakes. I had a few years of experience by that point so I hung back, nodded, poured syrup coolly. Dave went back to New York.

I wasn't sure if we would see him again. You can never be sure. But he came back the next week with a real offer and real money.

Everybody was excited. My parents went to a big church event and told everyone that Sly and the Family Stone got a record deal. They said it that way, official name for official news: Sly and the Family Stone. That was us! Rich Romanello was even excited.

We were signed to Epic, which was a part of the Columbia

Records puzzle. It was an odd-shaped piece that had been broken off back in the early fifties for jazz and classical acts that weren't the usual thing. Within a couple years, they were starting to figure out pop. Roy Hamilton was a good example. He sang somewhere between classical and gospel and had huge hits for them with "You'll Never Walk Alone" and "Unchained Melody." They had Bobby Vinton, too, and the Dave Clark Five. Toward the mid-sixties they were looking more toward American rock music, and there we were.

Epic meant Columbia, and Columbia meant Clive Davis. At this point, it's hard to think that there was ever a moment when Clive wasn't a legend, but back then he was new to the record business, at least the talent side of it. He had started out as a lawyer doing work for CBS and had just been put in charge of Columbia's record division.

When I first met Clive, I immediately felt a sincere and serious vibe, sensitive. "Tell me about the group and the direction you see yourself going," he said. Up, I hoped.

We started recording our debut. I had pieces of songs that I had been collecting for years. Some were new things I hadn't tried out yet but that were in my pocket. Others were reworked from songs I had written with Billy Preston or Autumn acts.

We rehearsed wherever we could: at Winchester Cathedral, at Urbano. Somewhere in there I moved into an apartment in a building at 155 Haight, between Gough and Laguna. I remember girls coming to see me there too, some staying the night. We got booked into clubs and practiced as we played. There was a place in Sunnyvale named Wayne Manor ("after Batman's straight self," the ad said). They had girls in Robin costumes in glass booths dancing the Batusi. By the time we got there they had switched over to an outer space theme ("soar on a spectacular interstellar excursion"), complete with a light show and a floating astronaut. We were also at Frenchy's in Hayward, where we were "Sly and the Family Stones." (That wasn't the best misprint—a handful of times we got called "Sly and the Family Store.")

Every band wants a regular gig, and we got ourselves one at the Pussycat a Go Go in Las Vegas. It was one of the hottest spots on the Strip, one of the first places to go past lounge acts into rock and roll. There were two stages, at least, along with go-go dancers, a restaurant, and a small casino.

Vegas was wild. We stayed up all night getting into everything. But it also put the eyes of others on us. April Stevens and Nino Tempo came onstage with us. Bobby Darin loved our act and said so. James Brown brought his whole crew around one night.

We were there for three months, going back and forth to L.A. to record. They put us with producers and the fit wasn't always right. One engineer in L.A. started in talking about how we were wasting his time and his tape. Wasting? I had been doing what he was doing for years, and I had put songs on the chart. We would get our work done and then head back to Vegas. We got most of our first album recorded that way.

Vegas ended like a short sentence. I was seeing a white girl named Nita who had, before me, been seeing the owner of the club. She sat up in front and watched the band, which made him angry. He tried to put her out of the place. I told him to leave her alone. He wouldn't so I told her to leave, alone. "Get your shit and get in the car," I said. Then I went out onstage and explained to the crowd what had happened. The club owner was pissed and we had to get out of town that same night, with a police escort.

We went on to New York City to finish the record. The first time we flew, Cynthia was late. We were already at the San Francisco airport by the time she got in touch with me. She told me, tears in her voice, that she wasn't going to make it. "Don't worry," I said. "I'm not leaving without you. Just get here when you can."

I waited for her. We flew to New York together, not saying a word—I wasn't angry but she was afraid I might be, and that made her even more quiet than usual. We landed and rejoined the others. She always said that she was surprised that I never brought it up in front of the rest of the band, that I never held it over her head. Why would I? She already felt bad enough.

The label tried at first to put us into a hotel downtown, but it was already full, with rats. We kicked up an objection and got moved to the Park Sheraton. Cynthia was with Freddie, and I was with Nita. We had kitchenettes in our rooms so we could make our own food. Cynthia and Jerry went out to buy some groceries. On their way to the store they passed by a barbershop, Jerry with his long hippie hair, Cynthia with her afro blown out big. Some guys from the shop came out with a straight razor and started asking too many questions. They scared Cynthia and Jerry, which they told me when they came back. "What happened?" I said. I was trying to keep my voice low.

I grabbed Freddie and Larry and went back to the shop. We had some words. I tried to explain how it was wrong to pick on peaceful people. We had some words and some more. I can't fix a picture of those barbers in my mind. But I do know that Cynthia passed by that shop a bunch more times during our stay there, and no one ever bothered her again.

The city was San Francisco times ten, in population, in energy, in everything. One street was just shoe store after shoe store for what seemed like miles. But those streets had more hard stories and more drugs. It's not that San Francisco had been clean. The Bay Area in the mid-sixties had plenty of weed, some coke, was starting to go psychedelic. But New York was a tougher game, with a higher grade of coke.

Drugs came in. There were reasons. There was a culture and there was a mindset, but there were also demands. I was trying to write, trying to play, trying to record. All of that needed to be fueled. But how did that fuel make me feel? A drug is a substance and so the question has substance. A drug can be a temporary escape and so I will temporarily escape that question.

In 1967, we got booked into a place called the Electric Circus on St. Marks. Jerry Brandt, who had started in the William Morris mailroom and handled everyone from Sam Cooke to the Beach Boys, had opened the place. It really was a circus, jugglers and fire-eaters and trapeze artists, smoke and fog and lights. The Electric Circus booked the Velvet Underground. Muddy Waters. The Grateful Dead. Cat Mother and the All-Night Newsboys. And they booked us.

We brought a different kind of energy. Some of the other groups didn't get people dancing but we got them up all the way. The place might have held five hundred but when we played there were lines around the block. We had long shows there because no one wanted us to stop.

Introductions were made during those shows. The label sent a photographer to take pictures of us. That was Steve Paley, who would be around the band for years and would be important the whole time he was.

That was also where we came to the attention of Bill Graham. Bill was a major figure around San Francisco as a club owner and promoter, booking acts, making names, helping to define and then refine the scene. He knew of us from Winchester Cathedral, and while he liked us well enough, he didn't see a group that could carry the Fillmore Auditorium, the place he ran on Geary. In early 1967, he booked us for a benefit at the Fillmore along with other Bay Area bands like the Grateful Dead and Moby Grape. But the Electric Circus showed him that we could star.

* * *

We worked all summer. In the fall our record came out. It was called *A Whole New Thing*. The cover showed me in a yellow shirt looking down at a tabletop, where the rest of the band was in dance poses. The outfits were eclectic. Freddie was in blue and yellow with white boots, Cynthia in a patterned dress with pink heels, Larry with a big red tie hanging down, Greg in a suit, Jerry not. Greg was the exception that proved the new rule. Go back five years, or even three, and you'd see black artists in suits and ties, like slick preachers or insurance agents. Black music was stuck there for the purposes of formality and respectability. But we were crossing over, away from the idea that we needed the former for the latter. Clive Davis asked me around then if I thought that our fashion might distract people from the music. I considered the question, really gave it thought. "No," I said. It was fashion but it was also feeling. We could be who we were.

The album notes were written by John Hardy, a longtime Bay Area DJ who had spun blues and jazz at KSAN and then moved over to KDIA. "Sly takes us on a trip that makes stops at all the musical ports of planet Earth's hip circles," John wrote. He made special mention of "lyrics that say more than 'my baby loves me' or 'my baby don't love me,' as the case may be" and "arrangements that swing with melodic variation and the unexpected." I trusted John Hardy in the matter of arrangements. He was friends with Duke Ellington, and he and his wife even had Ellington songs named after them ("John Hardy" and "John Hardy's Wife": simple). There was a long paragraph that established my credentials, reminding people about "The Swim" and especially the radio, and he ended up with an instruction: "Open your ears and dig it all!"

That was the record from the outside. Then the vinyl came

out and the needle got dropped. The first song, "Underdog," had been written for the Beau Brummels back at Avenue. They had recorded but not released it. "I know how it feels," which started every verse, was a kind of answer to Bob Dylan's "How does it feel?" from "Like a Rolling Stone." Sal Valentino sang it fast and dirty, garage-style. I reclaimed it as a soul song. The underdog was anyone in society who wasn't getting their due. It was partly about black and white, but it wasn't limited to that. It was about anyone who was treated unfairly, stared at on the street, kept down, forced out. That was how we were going for something more than "my baby loves me." As for the "arrangements that swing with melodic variation and the unexpected," "Underdog" started with a nursery rhyme played by the horns. I shouted "Hey, dig!" and the whole band came crashing in, energy everywhere.

The record slowed down a little with "If This Room Could Talk," a pop song about a bad breakup, and then it sped back up again with "Run, Run, Run," which was the generation gap, young longhairs and old squares eyeing each other uneasily. "Advice" had tumbling horns and sharp drumming. "Trip to Your Heart" went from a swirling freakout to a love song with deep harmonies. There were also nods to other songs: "Run, Run, Run" opened with a toy version of the Rolling Stones' "Satisfaction," and "Turn Me Loose" wasn't a cover of Otis Redding's "I Can't Turn You Loose," but another kind of answer record, rushing forward like Otis on speed.

It was my first real chance to show what I had learned, from Autumn, from KSOL, from Mr. Froehlich, and so I wrote and I wrote and arranged and arranged, put parts over parts over parts. I wanted every instrument to do everything. It wasn't just *A Whole New Thing*, but a whole bunch of new things all at once. As I said in "Only One Way Out of This Mess"—quoting Lord Buckley's "The Nazz"—I was trying to knock the corners off every square. (That song didn't even make the record. "Life of Fortune and Fame," another one that the Beau Brummels tried their hand at, got rerecorded but not released.)

*A Whole New Thing* didn't do a whole lot on the charts. And my first *Rolling Stone* review was nothing to frame. It was two paragraphs, the first one mostly just repeating what John Hardy said about my history as a producer and DJ, the second declaring that the group's approach was "interesting but not entirely effective," that "none of the tracks [stood] out as strong," and that our sound was "still in the experimentation stage and has not yet come to a satisfactory conclusion."

In general I don't like talking about reviews. They are one mind frozen in time. But what I took from that one was that I hadn't completely figured out how to reach people. When I listened to Bob Dylan, I heard how he made his music straightforward so that he could get to people with his lyrics. He cleared out space for thought. I was filling space. People heard clutter. They were tripping over it instead of tripping on it.

I had been missing shifts at KSOL because of gigs and the band. When we came back after the first record, I moved over to KDIA. But spirits weren't as high there, either on the air or in my mind. We signed to William Morris, where an agent named Al DeMarino promised he would get us better gigs. But there were lots of promises.

I wasn't sure where it was all headed, or what it might mean for me, but life popped up with perspective. Vet was in the hospital. She had gotten pregnant the year before, at seventeen. Her boyfriend came from the church world, and even though my parents thought she was too young, they supported her. She carried the baby for more than six months and then went into labor. One story says that it was Thanksgiving Day, when she was eating pie at Urbano.

My parents took her to the hospital—supposedly she brought

the pie along—so she could deliver the baby. Two things happened. The first was that they found out two things were happening: she was having twins. The second was that she slipped out of the bed and hit her head hard. In the confusion of the labor, they ignored the headache that she told them she was feeling. When the babies were out and they got around to asking her about her head, they discovered that the fall had caused a brain bleed. She had seizures and then slipped into a coma. The doctors did brain surgery to clear the clots. My parents put all their faith in the power of the Lord. Vet says that they stopped eating and had the whole church stop, too, believing that fasting would get attention from above. I don't remember that, exactly, but I remember that everyone in the congregation prayed for her. Some of the church members went to see her and all of the family did.

When I visited, I couldn't believe that the frail body in the bed was Vet. It was like the fade-out of a song, but this song couldn't be ending. I asked a doctor if she could hear me. He said that he didn't think so. I put my hand in hers and told her to squeeze. Nothing. I said it again, willing her to hear me, and that's when I felt life pressing back. It took her a while to get back to full strength, but she got there.

# 5
## *

## Dance to the Music
### (1968)

**I** **wasn't happy that** *A Whole New Thing* **didn't make the** right kind of splash. We had worked so hard only to feel like the first step we took might have been a step backward.

But the record's reception was a matter of perception. Though audiences and critics played it cool, musicians warmed up to it immediately. Dave Kapralik told me that whenever he would speak to a singer or player or producer, they would say good things. Jon Hendricks, the jazz singer, loved it. So did Teo Macero, who produced Miles Davis. I liked that because I liked the jazz guys. Even when I was young, I preferred jazz to blues. It could be interesting even if it was boring.

But artists recognizing artistry didn't put wind in our sales. Dave Kapralik told me that also. "You're not making music for those people," he said. "You have to make it for everyone, to get people dancing to your music." I wasn't against hits. I had gotten one for Bobby Freeman. So I went right back to work. I had an idea in mind with the catchiest melody, the most obvious rhythm, and the simplest words.

Soon it was a song, and soon after that, a record. The band started out at full speed, horns in fanfare, Freddie and Larry fuzzing and slapping, Greg handing and feeting. I played organ, a Hammond, which was big and heavy and expensive and had a churchy sound, even though it wasn't in too many churches because it was big and expensive. But if you had one—like Billy Preston, like Ray Charles, like Booker T., like me—you could draw a crowd.

Right into that hurricane of sound, Cynthia shouted an order: "Get up and dance to the music! Get on up and dance to the music!" That was the name of the song: "Dance to the Music." It was both a title and a description of itself.

Freddie and Larry and I followed with a cappella harmonies, and then we all introduced ourselves, musically and instrumentally. Greg was the drummer, for the people who only needed a beat. Freddie added a little guitar, to make it easy to move your feet. Larry added some bottom, so that the dancers wouldn't just hide. Then it was my turn: "You might like to hear my organ—I said ride, Sally, ride." Sally rode. After the horns soared, Cynthia came back in with a message, a famous one: "All the squares, go home!" Then she said, "Listen to the voices," and we broke back in with an a cappella breakdown before the song's engine roared to life again.

"Dance to the Music" was pure energy beamed out for exactly three minutes, perfect pop-song length. The finished product did its job, but it was also a product. Jerry Martini had a famous quote, which was that it was "glorified Motown." Someone else said it was nowhere near as hip as the rest of our music. I didn't disagree completely. My name was spelled wrong on early pressings of the single, as "Steward," which maybe made a little sense. I was tending to the needs of passengers. But even in such a straightforward song, there was a second message behind it. Giving people energy was an interesting business. Once they were up you couldn't necessarily control what they were going to do next.

Released toward the end of 1967, "Dance to the Music" was quickly a Best Record Bet, a song to watch, an up-and-comer, and it ate well through winter and spring. We were right there next to Aretha singing "Since You've Been Gone," the Beatles singing "Lady Madonna," Cream singing "Sunshine of Your Love." Suddenly, we had a signature song.

The bigger it got, the more places it went. Clive wanted a French-language version of it and I gave him one, though "Danse à la Musique" wasn't exactly like the original single. It was ten times harder and louder, with the vocals sped up. It ended up not even being credited to us, but to the French Fries.

The B side was another French Fries song, again with sped-up vocals. But this wasn't a French-language version of an American hit. It was a new English-language song, "Small Fries," the story of three teenage pigs. Freddie, Larry, and Sylvester were their names. Each of them had wandered out into the world, where they found work and wages, but then letters started coming in from "Uncle Samuel" telling them they had to join the service. They felt unfit. Freddie the pig was religious. Larry the pig was lazy and only liked food. Sylvester the pig "hated to be told what to do." But each of them ended up answering the call. The song was current events, sarcastic and patriotic both, with layer over layer—everything that "Dance to the Music" wasn't. When I went down to the draft board myself, in real life, I got classified 4-F for flat feet.

"Small Fries" made a point. But "Dance to the Music" was the point. It let us play in bigger and bigger places, ballrooms instead of clubs. The song needed an album around it, and by spring we had one. We took the cover photo of the *Dance to the*

*Music* album sitting on top of a sculpture in a park in Oakland, the one people called the "Mid-Century Monster."

There was one major change for the Family Stone at that time, which was that Rose finally came aboard. She wasn't completely comfortable leaving behind jobs and steady pay, but I gave her the courage to do it. She did, and she was surprised that she sounded so good. She was okay after that. As a person, she was a different color of the rainbow, too: quiet, the quietest one in the group. Where Freddie might go up in volume she went down, but that only made her easier to see. She was as loud as a flower. And she helped us onstage and on record. But she sang her ass off without a second thought and she had a perfect memory for what had to be done. You could play her a song and she'd listen once and come right back with her vocal. One-Take Rose. Pretty soon after she was in the band, she was also in a thing with Larry.

Rose's appearance changed the balance of the band. Cynthia was a strong vocalist but nothing close to Rose for pitch, for tone, for control. Cynthia knew it, too. She wasn't filled with false ideas about herself. Whenever she started to sing, I stopped her, pointed her in another direction. What she did with "All the squares, go home" was that direction.

"Dance to the Music" wasn't just the hit and the title. It was also a model for half the record: leads traded off, tight solos, keep everyone's feet on the dance floor. Side one ended with a medley of variations on the theme: "Music Is Alive," "Dance In" (as in "Meet me at the . . ."), and "Music Lover." Some people said "formula," but formula was something you fed to a baby. We were feeding people of all ages.

A few of the songs kept the sophisticated feel of the first record. "I Ain't Got Nobody (for Real)" had little moments of jazz and even classical mixed in with pop, rock, R&B, and Latin. "Are You Ready" put race in its place right off the top, arguing against seeing things as a matter of color and instead seeing them as matters of what mattered: There was "Don't Burn Baby," a response to urban unrest, and "Color Me True" listed off ethical questions to help people become their best selves. Did people talk the same way to people in power as to people they had power over? Did people take credit for their own work or for the work of others? (I can't say that I was thinking back to George Motola, but I can't say I wasn't.)

Because it was a second record, put out so soon after the first, I had to dig a little deeper for material. One song on *Dance to the Music*, "Higher," was a remake of Billy Preston's "Advice" with the same lyrical hook about taking the audience higher. Even though that line came from the past, I also felt like it was pointing to the future. I just wasn't quite sure how yet.

Just as the album was coming out, Martin Luther King, Jr., was murdered in Memphis. I wasn't driving when I heard, like I had been with President Kennedy, but my reaction was the same: stunned, tears, time alone to think. I liked Martin. I saw the kind of peace he was trying to achieve. I liked Malcolm X, too, for his intelligence and clarity, but I felt more for Martin.

Both approaches to the problem of race were needed. There was plenty left that needed approaching. We were touring that year in the Midwest, the whole band in a van along with Big Daddy and Nita, Jerry at the wheel like usual. Jerry and I were probably talking. He was the source of the most interesting conversations on the road: news he had heard, books he had read.

We were running low on gas so we pulled off the highway somewhere in Michigan. The whole town was dark, no traffic lights and no traffic to stop at them. "Is that a military truck?" someone said.

"Sure is," someone else said.

I realized what was happening. The town was under curfew.

It had started after the riots that summer. Social unrest led to some parts of society controlling the rest.

The trucks had guardsmen in them, and they pulled us over and took us out of the van. They told us we were out of line to be out on the street. One started pushing Big Daddy around. I didn't have any interest in that and said so, loudly, but Big Daddy put up a hand. "Don't worry about it," he said. He had a clear sense of where we were and thought I didn't.

They took the girls—Rose, Cynthia, Nita—and put them on a panel truck. One of the uniforms, maybe the same guy, walked by them, stopped at Nita, and said "nigger lover" to her. She was ready to yell, maybe even fight, but this time Cynthia was the one who put up a hand. "He's just trying to get a reaction from us so he can beat our ass," she said. "Don't respond." We got out of there without too much trouble, other than all the trouble.

People ask if we ever played at the same place as Jimi Hendrix. Yeah: Woodstock. But it happened even before that.

Bill Graham had his western spots but then went eastward ho. The Fillmore East, which opened in March 1968, followed the Electric Circus model in some ways—there were Joshua Light shows, trippy visuals to set the tone for the bands—but in other ways it was pure Bill Graham, with bills that reflected his tastes, which meant that they moved in all directions at once. He opened the place with Janis Joplin, Tim Buckley, and Albert King. The Who was there with Buddy Guy and the jazz-rock group Free Spirits in April. In May he booked us along with the Jimi Hendrix Experience. It was a rock show, but because of us we knew it would also be a soul show and a dance show.

That night, one of the musicians backstage had a sore throat. Singing was going to be rough going. He was looking grim. A guy came up and asked after his health. The man nodded, hand went in pocket, hand came out. It wasn't Vicks drops. It was coke. It cured the sore throat in a minute, restored energy and then some. Many musicians had stories like that: a little shot of something helped you out, gave you pep back in your step, so you stuck with it for weeks into months into years, whether or not the help had turned to hurt.

We played a short set, five or six songs, starting with a cover of Otis Redding's "Try a Little Tenderness," special placement for "Dance to the Music," but by the end of it half of the band (me, Freddie, and I think Larry) were in the aisles, hamboning, and then we pied pipered the crowd out of the theater onto the street. When we were doing that, someone had to play the bass, and we picked Cynthia. She could hold it down for a while.

They had to put the place back together after our set and then Jimi came on and tore the place up again. He was already something special. You could tell that on his records and you could tell it in the room. He had the ability to make sounds come out of his fingers that I could not even have imagined before I heard them.

When we were done, when Jimi was done, we went outside, where limos were lined up to take us to the after-hours shows. I can't remember if Jimi and I rode in the same car but we went to the same place.

Jimi and I hung now and then, never too much, but I had a real good feeling about him, and not just because of his talent. He was so even in his temper, maybe even too even. People would come up to us, get up on us, start crowding him and demanding his attention, and my impulse would be to get into it with them, to push back. But Jimi would get a faraway expression on his face and say "That's cool, man, that's cool." It frustrated me. It was like he didn't know what the world could do to him.

Once I went to a girl's apartment. At some point in the evening, she told me that she had a film of herself and Jimi having sex. "Let me see," I said. I didn't want to see the movie. I just wanted to get eyes on it to make sure it was what she said it was. It was. When I left, I took it with me. I figured that Jimi didn't know about it and I didn't think it was right to have it out there in the world like that, where it could appear suddenly and do him harm. I gave it to someone who wasn't in the business, who I knew would never do anything with it other than throw it away.

The year went so fast and we sped up with it. By the end of summer we had our third album, *Life*.

If the second album was a step toward basics, the third one tried to get back into the bag of the first. I was finally making the shortest, sharpest songs I could imagine: "Into My Own Thing" and "Chicken" were a touch over two minutes. But they were packed full in terms of influences, dynamics, references to other songs. "Plastic Jim" picked up a little bit of the melody and lyrics of "Eleanor Rigby."

This time, *Rolling Stone* had plenty to say. Back in 1967, *A Whole New Thing* had gotten a blink. *Life* got a long stare. The piece paired us with the Chambers Brothers as bands that are primarily black, but have white members and spend more time on the white rock circuit than in the black clubs and theaters." Maybe that's why *Rolling Stone* paid so much attention.

The opening track was called "Dynamite!" Dave Kapralik had us cut it with a singer named Johnny Robinson, but we repossessed it. The review put a microscope on the track. It talked about the "unaccompanied blues guitar lick," the "fuzz guitar out front," a "melodic line and progressions" that were "fairly standard soul" over a "radical way" the vocal lead was "split up between at least three different singers." Then came "a building drum roll that amply suggests the impact of an explosion." That was just the beginning of a long review of a short song, the conclusion being that it was "ecstatic listening in any situation."

The rest of the review reached out its arms even further. It compared us to Lambert, Hendricks, and Ross (for vocal arrangements), to Count Basie (for big brassy riffs), to Frank Zappa and the Mothers of Invention (for subject matter—the record included "Jane Is a Groupee," which was similar to songs that Zappa had written about groupies but which was, according to the magazine, "the most incisive song ever written about rock's camp-followers"). The reviewer seemed to understand that the arrangements were meant to work like a kaleidoscope: many colors making the same pattern, coming in from all directions.

The title track got brushed off: "Despite a fine flash in which a 1900 brass band becomes a soul horn section, and some brilliant effects on organ, it's not quite the best cut." Even this was sold as a silver lining ("This itself signifies a welcome change from all those R&B albums that sink or swim with their hit singles"), but it also meant that the review missed one of the main lyrics on the record: "Look at Mr. Stewart—he's the only person he has to fear." All my life people had been telling me to watch out for this one or that one. But then later, at home, I would think that this one or that one didn't scare me, that they couldn't scare me unless I let the fear come through.

The world was testing that theory every day. Life, and *Life*, were sometimes hard to hear with all the death around. In the wake of Martin Luther King's murder there had been riots across the country. In June, Bobby Kennedy had been assassinated at the Ambassador in Los Angeles. Even smaller headlines burned: Glenville, a neighborhood in Cleveland, Ohio, erupted after a gun battle between cops and Black Panthers.

Some of the darkness happened close to home. Epic was part of the Columbia family, and I became friendly with Terry Melcher, who was A&R at Columbia and friends with Dave

Kapralik. Terry was an important figure in the Southern California rock scene—he produced the Byrds, worked with the Beach Boys—and was also Doris Day's son.

When I was down in L.A. recording, I would hang out with Terry. I met Doris, a nice lady. One of the other people in Terry's circle was a short, intense guy who had kicked around the music business for a few years and kept auditioning for Terry. His name was Charlie Manson. I crossed paths with him a few times. Sometimes he would give an opinion and I'd give the opposite and we'd have a little disagreement. They weren't even about songs. They were about nothing. Turn the lights brighter or darker. Open or close a door. Whichever way I went, he'd go the other way.

Terry wasn't going to sign him, but he also didn't tell him to leave, partly because Manson made everyone uncomfortable. I remember once getting the feeling that he shouldn't be there anymore. "We have to get out of here," I said, "it's time to go." I went to the door, walking real slow, making sure Charlie came along. When he was out the door, I turned and went back in and worked on some songs with Terry.

I didn't put it all together until later. Manson had his family and I had mine. One of his, Tex Watson, was really named Charles, too, but they called him Tex because he was from Dallas, and had even lived in Denton for a minute. Small world. Sometimes too small.

**✳ ✳ ✳**

We kept at it. We went back to the Electric Circus in August and got even bigger crowds who made even longer lines around the block. In September, we flew to England. Larry got busted for a joint at the airport. "A velvet-clad member of the American pop music group," the press called him. Around that same time we had a theater show scheduled. Our equipment got lost in transit and I got a fucked-up organ with four or five keys busted. I wouldn't play it. I went out and talked to the people instead, told them that we could not possibly satisfy our commitment without the proper instruments. They seemed to appreciate the explanation.

We were back in New York in October, at the Fillmore East, opening for Eric Burdon and the Animals, even though we all felt that our days of opening were closing.

Bill Graham and I ran into each other there. Meaning that we had a run-in. Bill was tense. He would do intense things. I was backstage with a girl. She went outside for a second and tried to come back in to see the show. Bill had his security keep her out. It pissed me off. I made him apologize to her and then to me and then to Big Daddy, too. But once he apologized everything was cool.

We played "Dance to the Music" in every set, of course, along with "Life" and "Color Me True" and "Are You Ready." We played "Turn Me Loose" in medley with Otis Redding's "I Can't Turn You Loose," linking them back together. We played "St. James Infirmary," still a Cynthia showcase. We played the riffs. And since there was a presidential election only a month away, we left the crowd with some valuable information: their choice was "Humphrey, Wallace, and eeny, meeny, minie, moe." For some reason, we didn't play "I'm an Animal."

The year ended with an appearance on *The Ed Sullivan Show*. I tried to say hello but Ed wasn't much for conversation. He just went out onstage, gray suit, hair slicked flat to his head, and introduced us. "Now," he said, more flat than slick, "here for the youngsters who undoubtedly by now are oldsters, Sly and the Family Stone."

The camera came to me first, and I recited the color-blind lines from "Are You Ready." Our performance was a medley: a full version of "Dance to the Music," some of "Music Lover," and also pieces of new music. Some wouldn't flower fully for a year or more. Rose and I went up into the crowd during a jam built around the lyric "I want to take you higher," and in the closing moments I waved goodbye to the crowd and said "Thank you for letting us be ourselves." Those were shapes of things to come. But one of the new songs was ready to be brought into the light, and we got to it right at the beginning of the night when Rose sang "Different strokes for different folks" and I came in after her: "I am everyday people."

That song, "Everyday People," was the new single from what would become our fourth album. "Everyday People" was two minutes and twenty seconds, not much longer than "Hit the Road Jack." But I kept it short with the idea that it would have a long life. I didn't just want "Everyday People" to be a song. I wanted it to be a standard, something that would be up there with "Jingle Bells" or "Moon River." And I knew how to do it. It meant a simple melody with a simple arrangement to match. I think Larry played a single note through the whole song.

Writing a standard also meant writing lyrics that people would remember even when the song ended. That's how I got to lines like "Different strokes for different folks." Even more than the title, that was the phrase that stuck, to the point where the label put it on the record sleeve of the single, right under the name of the song. I don't know where it came from. I think I thought of it. It could have been in the air. But it carried the same message I had been conveying since "Underdog," since the swimming pool in Vallejo, since always. You couldn't take turns with freedom. You couldn't have one moment where freedom went with the majority and one where it went with the money and one where it went with one skin color or another. Everyone had to be free all the time or no one was free at all.

"Everyday People" came out in November. The chart was filled with soul songs that would later on be classed as classics:

Marvin Gaye's "I Heard It Through the Grapevine," the Supremes' "Love Child," Stevie Wonder's "For Once in My Life." The Beatles' "Hey Jude" was there too. "Everyday People" joined them in the Top 100 by Thanksgiving and made Top 40 by Christmas. By mid-January it cracked the Top 20 and in February got the top spot, where it stayed there for a month. We had never reached the peak before, so I was proud, but I was most proud that I had written a song that I knew would last, not just because we had recorded it, but because other people would, too. (Almost immediately other groups and singers started covering it: the Winstons, the Supremes, the Staple Singers, Peggy Lee.)

Around that time I gave an interview about how pop music was discovering gospel. What I meant wasn't Stewart Four–style gospel, but the larger idea of music as a spiritual force. Rhythm, melody, and lyrics carried inspiration to the people. Sound pulled the soul upward. "There's nothing wrong with feeling religious out of church," I said. I pointed at Aretha Franklin but I could have pointed right back at us.

# 6
## ✳

## I Want to Take You Higher
### (1969)

**P**acific High Studios had opened in a building on Brady Street that used to house a plastics factory. The door was painted as purple as a car. Pacific High was off Market, near the Fillmore West, right in the line of sight for the bands of the time. Quicksilver Messenger Service was there the same month as us, Jefferson Airplane a little later, and within a few years they were broadcasting in-studio sessions by artists like Van Morrison and Jerry Garcia.

Our fourth album had to think about the first three. *A Whole New Thing* showed off my ambition and our desire to do something timeless. *Dance to the Music* showed me that simplicity could reach the largest number of ears. *Life* showed how we were improving as a band, getting quicker and smarter. Past performance was no guarantee of future results, but I didn't want to ignore it either. I went into those fourth-album sessions with Walter Piston's books. I had studied them with Mr. Froehlich and I took them up again.

It was the right time and place for a big leap forward. It was America in 1968, a year where everything happened—Khe Sanh and Tet, King and the riots, Bobby Kennedy, the Democratic National Convention, Tommie Smith and John Carlos with their fists up in Mexico City. There was no shortage of circumstance. The trick was not to become a victim of it. Being an artist meant more than just traveling through events. It meant channeling them.

That's what had led me to "Everyday People." I busted up my finger while we were recording that song. I hit the piano too hard and my finger just went out of its socket. It hurt so bad that my eyes bulge out just remembering it.

That's also what led me to "Stand!," which became the second single and the album's title song. Snare drum in, and then it was lift and uplift. There were some lines about personal pride that took up where "Underdog" had left off (only two years before, hard to believe): "There's a midget standing tall / And a giant beside him about to fall." I know right where I was when I first wrote that song. I was in my mind. But it had to meet the world. One night I took it to a club to play it and saw that it wasn't producing the necessary effect. I went back to the studio and added in a funky breakdown with me and Freddie and Larry singing "Na na na na na na na na." That was a booster engine, and the whole song took off.

"Stand!" was backed with "I Want to Take You Higher," which was proof of evolution. That was the song that had been with me for years, in some form, starting out as a Billy Preston song called "Advice," resurfacing as "Higher" on *A Whole New Thing*. Here it was again, new clothes on a stronger body. Freddie opened up with a tight, strong guitar line, and there was shouting, stabbing horns, and the "boom-shaka-laka" chant. What did people think of that? Was it supercharged doo-wop?

Something African? Nonsense? No matter how it seemed, it pushed at what they knew or thought they did.

"I Want to Take You Higher" was a song I especially liked to play live. It was always one of the last songs in the set, which meant that we could bring the crowd up to where they needed to be and leave the place still vibrating.

"Sing a Simple Song," which had been the B side of "Everyday People," was one of my favorites on the whole record, deep soul with a simple message. All the notes were identified by name as they were sung: do, re, mi, fa, sol, la, ti, and back to do. It had a joke in it—with the song fully rolling along. Larry made a joke about overdubbing, followed by spontaneous (or was it overdubbed?) laughter.

The album ended with maybe the most optimistic lyric, "You Can Make It If You Try," another recipe for rising. But there were times, too, of sinking, moments on a mostly sunny record of clouds covering up the light. Between "Stand!" and "I Want to Take You Higher" we added a song called "Don't Call Me Nigger, Whitey." That song was a simple message: Don't do anything that pisses me off and I won't do anything that pisses you off. It was the Golden Rule. The song wasn't only black warning white. It was "Don't Call Me Whitey, Nigger" too, which wasn't part of the title but was part of the lyrics and the message. Come at bad blood from either side and blood was what you'd get.

The other shadow on the album was "Somebody's Watching You." It was a short pop song that looked at the process of being looked at: because of fame, because of fortune, because of the rest. It was also a statement about the world in general. Every day, people (and everyday people) got watched—could be the boss, the landlady, COINTELPRO, any prying eyes.

One of the best songs on that record is the oddest man out: "Sex Machine," almost fourteen minutes of groove. There was something about that track. It took so long to get it right. People think it's just a loose jam but it was work getting it there. Much of it came from Freddie. He had a big part in that song, and he spent days and days planning out what he would do, practicing, playing other musicians' records and playing along with them. He was driving himself crazy. I finally had to take him aside. "Fuck everyone else," I said. "Just be you. Just be Freddie."

That's all it took to get him to deliver. He could play like a motherfucker and he did. That was much of the battle much of the time, giving people permission to be themselves. It worked for Freddie on guitar just like it worked for Cynthia or Rose on vocals. James Brown had an album with the same title but that was a year in the future at least. In 1969 ours was the only machine of this kind in operation.

I had so many ideas for songs that year: simple songs, complicated ones, songs I thought could be standalone singles, experimental things. Mostly I'd get hold of a rhythm, get it down, and then listen to it again and again as the song grew around it. Words would come in, countermelodies, ideas for arrangements. One day, with an idea hot in my head, I called Steve Paley, who had gone from a photographer sent to take pictures of us to one of our inside guys at Epic. "Steve," I said. "I need studio time."

"It's Friday night," he said.

"So?"

"That means tomorrow is Saturday," he said.

"So?"

"It's not a workday, is it?" I explained that ideas didn't have a workweek. "But people do," he said. I needed the studio and said so. He said it was impossible. I said it again, not as nicely. Finally, he arranged it.

I got there early on Saturday. By the time Steve and the engineer showed up I was asleep on the console table. Steve got pissed. If I was just going to sleep, he could have gotten me a hotel room.

"Fuck off," I said, or "kiss my ass," or something of that flavor. I had to make some calls to smooth things over. What song that was, or would have been, is lost to history. But when a song is knocking at your head, you have to open as many doors as possible to try to let it out.

*Stand!* went off like a rocket. I was riding high on the album, but not just on the album. High on life. High on coke. High on everything. I had a Winnebago that I took around town, and one day I saw a pretty girl with long black hair walking down Ocean Avenue in San Francisco. She was dressed like a student. I figured she was coming from City College. I followed her up the street for a little while and then pulled over so that we could have a conversation. She was a student, like I thought, but not a college student. She was still in high school, eighteen years old, named Debbie King. I liked her and said so. She knew who I was but didn't say so right away.

I got her number and that night or the next called her at her house to ask her out. We set a date. On Friday, at the appointed time, seven on the dot, I went to pick her up, knocked on the door of her parents' house. I was wearing giant glasses, goggles almost, over most of my face and a purple shirt that matched the scarf in her hair. That was just coincidence.

I met her parents that first night. It was what you did, even if you were wearing goggles. "Nice to meet you," I said. The point was to be respectful. Her mom, Jo, was white, worked for the state government or something. Her dad, Saunders King, was black, a musician and another Texas-to-California transplant, Houston in his case. He had sung with his father's church like me and gone on to have one of the first blues hits in the Bay Area, "S.K. Blues."

I took Debbie for seafood on Polk Street. We didn't take the camper that night. I drove one of the other cars, the Cord. It had two doors but only one seat, a driver's seat, and anyone else riding had to sit on a big pillow. We had a night on the town and I had her home by midnight, Cinderella curfew. Debbie and I saw each other all the time after that. We didn't take it too fast. We took it pretty slow.

* * *

Over the summer of 1969, we went east for a bunch of performances. We played Mount Morris Park in late June for the Harlem Cultural Festival. The festival was running all summer, six weekends, and we headlined the first one, which also included the Fifth Dimension and the Edwin Hawkins Singers. The New York City police wouldn't work security for the show, so the Black Panthers filled in. Black Panthers, black audiences wasn't our usual situation—most of the time we were playing for crowds that were mixed in every way except age—but it was a situation I liked. The crowd seemed to agree. We got down into the audience again to dance. *Hambone, hambone, pat him on the shoulder, if you get a pretty girl I'll show you how to hold her.* That performance was edited into a set with others in the series and broadcast later that summer on CBS.

From there, we went up to Newport, Rhode Island, for the Jazz Festival, which wasn't only jazz anymore—Jeff Beck was there on Friday and James Brown on Sunday. We played on Saturday. The show was oversold and kids kept trying to scale the wooden fence around the grounds. Some ended up perched on top like birds. Some surged toward the stage. "Only a sudden cloudburst coupled with restraining words by rock performer Sly Stone averted further disaster," the paper said.

Then it was on to more festivals and shows: Philadelphia,

Baltimore, Detroit. St. Louis, Chicago, Montreal. In Cleveland, the kids got up onto the seats and broke and ripped them. Dave Kapralik had to take out an ad in apology. It ran in music newspapers near ads for our new single, "Hot Fun in the Summertime." If the song had come out the year before, it would have felt like a funhouse mirror of what was happening, cities in flames. But in 1969, with riots across the country mostly over, it was promoting a good feeling that was needed in the world.

We had a weekend of shows at the Apollo Theater in New York with Redd Foxx opening. The night of the first performance, Jerry and Greg told me they wanted to go out to 125th Street to buy some food. I warned them not to experiment with being white guys in Harlem. They came back scared, having seen some things. Onstage there was some resistance to them too, but I had Jerry play a solo to show that he had every right to be there. That quieted down the crowd. While we were at the Apollo, the world was thinking about another Apollo: the one that was landing on the moon the same Sunday we were finishing up our run. Neil Armstrong put a foot down on it right around the same time we stepped onstage.

The moon landing was the biggest thing to happen that summer, for a little while. About a month later there was a three-day festival in upstate New York. The organizers were calling it an Aquarian Exposition, and then they were calling it Woodstock, after the first town where they wanted to hold it. That name stuck even when it bounced from place to place, even when it ended up more than an hour away on a farm in the town of Bethel. In July we got added to the acts. The first day was scheduled to be mostly folk acts: Richie Havens opening, Joan Baez closing, Tim Hardin and Arlo Guthrie and others in between.

The second and third days shifted over to rock, blues, and more. We were the more, playing late Saturday or early Sunday depending on how you decided to look at it.

Santana was also playing, and Janis Joplin, and Creedence Clearwater Revival, and Jefferson Airplane, though I didn't spend time with any of them beforehand. I came up from the city. They sent an Army helicopter to get me, or at least an Army-style helicopter. As I flew in I couldn't see the whole crowd, but you could see enough people dotting the landscape that it was hard to believe that there were even more. *Goddamn.* I said to myself. *Goddamn. What the fuck is this?* So many people, an ocean of them without any land for miles. When something is that big a deal, be sure you're ready—and I doubt that you will be.

That was still my thought onstage. Did I feel the moment as pressure? I knew we had to live up to it, not to mention rise to the level of the other artists. Janis Joplin was on before us, and then there was a break, and it was like the sky split open with rain. Now the dots in the crowd had dots of rain in front of them. More than one of us was afraid to touch the equipment because of the danger of getting shocked.

We went on around 3:30 in the morning and opened with "M'Lady," Freddie playing his licks, Larry holding down the bottom and then some, a big vocal breakdown at the end and then the band storming back in to finish it while the weather did the same all around us. But I had heard something, or not quite heard it, and that meant I had to rap to the audience. "See . . . ," I said, "the problem here is that we have some equipment . . . wait a minute, man . . . we have some equipment that is not working properly. So what we can do is try to hurry up and play to avoid hanging you up or we can try to wait until the shit works right so we can play for you the way that we would like to."

I wasn't really giving the crowd a vote. I knew we'd keep playing. "Check," Rose said into her microphone.

We rolled into the guitar-and-organ intro to "Sing a Simple Song," and rolled through "You Can Make It If You Try." If the equipment wasn't perfect it didn't matter anymore. We were leaving a record behind in the air, in the minds of the people who were there. You've seen the pictures, me wearing a fringed white jacket, looking like a giant bird? We flew onstage so early in the morning—or was it late at night?—that the film crews weren't set up yet, though they captured the audio. Next we played "Everyday People." We were building to "I Want to Take You Higher." By now it was past four in the morning, still dark, but I could see more of the crowd in the predawn light. *Goddamn.* Even those I didn't see I could sense, between the smoke and the sound. I was thinking what would happen if I said something and they all said it back. What would that sound like? What would it be like? So I tried it. I took the microphone and spoke to everyone.

"What we would like to do is sing a song together. And you see what usually happens is you got a group of people that might sing and for some reasons that are not unknown anymore, they won't do it. Most of us need approval. Most of us need to get approval from our neighbors before we can actually let it all hang down. But what is happening here is we're going to try to do a singalong. Now a lot of people don't like to do it. Because they feel that it might be old-fashioned. But you must dig that it is not a fashion in the first place. It is a feeling. And if it was good in the past, it's still good. We would like to sing a song called 'Higher.' And if we could get everybody to join in, we'd appreciate it."

I sang, "I want to take you higher," and they sang back the last word, "higher." All of them. Damn.

We kept it going. I kept it going.

"Just say 'higher' and throw the peace sign up. It'll do you no harm. Still again, some people feel that they shouldn't because there are situations where you need approval to get in on something that could do you some good."

*Want to take you higher* went out. *Higher* came back. What the word meant widened. It wasn't just keeping yourself up with a good mood or good drugs. It was defeating anything that could bring you down. It was an instruction how to go over your problems. It was a solution.

"If you throw the peace sign up and say 'higher,' you get everybody to do it. There's a whole lot of people here and a whole lot of people that might not want to do it, because if they can somehow get around it, they feel there are enough people to make up for it. On and on. Et cetera. Et cetera. We're going to try 'higher' again, and if we can get everybody to join in, we'd appreciate it. It'll do you no harm."

*Want to take you higher* / *Higher.* A wave crashing onto the shore of the stage.

Way up on the hill . . .

*Want to take you higher!* / *Higher!*
*Want to take you higher!* / *Higher!*
*Want to take you higher!* / *Higher!*

The call, the response. It felt like church. By then the film crew was fully in place. The horns went up into the sky.

The set closed out with "Love City" and "Stand!" Chip Monck, who was the official announcer of the festival, came on the PA to tell people not to lean too hard on the fence. A wallet had been lost. Anthony Penza, go to the information center.

When the show was over, we were wet and cold. Cynthia was shivering. I gave her my jacket to keep her warm. We wandered off to try to find some food. All we could locate was a table of sandwiches but they were already spoiled. You could see the meat walking. I don't remember how I left, maybe the same way

I came in, but I wasn't there to see Jimi (not Roy Rogers) close the festival.

By the next day it was clear that the festival had been a big deal, and that we had been a major part of that deal. I hadn't thought of it as a competition until the results started to come in. The festival had put a spotlight on lots of groups, but us and Jimi the most. I was getting phone calls nonstop. What really made it clear to me was when David Kapralik gave me a Stellavox tape recorder, one of the best in the world. *This is a nice motherfucker,* I thought. *Why would you give that to me?* But I didn't ask him. I asked myself. And then I answered myself: Because I kicked ass.

After Woodstock, everything glowed. The band's price went up, which meant that we didn't have to limit ourselves to the kinds of gigs we were playing before. No more nightclubs if we didn't want.

We all got a boost. Everyone bought cars and houses. But I was singled out: front man, songwriter, rock performer. If there was a picture next to an article about us, more and more often it was a picture of me.

I stayed around the Bay Area when I could. Lou Gordon, nice guy, good talker, came up to Clear Lake, where I had a seventeen-foot runabout, and the two of us spent the afternoon out on the water, watching the sun bounce off the surface of the lake.

But it also felt like it was time to be on the move. I sent Debbie down to L.A. to set up an office. Her sister Kitsaun moved down there too. L.A. was making more sense as a place to be. It had studios and musicians and executives, the spine of the industry. I remember once being there, either for a gig or a recording session, and playing basketball with Clive Davis at the Beverly Hills Hotel. He played real good, too.

Debbie and I were still a going concern, but that didn't mean I wasn't also seeing other girls. One of them, Stephanie Swanigan, came to me when David Kapralik hired her to work with the band. She was a beauty queen. That's not just an opinion. She had won Miss Bronze and Miss Seal Beach. Stephanie was my secretary. She had a professionalism to her. She got to setting the office in order.

By that point, more people had joined the inner circle. Along with the glowing, there was growing. I had met a guy named JR who was working at Madison Square Garden. He came aboard for help and security. JR knew some guys, but was a lawyer, too. He had a big laugh. "Sly," he'd say, "ha ha ha." Or sometimes "Freddie, ha ha ha." Or "Larry, ha ha ha." He was loads of fun. If we were in New York he might have us over to his mother's house for a big spaghetti dinner and he'd leave in the middle, with the rest of us still there, to take care of business. Whatever needed done in any area, that's what JR did. Some things were spoken about and some were not. He carried a .32 caliber revolver with him, a shining silver Smith and Wesson. He handled that as well as he handled everything else, which was perfectly.

I kept an apartment at Sunset and San Vicente in West Hollywood. Debbie and Stephanie used it for management and stayed there as well. Jim Brown, the football player and actor, used to come by with his motorcycle at night and try to get the girls to come out with him. He was trying to get them onto his bike and then, after that, off of it. When I heard about it, I wasn't in town, but I sent word that I wasn't happy.

Then I was in L.A. for a few days and saw him out there, revving in the dark. We had a talk. I thought I had been clear, but it was clear to me that he didn't care what I thought. JR came out of the apartment on my behalf. He told Jim Brown, in his own special way, to go fuck himself. "Whatever you're doing, don't,"

was one of the things he said. Jim Brown was a tough motherfucker. I don't know if he made a habit of letting other people tell
him what to do. But he caught the habit that night. He nodded.
"Okay," he said. He started his bike and drove off.

After a few months at that apartment, I moved into a house
near where Coldwater Canyon comes off Mulholland. It used to
be Isaac Hayes's place but after his movement it was mine. I
moved in with my equipment, my clothes, my cars, and my guns.
It's how my daddy had been raised, gun in the house, gun in the
car, so it's how I was raised, too. I started with a few and added
more and more: a .38, two 16-gauge shotguns, a .22/410 over/
under. I liked collecting them, but they also made me feel safer.
There were lots of people coming in and out of the house and not
all of them were bringing flowers.

That place was a party. At first, my older sister, Loretta, came
down to help me manage the house and keep things in order, but
they got out of order and unmanageable pretty quick after that.
Drugs were accelerating by that point. I didn't even have to buy
them. People gave me powder or pills because I was famous or
they wanted my approval or they were trying to establish a
relationship on that basis. It would have been rude to refuse. I
had a violin case filled with cocaine that I would carry around
town with me. We found a doctor to sell me pills, Placidyls in
batches, and I would keep them in a safe. Depending on the time
of day I was in some kind of way, coming from or heading back
toward powder or pills. I never used in front of my parents, but
they still had advice: "You got to put that nasty stuff down, boy."
I didn't put it down. It picked up.

Bubba had been in jail. When he got out, he came down to
L.A. along with a friend of his named JB. They moved in at
Coldwater to keep the house running smoothly. Bubba had always been interested in Rose, and he got interested again, even
though she was still with Larry. That was fine with me. It wasn't

because of the way that Larry was acting, making a spotlight around himself. Some people took exception to it. I saw it but it didn't bother me. I just liked how Bubba and Rose got on with each other and liked it more the closer they got.

Everyone's heart was beating: one of the other arrivals from San Francisco was Eddie Chin, real last name Elliott, but he used to tell girls he was part Chinese, because some of them were and he wanted to make a good impression. One of the girls he told was Vet, who wasn't, but he made a good impression on her anyway.

That was the era of the knit hat. Women around the band made them constantly. It was an occupation of the times, especially if you were a girlfriend whose boyfriend was a musician. Stephanie made mine.

It was also the time that PCP entered the picture, angel dust in the City of Angels. I don't know who brought it around first, maybe a guy who knew a guy who knew someone in the house. You could snort it as powder or smoke it in dipped cigarettes. It threw your perspective off, which I liked. But it wasn't for everybody. It could send people down a road. The PCP completed the picture or maybe it just cluttered up a scene that was already crowded with coke and pills.

There are many tales from that time that people like to tell, that have been told over the years. Freddie said that at a party I appeared at the top of the stairs and announced to guests that they were welcome to my cocaine but should be careful about using what other people brought around, meaning the PCP. "That'll be trouble," I said, and two people who didn't listen ended up in the hospital. Bubba said that once I was walking around the house like I was in a trance, stiff as a plank, asking about my phone book in a voice that he didn't recognize. He went upstairs and got a pistol to keep the peace, and when I saw the piece I ran upstairs to my bedroom and stayed there for the rest of the day. Stephanie said that the group at Coldwater briefly included a young rich white girl, nineteen or twenty, who owned horses and drove a Mercedes but preferred hanging with musicians and using drugs. She had taken too much PCP and broken down completely, to the point where she needed to relearn even her own name. When Stephanie heard about that, she flushed my stash.

What can I say to all of that? Yes, no, no? No, yes, no? Maybe I was standing on a chair instead of the top of the stairs when I came down to warn people about the other dealer's stash. Maybe I asked Bubba to get me a lighter instead of a phone book, or maybe he was holding a newspaper instead of a gun. Maybe the girl was half-Japanese. The details in the stories people tell shift over time, in their minds and in mine, in part or in whole, each time they're told. That's what makes them stories. Telling stories about the past, about the way your life crosses into the lives of those around you, is what people do, what they have always done. Those people aren't trying to hurt you. They're trying to set the record straight. But a record's not straight, especially when you're not. It's a circle with a spiral inside it. Every time a story is told it's a test of memory and motive. Telling stories isn't right and it isn't wrong. It isn't evil but it isn't good. It's the name of the game but a shame just the same.

In October the Family Stone taped an appearance for *Music Scene*, a new ABC variety show. The first episode, about a month before us, had a concept performance by James Brown, who sang his new song "World" while he walked through a crowd, appealing to people of all races and ages for love and understanding. Each person he reached out to turned away.

We played it straighter, a pair of medleys on a small white stage. I was late to the taping but Dave Kapralik had told me to take my time, even pretend I was at the doctor, because our set list had a song on it that might give the censors pause. The problem song wasn't in our first medley, which included "Everyday People" and "Dance to the Music." The second medley started easy, with "Hot Fun in the Summertime," but then switched midway to the problem: "Don't Call Me Nigger, Whitey." I wanted people to hear its message, which I explained to a magazine a few months later: "You can't scream that because you are a color you are anything. You are black—you are black, that's all. You are among people who've been mistreated a lot. But it doesn't necessarily mean a white person next door is responsible. His grandfather may have killed yours, but he himself may love you."

Not everyone agreed. The Black Panther Party had come up in Oakland around the same time as us and the rumor was that they didn't like the way I was doing things, that I was stepping too much toward what White America wanted, that they didn't like that I had Jerry and Greg in the band, not to mention Dave Kapralik behind the scenes. Maybe they said something to someone else but not to me directly. I knew Huey Newton. We hung but we didn't really rap. Eldridge Cleaver once sent word that he wanted me to make a substantial donation to the cause, substantial meaning six figures. I didn't have an issue with being black. I was proud of it. But I couldn't get behind the way the Panthers expressed their message, the calls for violence.

The funny thing was that some white people thought we were too militant. Where were we really? Somewhere in the middle, which was the best place to be if you wanted to keep on finding solutions. If you got far out on one side or another, you were a threat, and threats were being eliminated. That thought did cause me to spend more time at home than I otherwise might have. And as for changing the band, even if they had asked, I wouldn't have done it. That was the entire point, to rise above that. Divisions were subtractions.

The end of the decade rose into sight. But things were falling too. In December Fred Hampton was assassinated in Chicago, in his own apartment, during a raid by the FBI, the Chicago cops, and the Cook County State's Attorney's office. Hampton was sleeping—probably drugged to defenselessness by his bodyguard William O'Neal, who was acting as a double agent—and his girl-friend, Deborah Johnson, nine months pregnant with their first child, was asleep next to him when officers came in. The cops took Deborah Johnson out and then shot Fred Hampton in the head. Two days later the Rolling Stones played at Altamont Speedway and hired the Hells Angels as security. The crowd was rowdy and one of the Angels stabbed a black kid named Meredith Hunter to death. Eighteen years old, younger than my youngest sister. People analyzed these things as the end of the year and also as the end of the decade and also as the end of everything that the decade had meant. I had a simpler reaction. I hated that they happened.

We said goodbye to the sixties with a new single, double-A like a battery. One side was "Everybody Is a Star," smooth and gentle like "Hot Fun in the Summertime," vocals traded off among the band. The message was real. You could look up at the sky, and everything up there was a star, or you could look across you on the earth and see the same thing. If people could all be light, they would be all right.

The other song on the single, "Thank You (Falettinme Be Mice Elf Agin)," came in quicker and thicker. Larry had the bass down, thumbing and thumping. Cynthia's and Jerry's horns sometimes stabbed like a Morse code message, sometimes slid across the groove like a siren coming closer and then going away. Freddie played like a motherfucker. Rose sang like a mother-fucker. Greg held the whole thing down.

Like so many other songs it meant what it said. I wanted to

thank people in general, the everyday people, if they let me be me, if they let others be others, if others let them be them. We exist to coexist.

But there were other things in there, too. The way I spelled the title was one of them—mice, elf, small humble things that were reminders of how big the rest of the world was. You had to stand up straight to be seen at all.

And there were forces working against standing up straight. I tried to get to them in the lyrics. The song started with a wrestling match between me and the devil. Was I trying to get out from under celebrity or trying to get over on it? It was hard to enjoy pleasure when there was business to be done: "Thank you for the party but I could never stay / Many things on my mind, words in the way."

After the first two verses, there was a bridge where I crossed back through old song titles and lyrics. I wanted people to listen to the old songs, and not just listen, but really hear what they were saying. Instead, people had used the songs as bricks to build up our fame. And fame had brought appreciation and admiration, but also envy ("flamin' eyes burning into you"), because some people were unhappily trapped by obligations ("many men missin' much, hatin' what they do"). Could people use the messages of the songs to set themselves free? And what if they couldn't? I had an idea of what if they couldn't: "Dying young is hard to take but selling out is harder." That line stuck in people's minds like "different strokes for different folks" had the year before. It was a cutting song that refused to stitch itself back up.

During the recording, when the song sounded like it was where it needed to be, when more work on it would have just been more work, I called the band over. "That's about all I can do today," I said, "if you don't mind."

**PART TWO**

# Listen to the Voices

# 7

✳

## Hot Fun in the Summertime

### (1969–1970)

**W**e were on the air already. Dick Cavett handed me a glass of water, remarked on his show's entertainment budget. "Free water for those who request it," he said. I drank it and then laughed. (It was 1970 on the screen but 2020 in the room. I was watching the interview back, not for the first time. Of course I watched old interviews. Who wouldn't? When there's a record kept, play it. Time moves forward and also stays where it was. Two different times at the same time. I laughed again at Cavett's joke. Free water upon request!)

"Mr. S. . . . ," Dick Cavett said. Then he said "Mr. . . ." again. "What'll I call you, actually?" (This was the first question he asked me, and in some ways the best. It got to so much so quickly.)

"Mr. S. . . . Mr.," I said back to him. (I wasn't mocking, just mirroring. The audience took it for comedy, burst out in laughter of their own.)

"I'm going to be put on," Cavett said. The audience laughed, but I was a little serious, too, so I went on. What he called me didn't matter, I said. It was only for means of identification. "A person wants to be known by his name or something similar to it," Cavett said.

"I can feel when you're talking to me," I said. "I don't care what you call me." (I meant it. Names were only labels on containers. But now, fifty years later, he had me thinking. What in fact should he call the man sitting opposite him, not just in a chair but in black leather pants, black fringed jacket, tall hat that looked like a big black bell, gold metal pin fastened to the side of it that matched the gold chain around his neck? That was Sly, right? Look at Mr. Stewart.)

Of the talk-show hosts, Cavett was my favorite. He was in order. We weren't exactly friends but like I said, I could feel when he was talking to me. Even so, I was a little nervous, which he noticed. (It was a miracle I was there at all. Earlier that week, I had been in Cherry Hill, New Jersey, visiting Muhammad Ali. Ali had been on ice as a boxer since 1967, when he was stripped of his title for refusing induction into the Army. In 1970 he was going to court, trying to get back in the ring. After Cherry Hill, I didn't want to go to New York, didn't want to go to the show. It was nerves and it was exhaustion and it was a question: What did I need with another appearance? But everyone told me I was making a mistake. Go on the show, they said. I ended up on the show, on the set, in a chair next to Cavett, nervous, noticed, feeling it when he was talking to me.)

Cavett and I bantered and then got down to it. "Tell me something," he said. "I know you're responsible for all the music, that you write it. Do you sit down and write it?"

"Sometimes I stand up." Another laugh.

"Yes," he said. "You know that Hemingway wrote on top of the icebox."

I wasn't trying to match wits, and I told him so. "I write in a mirror," I said. His head tilted in a confused direction. "The reason why I do that is that I can critique myself. I can react spontaneously before I realize that I'm going along with what I'm doing, dislike it or like it before I know I'm doing it."

This time the audience laugh got under my skin a bit.

"I'm serious," I said. "You don't have to write it down. I'm writing notes and words, melodies and rhythms and things. And I sit in front of the mirror and I write and then I look up and something happens and I go 'ohhh.'" I made a disappointed face to illustrate. (Fifty years later, watching myself across the distance, I tried to make the same face and failed. Disappointing.)

The interview picked up speed. Cavett asked about my history studying composition. He asked about my DJ days. He also asked about how I felt about influencing young people. "Everybody's an influence, I guess," I said. "Everybody has an influence on a number of people. I don't think in our case it is necessarily the young. It's more the young of mind, you know, and some of them are chronologically much older than yourself but they are younger than the both of us."

"How old would you say you are?" he said.

"Would I say?" I said. Now the head tilting in confusion was mine. "Just ask me."

"How old are you?"

"Twenty-six."

"I would have guessed, I don't know, a year or two older. I don't know why."

"I sound kind of heavy to you?"

"It's not that. Listen, if I was to join your group . . ."

"What is it, then?"

"I wanted to ask you a serious question."

"I know. I wanted to ask you one, too. I was first."

Cavett looked out to the audience. "He's right about that." He turned back toward me. "You want to ask me a serious question?"

"How come you thought I was two or three years older?"

"I don't have the slightest idea."

"Some people don't know anything," I said. "Some people don't have the slightest idea." The audience inhaled a little or was it my imagination.

"Name one of them," Cavett said. The audience exhaled a little or was it my imagination. "But if a guy like me . . . suppose I had a background in music and wanted to play in your group. This is kind of a serious question, kind of silly question at the same time. Could I dress like this and play with your group?"

"Any way you like," I said.

"Wouldn't it look funny, though, somebody dressed with a tie?"

"If people were judging the way you were dressing," I said.

"There'd probably be a certain pressure on me."

"There's a pressure on all of us," I said.

✳ ✳ ✳

There was a pressure on all of us. Mine was Epic pressure. The label was waiting for a follow-up to *Stand!* Sitting there in Cavett's chair, I was a year past Woodstock. Was that enough time to put a new record together? During the first half of 1970, James Brown released three albums (*Ain't It Funky* in January, *Soul on Top* in April, *It's a New Day—Let a Man Come In* in June) and would have two more before Christmas (*Sex Machine* in September and *Hey America* in November). But James Brown wasn't having the year I was having.

The single we had released at the end of December, "Thank You (Falettinme Be Mice Elf Agin)" and "Everybody Is a Star," reached the top of the charts in February 1970, exactly a year after "Everyday People." The next month, we made the cover of *Rolling Stone*. The caption for the cover photo said "The Sly

Stone Family," which put a little different spin on things. The article covered a wide range of topics: how I felt about the crowd at our *Music Scene* appearance back in December ("I don't care if they rush the stage. We love it. Even on TV, if they rush us and they can't see us on camera, I don't care"), high school ("It was boring for me 'cause either I was too smart, or too dumb to realize what I could learn"), the next record. The label wasn't just asking for it anymore. They were naming it—they had a title, *The Incredible and Unpredictable Sly and the Family Stone*, that was starting to appear in ads. The way they wrote it left at least one question open. Where was the adjective attaching? Was the whole group unpredictable or just me?

And what would a new record be, exactly? "We could do some good songs," I told *Rolling Stone*, "but that would be just another LP. Now you expect a group to come out with another LP and another. There's got to be more to it. But what else can you do? The only thing that sounds interesting is something that ties in with a play that finishes what an LP starts to say, and the LP will be important on account of the play." I shrugged at my own idea. "Maybe it's impossible. What can you put on vinyl or acetate or plastic? Not just something like a funny-shaped LP cover. Gotta be something it says or does. Maybe melt the LP and turn it into something. Like hash you can smoke."

That week after the *Rolling Stone* story hit newsstands, the *Woodstock* movie hit theaters. Appeared and stayed: It ended up being one of the biggest movies of the year. I didn't see it but someone told me I was the star.

Suddenly our music was everywhere, not just in the form of our songs on the radio but in the form of our sound in other people's songs. Motown seemed especially interested. The Jackson 5's second single, "ABC," used our blueprint (back in 1968, in "Harmony," we had even had a simple as one-two-three and easy as A-B-C moment), and the Temptations and Norman

Whitfield had moved on from classic Motown to what people were calling "psychedelic soul." It sounded familiar: cloud mine.

If other people were going to build on my sound, I figured I might as well do the same. David Kapralik and I set up a record label where I could sign and produce groups other than the Family Stone. We named it Stone Flower. I liked the balance of it: hard things and soft things, dead things and living things, heavy things and light things.

We got distribution from Atlantic Records and offices on Vine Street and I went in search of new acts. I started close to home with Little Sister, a vocal group that had been backing us since the early days: my actual little sister Vet along with Tiny Mouton and Mary McCreary. Tiny had the biggest voice.

I gave Little Sister a song called "You're the One," about personal responsibility—this time, the underdog wasn't behind because of other people's hang-ups but because he was holding himself back. I arranged it in bright colors, warm electric piano and soaring horns held to earth by a knot of guitar and bass. Another song, "Stanga," used a drum machine and guitar like stretched-out fingers to set off downbeat lyrics. Their third song was an almost churchy cover of "Somebody's Watching You" that sounded like it was done under cover of night.

We also had a band called 6ix, pronounced "Six." There was a rumor about how we came up with the name—that the "ix" was 9 in Roman numerals and the overall name meant 69. That wasn't true. Nine was my favorite number, for many reasons. "Sylvester" has nine letters. Cats have nine lives, including Sylvester the cat. "The Cat" has six letters. Flip that number upside-down and it's nine again. And nine is the highest single number. But 6ix got its name for a simpler reason: there were six people in it. The band came together around a harmonica player named Marvin Braxton, who had grown up in Cleveland, worked as a hot walker at racetracks, and ended up in the mailroom at CBS. His nickname was Crazy Marvin Braxton, because of how he acted onstage. We used 6ix to back Little Sister live and put out singles under their name, too. "I'm Just Like You," a cage of beats with vocals poking through the bars and harmonica hanging there, went on a single with "Dynamite," a slow-funk cover of a song from our debut.

After 6ix came Hicks—Joe Hicks, a singer from San Francisco who I met in L.A. Joe was laughy and not in the same way as JR. He would ha ha for no reason at all or tell a joke and then ha ha quick before anyone else could react. I gave Joe a song I had written called "Life and Death in G&A," and it was filled with philosophy. Do opposites attract or do they dissolve each other? Is what matters the way things are or the way they seem? Do you always understand your own feelings well enough to communicate them clearly to another person? Joe's version sounded like the other Stone Flower material, a drum-machine frame with vocals stretched over it. There was a full-band cover version by a group called Abaco Dream rumored to be the Family Stone in disguise. Rumored.

To find new artists and more musicians to back our acts when they played live, I held open call at a rehearsal space out on Santa Monica Boulevard, right near the Hollywood Freeway. That was the project the *Rolling Stone* article mentioned. I ran the room and brought some people with me. Buddy Miles was there, just a few months before the New Year's show with Jimi Hendrix that would be *Band of Gypsys*. At that show, Buddy and Jimi played a song that Buddy wrote called "We Gotta Live Together," which borrowed a section from another song I did with Joe Hicks, "Home Sweet Home." Buddy made noise, lots of it. He wasn't that funky but he was around often.

Stephanie was there, too, as recording secretary. We saw a bunch of players, and I tried to get down in it with them. If they were playing bass, I would join in on organ. If they were playing keyboard, I joined in on bass. We took a few names and then I drove back to Stone Flower in the Cord, went into my office, where the desk was covered with a purple rug, shag the color of my Jag.

New friends started to come around. I began to hang with Jim Ford, a white dude who wrote songs that some people called country, but to me were just songs. I said on a talk show once that Jimmy was "the baddest white man on the planet" and that songs like "Dr. Handy's Dandy Candy" and "Niki Hoeky" were "destroying the minds of people who have been led to believe that the world was flat."

Jimmy and I were close for a while off and on. He was more raw than he seemed. He thought I would hit it off with Bobby Womack. Bobby had been singing since he was a kid, like Billy Preston, like me, first with his brothers as a gospel group and then behind Sam Cooke, who changed their name to the Valentinos and produced hits for them like "Lookin' for a Love" and "It's All Over Now." When Sam Cooke died, Bobby married Sam's widow, which made people mad. Record stations would throw his records in the trash. He toured with Ray Charles and was just getting his solo career going.

Jim put me and Bobby together. According to Bobby, at our first meeting he was dressed like R&B singers used to dress, in a suit, carrying a briefcase. He said that I told him that he wasn't a businessman and didn't need to dress that way, that he should dress natural, and that I opened up his briefcase and what fell out was a muffin and a sandwich. I don't know what fell out but Bobby and I fell in together. We got on well. He had a hell of a soul yell and he could play guitar like a motherfucker.

The Family Stone was in higher demand than ever. We rolled like thunder through Detroit, South Bend, Gainesville, Phoenix, San

Antonio. A travelogue sounds easy when it's just words on a page. Even if you're looking at a map, you can just move your finger from place to place. But if you have to actually be located at those locations at the times specified, it's complicated, draining, and boring, with only the energy of the shows to keep the whole thing lit. Sometimes I didn't make it and shows had to be rescheduled.

Woodstock was still a recent memory, and every city wanted its own version to see if lightning could strike twice. There was a July festival on Randall's Island in New York designed as a large liberation event, with participation from groups like the Black Panthers, the Young Lords (the Latino version of the Panthers), the Yippies, the Gay Liberation Front, and more. They booked lots of acts that had been at Woodstock: Jimi, Ravi Shankar, John Sebastian, Joe Cocker. When Cocker canceled, we were slotted in as his replacement, but they couldn't work out the contracts, and we pulled out. Kapralik had to take the message to the Panthers and the Lords.

In Minneapolis a few days later, there was another Bethel reunion, the Open-Air Pop Festival, with us, Richie Havens, and the blues guitarist Johnny Winter. I didn't know Johnny well but I liked his look, his long white-blond hair and ghostly complexion. His brother Edgar, who was also an albino, was funkier. A few years later, when Edgar had a big hit with "Frankenstein," I ran into Johnny at a hotel. "What's up?" Johnny said. "Edgar!" I said. Johnny laughed hard at that.

The week after Open-Air Pop, we played in Milwaukee, at Summerfest, not on a large festival bill but as sole headliners. The city knew that kids would turn out for that one, that they would bring their blankets and fire up their joints and line the shores of Lake Michigan. No one was prepared for how many kids, though—newspapers had the crowd at 125,000 people, something like that. A band named Yesterday's Children opened for us, and during their set, the crowd pushed forward and got their hands up right near the band. I liked that kind of thing. I even prohibited promoters from putting guards between us and the audience. But people were passing out.

We were at our hotel downtown, the Pfister, and we were getting reports about the show. We heard that babies had to be passed back to safety. "Fuck that," I said. I didn't want to head straight into a storm.

The promoters came up with a replacement plan. First it was limos but by the time the limos got to the hotel the traffic was too heavy to get us out to the stage on time, so they came up with a replacement plan for the replacement plan, which involved ferrying me to the concert site by police boat. Yesterday's Children had to keep on playing until they were today's children and tomorrow's too. During their second set, which partly repeated their first, people started climbing up on the speakers, and the organizers had to come on over the PA and tell them to get down or there would be no Family Stone. The venue didn't have enough staff to enforce the threat so the rest of the crowd booed them down.

We went out. We were late but we were there. The microphones were weird. I took a shock on the mouth. And then it was a little bit of an angry game between us and the crowd and the promoters and the security. One report said that I refused to play unless the band got more weed. I don't remember that but it's not impossible. We got the crowd up for "Dance to the Music" and "You Can Make It If You Try" but the sound was bad and the day was hot and the crowd was restless, and our set ended quickly. Afterward police with nightsticks had to hold the crowd back so we could make our getaway. Hot time at the Summerfest.

The next day we were scheduled to play just down the lake, at Grant Park in Chicago, in a concert put on for free by the city as a show of goodwill. Many people got there early in the morning for a 4:00 p.m. show and started smoking and drinking.

The first group that went on was called Fat Water, a local blues-rock band. The crowd hadn't been told clearly to expect opening acts, and they weren't happy to see one. The assumption was that we were late or skipping out. Fat Water's set only lasted a few songs, and then the second act, the Flying Burrito Brothers, set up to play. They never got to start. Bottles and rocks started coming through the air. A piece of bench, torn clear, landed on the stage.

Because it was kids doing the throwing, because cops were watching, because it was Chicago, the unrest brought back memories of the Democratic National Convention two years earlier. Familiar habits took over. Cops started using nightsticks on the crowd and even throwing some of the rocks back at them. The crowd became a mob and the mob turned to mob violence. The final tally included store windows smashed, stores looted, more than 150 people injured, including more than 100 cops, and more than 160 arrests. A car was turned over and burned. A few people were shot.

The joke of it all was that I wasn't late. I was en route in a car with plenty of time to spare, hearing noises out the window, wondering what was up until someone told me. "Keep going," I said. I wanted to get onstage and calm the crowd. I would have hopped and switched to a police car to ride faster. But the cops wouldn't hear of it. There was no good way to get through, and anyway the riot had damaged the sound system.

After that, cities were suspicious of us, and not just us. Our Boston show was canceled because a Jackson 5 show a few weeks earlier hadn't been as easy as one-two-three and the mayor feared worse. At a summer festival at a ski resort in Connecticut, Powder Ridge, we were all ready to go when the locals got a judge to stop the whole concert. We had trouble with vans and buses, maybe not more than any other group, but more visible because they were feeding the story that I was the problem. Sly, late. Sly, missing. Sly, no-show. Stone, flown.

I tried to talk straight about it with a reporter, copped to the fact that while I was responsible for maybe 10 percent of the issue, the rest was road organization (or disorganization) and other circumstances beyond my control. But the issue didn't go away. It hung there around my neck. Somebody showed me an article with the headline "Is Sly Blowing Career?" Was that a joke about coke? Onstage Freddie might hand me a tissue if my nose was running or running away. I liked the last line of the article, which talked about the crowd's reaction when we finally came out onstage: "Anger toward the tardy performer is dissipated." But I only liked it for the language.

I spoke up, and not just to the press. I talked to promoters and managers. The problem was that other people talked right back, promising me that they would work it all out if I let them take charge. What they really meant was that they would charge me and take me. They were in business and that business was me.

I understood that I was being used. The problem was when I got misused. I was being asked to do more gigs in a month than there were days. Promoters would book me for two shows on the same night sometimes. It wasn't carelessness on their part. It was calculation. At a certain point we were required to put up a bond that would be forfeited if I missed curtain time. It might have been $50,000. So when I got incorrect information about when a show was starting, that money found its way into pockets. That was an incentive.

Lots of those things I didn't see clearly until later, but if I did catch a promoter pulling some kind of shit I would just walk away. I do regret leaving kids out in the audience without a show. What I should have done was to come out late and tell the audience what had happened and encourage them to get their money back. That way no one would make money: not me, maybe, but not the promoter either.

These stresses and others made a vise around me. Getting out of that required assistance. For energy, for traveling and performing, I took something to take me up. That was coke, mostly, and it could last all night if I played it right. But then I'd have to bring myself back down with pills. Sometimes, backstage, I would feel like I was swimming through something thick, but the second I hit the stage, I had a surge of sharpness. The crowd worked like its own kind of drug—and then I'd have to come down from that, too. I wasn't out in the yard, but I was still building a roller coaster.

# 8

✳

## Everybody Is a Star
### (1970–1971)

**N**ew York: Holiday Inn, Fifty-Seventh Street. Touring, tiring. Up the elevator to the eighteenth floor with Big Daddy, Larry, and Bubba. A few minutes later Freddie rushed into the room, out of breath, and told us that one of the bellboys who worked there had said something rude to Cynthia and then bumped her hard. An argument had broken out. Five of them had jumped on Freddie. Three more had jumped on Cynthia. I knew what to do immediately. Somebody had messed with us, which meant that I had to get a brick and make fo' sho' I left them quiverin' or still. I went back down with Freddie and Bubba and whoever else. Big Daddy might even have come down to see if we were doing it right. We found the guys and settled the score. Every time I saw one, I knocked him out. Bam! Bam! "It wasn't me," they'd say, but it was. Bam! At the end of the fight the police came to sort things out, see which bellboys got their bells rung. Somebody made peace with the cops—I'm pretty sure it was JR—and they went away.

\* \* \*

The record label wanted hits of a different kind. They were still asking about the album, a little louder each time. Kapralik kept telling me and I kept telling him that I understood. The record company had other things to do, other hits to handle: "I Never Promised You a Rose Garden," for example. I hadn't promised that or anything else.

When we wouldn't move, they did. Epic rereleased our first album, *A Whole New Thing*, with a new cover that showed me in the middle surrounded by a rainbow. In November, it was followed by *Greatest Hits*, which collected five songs from *Stand!*, four from before it, and the three recent singles ("Hot Fun in the Summertime," "Everybody Is a Star," and "Thank You [Falettinme Be Mice Elf Agin]"). I had said in interviews that I would never put out a greatest hits. I stood by that. I hadn't put it out. Epic had.

The cover art was a collage. On top were multiples of all the band members copied like rays of the sun—a bunch of Larrys, a bunch of Cynthias, a bunch of Jerrys. The bottom half of the image was the sun that gave off those rays, a picture of me in a car. It was my 1936 Cord, a car I loved. It wasn't an original. It was a replica I bought down in Los Angeles. But the replica was beautiful. On top of that, it *moved*. It was faster than dynamite.

I had moved, too, out of the Coldwater house to a place that fit even better. It was at 783 Bel Air Road. I got the house from John Phillips of the Mamas and the Papas. Right after I moved in, I was walking around the lawn and found a bunch of plastic bottles hidden like Easter eggs. Inside the bottles were pills. I could have called someone to come pick them up, but I kept them. That's how that place was. You might open a drawer or look in the back of a closet and find a stash.

I liked many of the houses I lived in, but I liked that one the best. It was across the street from where they filmed the *Beverly Hillbillies*, which was a turn-on: I could turn on the TV, tune in the show, and realize I was right there. And there was a hidden recording studio in the place. You went up to the top floor and pushed a panel on the wall at the top of the stairs, open-sesame-style. It had been built for John Phillips, red walls with lots of padding, thick carpet.

There were people around all the time. My dad was there for a while. The band came in and out, some staying for a party, some for a while. I had visitors: Bobby, Billy, Jimmy Ford, Buddy Miles, Johnny "Guitar" Watson, Ike Turner. We didn't keep a guest book.

There were, as always, dogs. Everyone in and around the band had them: Jerry had a Great Pyrenees, Larry had a Russian wolfhound. At Coldwater, I had a bulldog named Max, a great dane named Stoner, and a schipperke named Shadow. At Bel Air I had my favorite dog, a pit bull named Gun. He was my best friend. He was crazy. He would chase his tail in circles, not for a minute or for an hour but forever. He couldn't sleep. At first people thought he had been stung by a wasp but you don't get stung by a wasp forever. When it became clear the problem was something larger some of those same people said he needed to be put down. Then a suggestion came in that we dock his tail so that he would have less to chase. That settled him down, not completely but enough.

Gun was small when he was a puppy, like any dog, but when he was grown he was really grown. He must have weighed sixty pounds, and it was solid muscle. He and I ran the house. We would go through halls, him on a leash, me holding it, looking for people. It was a game of hide-and-seek, though the seeking happened before anyone could hide. Bobby Womack was afraid of Gun, so when he heard us coming he would go behind furniture or into closets. Once I went into a room and saw Bobby crouched up on a pool table. He put a finger to his lips to shush me up. I winked at him and walked out but I don't know what he was thinking. Gun could have gotten up on top of that table no problem.

I also had a baboon named Erfy, meaning earthy. I forget where I got him. Baboon store? Erfy used to tease Gun and then, just as Gun's temper was spilling over, leap away, higher than a pool table. One day Erfy jumped away too slowly. Gun lunged and got a baboon foot in his jaw and then more than that. He didn't just catch Erfy. He killed him. And he didn't just kill him. He forced him to have sex after he was dead. I didn't see it myself but I heard about it from everyone.

What I did see was everything else. Coldwater had taken things up a level. Bel Air did that again, on a bigger scale. You could walk into the house at any time of day or night and see coke cut into lines on a glass table or some motherfucker half-asleep with a gun on his chest or women in a room waiting for someone. I had a safe upstairs for Seconals, Tuinals, Placidyls, and since I was the only one with the combination I was the only one who could take a combination of them. Thank you for the party. I could never stop. But there were also days that were nothing but normal. Steve Paley might come over in the morning when I was cleaning up from the night before or having cereal for breakfast.

That music I made there had a different feel, and some people weren't feeling it. Greg decided to leave the band. What was happening around the house wasn't his scene, especially since I was putting down some of the drums with machines—I had a Maestro Rhythm King, which I liked setting up and programming. I brought in a guy named Gerry Gibson for a minute, though a minute after that he was gone, too. Most of the time a new song would start with me: I would pick up a guitar and lay down a track myself, and then add a bass line or some organ. I worked in the studio, at home, in my Winnebago. I knew that the new record was taking a while. I knew that we were taking our time and everyone else's, too. Some people said I didn't have any clocks in the house, and while I can neither confirm nor deny that, it sounds right.

Taking time, making time. Debbie was gone at some point, no hard feelings, just a feeling that things were no longer easy. Stephanie was still on the scene, and plenty of other girls came to hang or play. I met Claudia Martin, Dean Martin's daughter. She walked right up to me and made eyes. It was clear what she wanted but I didn't let it go any further. It wasn't that she was too young. She was right around my age. But I wasn't going to mess with it.

Some of the women weren't my age. Steve Paley visited me once and told me that as he had driven up, he had seen a bus with a bunch of old people, mostly women, parked out front. "What's up?" he said. "You have all these white-haired fans."

I laughed. "No, no," I said. "Jeanette MacDonald." Before the house had belonged to John Phillips, it had belonged to a Hollywood talent manager, and before that it had been the home of Jeanette MacDonald and Gene Raymond, Hollywood stars of the thirties and forties. They had called it Twin Gables and owned plenty of dogs as well. The buses were driving up to give their passengers a glimpse of the past.

Work visits, social visits. Many were both. Jeffrey Bowen came over to the house. Jeffrey had been a big man at Motown and with Holland-Dozier-Holland and had produced for everyone from Marvin Gaye to the Temptations. When he dropped in at Bel Air, he brought his wife, Ruth Copeland, a white girl, English. Ruth was a singer, first in London, then in Detroit. Jeffrey wanted to make her a star, and he wanted to give me a large sum of money to produce her. I liked Ruth, and I didn't always like how Jeffrey acted with her. I brought her back into the studio with me and left Jeffrey out with everybody else. A few minutes passed and a few more. Ruth and I stayed in the studio.

Jeffrey came knocking at the door. I sent for Bubba. "Man," I said to him, "put that motherfucker up out of here." Bubba carried the message. Jeffrey couldn't believe it. "I gotta go?" he said.

"You got to hit it, man," Bubba said. "That's it. That's all."

But Jeffrey didn't leave. He started moving toward the spot in the wall where the studio door was. Bubba got over to him and asked him what he thought he was doing. "I'm going to get my wife," he said.

Bubba told him to wait there. He came back and gave me the update. "Man wants his wife."

"She can stay," I said. "He has to go." Bubba went back to Jeffrey, gave him the bad news, and put him out. I never did make an album for Ruth.

In August we were at the Isle of Wight Festival, which was the biggest one yet, bigger than Woodstock, and again with plenty of echoes—Hendrix, the Who, Jefferson Airplane, Melanie. Many of the acts hadn't been at Bethel, though, from Joni Mitchell to Tiny Tim to the Doors to Miles Davis. Some people said that was when Miles started paying close attention to the music we were making. He may have already been heading that way— *Bitches Brew* had been out for a few months—but the *Jack Johnson* soundtrack he released the next year went even further in our direction.

We had a similar time slot to Woodstock, too, going on early on Sunday morning. I don't remember much about the performance except that Rose wasn't with us and the crowd wasn't always, either. At the end of our set a guy got up from the crowd and made a speech about justice or injustice and people all around him started booing. A beer can flew out of the audience and hit Freddie or at least his guitar. That settled it: no encore.

And then it was a continental affair, Germany, France, the Netherlands, then back to England, then Italy for Venice and Rome. If there were frequent flier miles back then, we would have owned the airlines.

In mid-September, we were in London to play at the Lyceum. After that—that night, the next night, hard to say through the haze of what was just about to happen—Freddie and I met up with Ginger Baker, the drummer from Cream. Ginger showed off some high-quality coke, pharmaceutical grade, and then he mentioned a big party that night where Jimi would be. He had an idea of sharing the coke with Jimi, only the best for the best.

I was eager to see Jimi. We were scheduled to have a jam session the night before, or maybe that night, but Jimi had gone to Ronnie Scott's instead to jam with Eric Burdon and War. And Jimi wasn't at the party either. "We'll catch him tomorrow," someone said. As it turns out, there was no tomorrow, at least for Jimi. From what the news said later, he had been out and around all day, buying clothes, drinking wine, taking speed, meeting with his manager about business, writing poetry and music, smoking hash, dropping in and out of parties. At around three in the morning, he had gone back to the Samarkand Hotel, the apartment building where one of his girlfriends, Monika Dannemann, was staying. Accounts after that are hard to follow or to figure, but at some point Monika woke up and couldn't get Jimi up at all. He was dead in the bed.

Someone called me in the morning. I heard the news but I couldn't take it in fully. By which I mean my head was already full. We had commitments: gigs in Newcastle, in Leicester, in Sheffield, in Venice, in Rome. Focus and energy were hard to come by. Wherever the breaking point was, we were right near it.

We did a show from the grounds of Kasteel Groeneveld in Baarn in the Netherlands. I think it was the week before Jimi died. It might have been the week after. If it was, we didn't say.

The world wasn't done being done with people. Less than a week after Jimi died, Janis Joplin did also. Bobby knew her—he had written a song on her last album and been to see her a few days before her death—and I knew her too. Once I was in my house and came outside and she was in my car. She told me she needed a ride. She had strong feelings about something she wanted to talk to me about. She was a good singer and a bad bitch.

Back at home we weren't getting booked any less, but I was missing more shows. If before it had been 90 percent bad booking and 10 percent me being tired, it had tilted another 10 percent toward tired. The weariness was spreading but I couldn't show it in the music.

We played Tanglewood in July at the music shed, not too warm for summer but windy and storms in the area. Marion Williams, the gospel singer, performed before us, and during the last part of her show the kids started crowding in to get better positioning. The shed held around five thousand but then there were ten, twelve, fifteen. I was late but not for any reasons other than weather: flights were hard to come by and I had to charter a helicopter from New York.

Work, play, play for work. It blurred the year. I have memories of faces popping up, though I can't pin them to a page of the calendar.

Richard Pryor came around that year. I knew him from way back. I was hanging with Redd Foxx's daughter Debbie so I went to Redd's club out on La Cienega. Redd didn't know about me and Debbie so I hung quietly in the garage area in the back of the place. "Hello," someone said. It wasn't a normal hello. It came in high and low at the same time, a funky wavering voice. That was Richard. Comedians used to open for bands, and Richard was one of the acts that went on before us at the Garden back in 1970. After that I would call him in the middle of the night just to come over and bring his energy. He was so funny even when he wasn't doing anything other than being. He would dance weird, speak weird. He was only ever him.

I was getting some weed and Marvin Gaye walked up to get some from me. I gave it to him. It was Marvin Gaye.

Jim Brown came by my house but didn't come inside. He stayed on the outside and played basketball.

At a party in London—not on the same trip where I saw Ginger and missed Jimi—Bill Cosby sat on a couch off to the side, a red couch, leaning back like a little king, shirt off and girls rubbing lotion on his chest. They seemed like they were doing it because they wanted to. But there was a feeling around him, a sideways vibe. Otherwise, he was just all right, cool enough but not with a capital C.

Bobby Womack and I were out on the road, in some city, at some hotel, and he had a backup singer I wanted to see. I asked Bobby which room she was staying in, and he got my drift, and we went down there, him and me and a couple of other guys. We got into the room somehow and saw her in the bed sleeping. She sensed our presence and woke up startled. She had a get-the-fuck-out look on her face, and so we got the fuck out of Pam Grier's room.

Whenever we went to Madison Square Garden, we had a Garden party. We sold the place out more times than I can count, and I can count to ten at least. We had some East Coast dates scheduled for the fall of 1971, Philly, New Haven, and three nights in New York.

The audiences might have expected that I would tell them

what to do, like at Woodstock, but I was past that. "Sit down," I said. "Stand up. I don't care." I wanted them to do their thing while we did ours. We put down a rhythm and the crowd picked it up. The shows earned their attention and also earned: I think the three-night stand grossed about a half million dollars. One paper said that I was in the "same class as Aristotle Onassis" but I wasn't attending class.

When you're at the top of the mountain, there's nowhere to go but down, and *The New York Times* had that idea in mind. Its review of the show was mostly an essay about how we were slipping, and it started with a crack about how we were late: "How does the old story go? When your girl friend's late, you flatter her by explaining that one waits 15 minutes for an ordinary date, a half-hour for a beauty queen and, ah, 45 minutes for a goddess." This was supposed to prove that we had an inflated idea of ourselves. I didn't know that old story.

# 9
✳

## You Caught Me Smilin'
### (1971–1972)

**I**n the fall of 1971, *Rolling Stone* **sent a reporter to interview** me. Not the same one who had come out back in January, and not for a cover story this time. The magazine wanted to take stock of everything that had been happening since. The year had kept me always in the spotlight but also sometimes put me in a bad light. People were saying (and writing) that I was missing shows, dragging my feet on the new record, isolating myself from my band. I had news about that new record—it was mostly done, due out before the end of the year—but I wasn't sure which parts of the story I told would be part of the story that got told. The words you said could be twisted before they were put down on the page.

And then there was the question of who the reporter would be interviewing. There was an idea circulating that I was two different people, Sylvester Stewart and Sly Stone. Sylvester was clear and calm, the kind of person you would want in the room, but Sly—antagonistic, unreliable, always with a joke and sometimes you were it—was the one everyone wanted to interview. Dave Kapralik had said that in more than one article, including one that the *Rolling Stone* reporter had read. I didn't agree with the two-persons-in-one theory. In my mind, there was only my mind, with different facets and edges like anyone's, and that was the mind that minded being probed and prodded, put to someone else's test.

It was also the mind that thought it all over and agreed, finally, to the *Rolling Stone* interview, which is why the reporter showed up one fall afternoon at my room in the New York Hilton.

The first time he came Richie answered the door. Richie was a guy who had worked around studios for a while and wanted to become an engineer. "I'll show you a little," I said, "and from there you can figure it out." I did and he did. In the hotel room we had a bunch of cassette recorders so we could move pieces of songs from one machine to the other. Richie told the reporter that I had gone with JR to his mother's house in Long Island and would be back later. That was true: It was one of those spaghetti dinners, and they took a while. Plus, we had a helicopter to catch, and a show in New Haven. But when later came, and the reporter returned, we still weren't there. We had started back to the city in a motor home but didn't make it all the way. Instead, we had pulled over on the side of the road to rest, and by the time we made it back to the hotel the reporter was already on his way home.

The third time was the charm. When the knock came at the door, it was late at night. Maybe that's when he figured he could catch me. I was in bed. I had JR answer the door and leave the reporter out in the front room with Stephanie and Cynthia. They watched TV, and I listened to them watching, until I was ready.

"Okay," I told JR, who brought the reporter back. He was a young guy, dark hair, glasses. There were many of him in 1971, and this was one. He came in and looked around the room like a . . . reporter. He looked at the burned-down joints and ash piled up in ashtrays and birth control pills scattered on the table. He looked at the remnants of a play-fight between me and JR, shaving cream and ice cubes. Love and war. He looked at me and took notice of my outfit ("white vinyl boots and red leather pants with fringe") and my hair ("several inches high and shaped like a Guardia Civil hat"). But did he see me at all? I asked him that but he didn't hear or he heard but didn't understand or he understood but didn't want to answer.

I spoke up more clearly. "I got to pee," I said, and went to the bathroom to do so, but also to smoke and to wait. I took my time because I didn't want anyone else taking it.

Eventually I went back out into the room. "Sorry for before," I said. An explanation was provided. I had missed the earlier meetings, I said, because of "valid negligence." That was, he said, a contradiction in terms. I think he was joking. But I wasn't. "Are you dense?" I asked him, enunciating sharply. Contradiction, diction. He put his tape recorder on the table and I had Richie put one of ours next to it, not for stereo but for coverage. I wanted our own record of what was said. I offered him some powder for sniffing—not even coke, but snuff. I offered to interview him instead. Then we got down to it.

The first question was about Kapralik's theory, and I answered plainly: "David Kapralik tries his best. And I don't think he has any malice in his heart. Whatever he said, he didn't know what he was talking about, I don't think. 'Cause I am who I am when I am it."

We went on from there. We talked about the fight at the Holiday Inn where I had gone down to the lobby to defend Freddie and Cynthia. We talked about the Black Panthers and whether they were leaning on me to change the way I did business. We talked about dogs, and how I had always liked them because they would be your buddy. We talked about the books I was reading: dog books and also books about Africa, but all of them carefully. I wasn't a big reader unless a book was a manual of some kind, I told him, because books tended to create a competitive mindset. People got their truths by pointing at other people's falses.

When the piece came out a few months later, the reporter said that it was difficult to talk to me. Maybe what he meant was that after a certain point I tried to show how much I wanted the interview to be over. It went on long enough that my answers got shorter and shorter.

I didn't only let my mouth do the talking. I had been playing with JR earlier in the night and I kept playing. I had JR soak a washcloth and then I threw it at the reporter, getting him in the face. He threw it back at me. I flipped a screwdriver in my hand like I might throw that, too, but it was only a joke.

On the other hand, I participated. There is significant evidence of it in the article. We discussed the music I was in the process of making, especially a song about Africa, and he asked why I hadn't made good on a plan I had announced to go to Kenya. "Can't make every gig," I said. "I don't wanna shoot any animals. I wrote a song about Africa because in Africa the animals are animals. The tiger is a tiger, the snake is a snake, you know what the hell he's gonna do. Here in New York, the asphalt jungle, a tiger or a snake may come up looking like . . . you." I was trying to explain the way urban life functioned or malfunctioned, how so-called civilization needed to call some people uncivilized to keep going. I wasn't sure he understood me and I wasn't sure I cared.

He also inquired after the current health of Stone Flower. On that last point, I gave him some news. "We got 6ix material, Little Sister material," I said. "*They* can't handle it. The record companies are pretty fucked up. And they try to fuck you around and fuck the kids around. The executives, on higher levels, they don't really associate with . . . well, you have to live the blues to sing about the blues. And honest to God, Clive Davis hasn't really been livin' a hell of a lot of blues." I wasn't knocking Clive. I had good feelings about him. I was using him to show how much lower the others flew.

And then it was done because I was done. "It's been a real pleasure," I said. "To the best of my knowledge." The reporter packed up his recorder and went. As he left, the same wet washcloth sailed through the air again, missed him, and hit the frame of the door, which was then bolted and chained.

I threw the towel but I hadn't thrown in the towel. I had been working steadily on the new album, the one that Epic had been waiting for since *Stand!*, and it was ready to bring into the light, even though the light had changed. As early as 1968 I had sensed a shadow was falling over America. It got better during the summer of 1969—the moon landing, Woodstock— but worse after. The possibility of possibility was leaking out and leaving the country feeling drained. The year the reporter came around, 1971, had "Joy to the World," but also "Slippin' into Darkness." It had "You've Got a Friend," but also "Smiling Faces Sometimes."

The new album finally arrived in stores in November. The label still seemed to be thinking mostly about how long it had taken. "Two Years Is Too Short to Wait" was one of the ideas for an ad for the record.

To wait for what? At first, the album was going to be called *Africa Talks to You "The Asphalt Jungle."* I had mentioned that during the *Rolling Stone* interview. That title started a conversation in the form of a series of questions. Was America looking back over its shoulder? Was black America holding up a hand or a hand mirror? Was civilization being honest with itself about its dishonesty?

The title changed but the questions stayed. The new title, *There's a Riot Goin' On*, did many things at once. It reached back to "Riot in Cell Block No. 9," a 1954 song by the Robins, the Leiber-Stoller group that would grow into the Coasters. It answered Marvin Gaye's *What's Going On*, which had come out back in January. It pointed toward Grant Park. But it was also deeply personal, about the riot that was going on inside each person.

For the cover art, I had talked to Steve Paley and come up with an idea. I wanted an American flag but not in red, white, and blue. I kept the white and added black, which were the flip sides of each other. White was the absence of any color. Black was the presence of all colors. I took out the blue and left the red, which was humanity and unity, blood in the veins of us all. I also wanted to do something about the stars. Stars blinked on and off. You had to go looking for them. I wanted to change them to suns, which came looking for you.

We had flags stitched, one for the record label, one for Steve, and one for me. The second part of the idea was that the cover art would be flag alone, no name of album, no name of band, nothing also. On some versions of the album, the label added a sticker that looked like a newspaper front page: *Good News* was the name of the fake newspaper, and the headlines identified us and listed the songs. The art included a collage of America: black faces, white faces, famous faces, unknown faces, beautiful young faces, beautiful old faces. More than a few peered out from under knit caps.

We hadn't released a single in advance of the album, but we needed one to accompany it. My pick was "Luv N' Haight," the opening track, a groove with a few lyrics about the qualities of living with quality of life. I had called up my mother one day to see how she was doing. "I feel so good I don't wanna move," she said. That went right into the song. Little Sister came in with woozy backup vocals.

Steve Paley wanted "Family Affair" instead. It posed like a band song, from the title on down. But most of the Family Stone was nowhere to be found. Bobby Womack played some rhythm guitar and Billy Preston impressed on a Pianet. Otherwise it was preset rhythms and One-Take Rose.

And me. For the vocal, I was downstairs in the house with others, partying, and I realized that I should be upstairs, by myself, making records. I had a drink. I had another one. I went up to the studio, where I had an eight-track recorder, and put down the vocal track. I was the only one in the room, the engineer and the audience and the performer. My voice was almost gone, so hoarse I had to ride in on it, but I made it do what I needed it to do. I was thinking not just about the Family Stone but about all families.

I wasn't sure it was the right song to release first, and some of the executives agreed. It sounded too stretched out and slowed down. That may have been because I worked the tape over too much, not just on that song but on the entire record. I sometimes sacrificed technique for feeling. But one day Steve told me that he had already sent "Family Affair" to stations and that they were already beginning to play it.

I made some of "Family Affair" at home, some of it some other places. I might have recorded in the Winnebago, even. The rest of the album was created under similar conditions. Some writers called it my first solo album and I knew what they meant. It was a record made by no one and everyone, made under the influence of substances and of itself. Is that a contradiction in terms? Contradiction, diction, addiction.

"Poet" was a little song about writing bigger songs. The organ bounced like the rest of the arrangement was a trampoline. "Time" was slow, even slower than the thing itself, filled with philosophy, questions, and paradox. Time gave me plenty to think about and I gave people plenty to think about time.

Others were about what happened when life waned. They were like someone soaked a rag—or a washcloth—and then wrung it out until it was almost bone-dry. "Brave & Strong" started scared ("Frightened faces to the wall / Can't you hear your mama call?") and passed into paranoia. "Runnin' Away" stacked up staccato horns and spoken laughter, and "(You Caught Me) Smilin'," was a blurry song about sharp regrets.

Some people pointed to songs like that when they said the album was dark, but that wasn't my intention. Other people didn't say dark. They said black instead. But then how did they explain "Spaced Cowboy"? I had always liked yodeling on records. A comedian whose name I forgot always made me laugh when he did it and so I tried myself: *Yodel-ayde-yodel-ayde-a.* On that one we were having some real fun.

If I had kept the original name of the album, the title track would have been "Africa Talks to You 'The Asphalt Jungle,'" a nearly nine-minute look at (black) life in America. The chorus was the opposite of "Stand!": "Timber! All fall down!" With the new name, I needed to come up with another title song. I put it at the end of side one. Track six. It was easy to fit because of its length, zero minutes and zero seconds. That was a message, too—don't give any time to violence. Don't give it the time of day. There's a runout going on.

I ended side two, and the whole album, with "Thank You for Talkin' to Me Africa," which was "Thank You (Falettinme Me Be Mice Elf Agin)" slowed down so that it needed another two minutes at least. Going slower like that gave everything more weight. I was digging down into a place where people hadn't been before.

But would they follow me there? When "Family Affair" went out as the single, I wasn't sure what would happen. What happened was our third number 1. One week, Isaac Hayes's "Theme from Shaft" topped the chart. The next week, we were the bad mother— (shut your mouth). I had moved into Isaac Hayes's house and now I moved into his spot.

The album climbed along with the song. People picked up on what I was putting down, put down their money and picked up the record. In December, *There's a Riot Goin' On* went to number 1. It was our first number 1 album. *Greatest Hits* had only gone to two.

Critics were more divided. They had waited so long since *Stand!*, waited through *Greatest Hits*, and maybe that's the kind of thing they wanted to hear instead of this kind of thing. "Muffled," they said, or "muted," or "lyrics ramble in strange corridors," or "jumbled, sometimes totally incoherent," or "obscure, meaningless, or just plain dumb."

Those reviews didn't hurt my feelings because I didn't see them. Also I knew that I was doing something different, doing something new to the old ways. I figured that people would see it sooner or later. *Rolling Stone* saw it sooner. "It's about disintegration," their review said, "getting fucked up, nodding, maybe dying . . . The music has no peaks, no emphasis, little movement, it seems to fall away like a landslide in a dream (you falling slowly too, not panicking)." Their review admitted that it wasn't easy to swallow. "At first I hated it for its weakness." But easy to swallow was something else. That was pop. That had happened. This was happening. The more *Rolling Stone* thought about the record, the more they saw that it was something to think about: "I began to respect the album's honesty, cause in spite of the obvious deception of some cuts, Sly was laying himself out in all his fuck-ups. And at the same time holding a mirror up to all of us. No more pretense; no more high-energy. You're dying, we're all dying. It's hard to take, but *There's a Riot Goin' On* is one of the most important fucking albums this year."

Nice to be heard.

We kept on touring: Louisville one night, Wooster, Ohio, the next; Montreal one night, Ottawa the next; Minneapolis; Tampa; Philly. Sometimes our opening act was Ruth Copeland, not at my home studio in Bel Air anymore but out on the road. Of the new songs, only "Family Affair" showed up on the set lists, which threw off some newspaper writers. Why should 1972 just repeat 1970? There were new sounds on the radio: Al Green's "Let's Stay Together," Bill Withers's "Lean on Me," Roberta Flack and Donny Hathaway's "Where Is the Love." I didn't like Curtis Mayfield's "Freddie's Dead" because my brother's name was Freddie and the song gave me a bad feeling. But I liked "Super Fly" and "Pusherman," especially those high harmonies. I was making new music in the studio and was happy to bring it to the stage, but I hadn't been able to rehearse the band on the rest of the record, not the way I needed to, every day without exception, bring a lunch. We did spin things differently, slowing songs down like I had done with "Thank You (Falettinme Be Mice Elf Agin)."

We had a few days off here and there. If I could, I would see a movie. I liked Bruce Lee. I watched him closely and then got my-self trained in martial arts. I had a bodyguard and driver named Teru Kawaoka, a bad motherfucker who knew karate in and out, including special forms like Gōjū-ryū, which focused on hard closed-hand strikes, soft open-hand blocks, grapples, breathing techniques. I got my hands strong and studied with Teru until I earned a belt. I don't remember the color: brown?

The number of shows hadn't decreased. Neither had the number of articles about my supposed trouble making them on time. In April there was a piece in the paper, partly a review of a show at the Apollo, partly a review of me: "A Has-Been at 26? Sly Stone Hits a Slump, Turns into Lackluster No-Show." The piece opened with a quote about inevitable downfalls, a quote taken from "Somebody's Watching You," and then tried to make the case that I had reached the end of the line. It also noted that I had made forty-one or forty-three shows since September of the year before. "Despite those statistics," it said, I was saddled with a reputation. (Why would you despite the statistics?)

The truth was that we were grinding at a grueling pace. I could push through in November and December, when there was a new album to promote, but by spring I was tapped. The road had taken its toll. I didn't miss many shows, but I was sometimes late, and when I showed the shows were sometimes as short as the candle I was burning at both ends. Once during a stretch where I felt especially tapped out I turned to my dad. "You going to have to leave the room," I said. I was desperate to use but just as desperate for him not to see me using.

Wick or fuse? It felt like an explosion was coming.

Dave Kapralik had burned his candle down, too, which meant that he wasn't taking care of business. That meant money failing to flow toward us at the proper rate, which meant missed payments on the Bel Air house, strain over studio time, a general feeling that bank balances were imbalanced. Ken Roberts, the concert promoter who had started to stabilize our tour schedule, stepped up, calling Epic to set things straight and also reaching out to the press to smooth over rumors. One article said, "Sly Defended by Producers." The picture showed me and Ken, white man on the right to keep the black man from being left behind.

The trouble around the band started to become trouble in the band. Larry was still making his own arrangements and plans, still hiring his own people. He had a guy who would walk a step in front of him, an intense look on his face like he was clearing the way for the president. And he was working with a side band, Hot Chocolate, and spending time with the group's singer, Patryce "Choc'let" Banks. (No relation to Bubba.)

And Jerry was unhappy to the point where he made it known that he wanted to leave. That was hard for me. He had been there from the start, from before the start, and though I wasn't worried about being lost where the music was concerned—I was doing more and more on my own—Jerry was a Family corner-stone. Still, I had my eyes and ears open for a replacement.

When we were in New York, at the Plaza, a young guy came to see me. He told me that he heard I was looking for a horn player. This kid—Italian, smiled easily—was from a musical family. His mother played concert piano. He had worked all around, club dates, straight jazz, a gig with Tito Puente, bubble-gum. I didn't want to talk to him around the other musicians, so I motioned toward the bathroom. We went in there. "You any good?" I said. He nodded, played me a little. That was the inter-view. That was Pat Rizzo.

I brought Pat into the band thinking Jerry would go, but Jerry stayed. The two of them had their jealousies at first, and I didn't try to stop it on either side. That kind of thing can make people better players, and they ended up being cool with each other. Pat didn't catch on right away. At one early gig I heard him playing too much to try to fit in. "Man," I told him, "there's plenty of people in this band." But he got there. He knew more jazz, which you could hear in his playing. And he knew lots of people. One of them was Jilly Rizzo, who owned Jilly's, one of Frank Sina-tra's favorite hangouts. Pat liked to tell a story about taking me to Jilly's, sitting at a nice table, eating, having a drink, watching a waiter approach, being told that Frank was on his way in and since we were sitting at his table we would have to move, moving, meeting Frank, saying hello, shaking hands, saying goodbye. I don't remember meeting Frank, which doesn't mean the story was a lie. When the spotlight was on you, blinding you, it was easy not to see people—even if those people had a bigger spotlight on them.

The follow-up to *Riot* was burbling by fall. We didn't have a name for the album yet but we had some full songs and plenty of pieces. We got down to assembling them in the Record Plant, not the old studio but a new one that had just opened up in Sausalito, near the harbor.

The new Record Plant was all done up in wood. The invitations to the opening-night party went out on wooden cards. It was a Halloween party. John Lennon and Yoko Ono were inspired by the invitation and came dressed up as trees. I didn't go. We were touring. But I had a presence at the place. The owners took one of the offices and converted it into a small studio room with red carpet, decorations all across the walls, fabric, the walls painted. The actual audio equipment was sunk down into a circular area in the center of the room. The musicians would stand up in a ring around that middle area. That arrangement gave the room its nickname, the Pit. There was also a bed that you got to through a big pair of lips, and it was wired so that you could record while you were in bed.

Even though I had helped inspire the Pit, I didn't always love working there. The separation between the musicians and the engineers was hard for me. I wasn't always able to concentrate, and sometimes a change of location was required. One afternoon I was recording with an engineer named Tom Flye, who we called

Superflye. I was laying down a bass part but it wasn't working for me. "Wait," I said. "Let's try this over at my mother's house." Tom got the portable studio and we went over there. It sounded better, but still not quite right. "I know," I said, "I want a different guitar for this one."

"Okay," he said. He turned to where the guitars were racked.

"No," I said. "It's in Los Angeles." He laughed. But then he saw I was serious and we packed up. A week later we were down in L.A., back on the song. I had the right guitar and was ready to go. Take it from the top, Tom said. "Why can't we just start where we left off?" I said. He was worried that it would sound strange, one sound changing into another one mid-song. But that was what I wanted. I think that song was "Let Me Have It All," but it could have been others, too.

The Pit wasn't perfect for me, but it panned out for others. A few years later, Stevie Nicks was at the Record Plant, recording with Fleetwood Mac. She got a melody stuck in her head, felt like the rest of the band was distracting her, and went out walking in the halls. A guy who worked there noticed the look on her face. She explained her trouble. He told her there was a secret room. She sat in there, connected with the energy of the place, and wrote "Dreams."

Madison Square Garden always felt like a place to recharge, fertile soil. Our 1972 shows, scheduled for the week of Thanksgiving, promised to be the usual—big crowds, big money, big news—though they also required a tight turnaround: When we were done in New York we were set to fly right back to Los Angeles for a benefit concert sponsored by KROQ.

The day of the first New York show I wandered in and around Times Square. The Macy's parade was that morning. Snoopy was in it, and Smokey the Bear. The Underdog balloon had to be twice as good.

I was always interested in gear, so I wandered into Harvey's, an electronics store on Forty-fifth Street. One of the clerks noticed me immediately. I had a buckskin jacket and a big belt buckle. None of that had anything to do with why I was noticed. That was on account of the silver holster on my hip and the silver pistol in it. I grabbed the gun out of the holster, set it back in, grabbed it out, set it back in, grabbed it out. And so on.

In my head I was clear on what was happening. The gun was a toy. The draw was a game. I thought I might run into Sammy Davis, Jr., later that night—he had sent word he might come to the show—and Sammy liked those kinds of contests. He had been in *The Rifleman* and sharpened his fast-draw abilities, but I liked to win.

Pistol grabbed, pistol replaced. "I'm from Fort Worth," I said, which was sort of true, and then "I'm a cowboy," which was also sort of true. *Yodel-ayde-yodel-ayde-a.* I didn't explain myself beyond that. No one asked me to do so.

The clerk who had taken notice of me put his hand over his mouth and spoke quickly and quietly to a clerk who hadn't noticed me. That second clerk called the cops, the cops came, the cowboy was taken down to the station, the gun and holster were taken away from the cowboy.

People said I was lucky the cop didn't just walk into the store and shoot me without asking questions. He must have known the gun was just a toy. It was obvious to me. I got out in time to make it to the Garden. The show, which must go on, did. The Staple Singers opened for us. I ended up not seeing Sammy that night—still undefeated in quick draw.

All things considered, that first night went off okay. The second night seemed snakebit. The cars were parked downstairs at the hotel in the afternoon to take us to the arena. We loaded in but we weren't moving. "Let's go," I said. We couldn't. Larry wasn't there.

Bubba called up to Larry and told him we were waiting, but Larry said he wasn't ready, that we should go ahead without him and send one of the cars back. Bubba didn't like that shit one bit. He went up to talk to Larry but Larry's guy answered the door with the same message as before: not ready, go ahead. Bubba kept a car back but made sure that he was in it too so Larry would see the consequence.

During the show and even after it, Bubba had Larry in mind. He couldn't get him out of mind. He went to Ken to talk about the problem named Larry. Ken suggested that whatever needed to happen also needed to wait until we got back to L.A. and did the benefit show. Bubba agreed and we flew back on an overnight flight. I wasn't awake so they put me in a chair and carried it down like they were moving furniture.

Back west, there was smoke and a little fire and when it cleared things were different.

There are so many stories about that time. That Bubba and Larry were set against each other in angry ways. That Bubba's second, Black, met us at the airport with a piece because he heard Larry's guy had a piece, or maybe Larry had a guy come carrying because he heard that Black was. All I can say is that I never saw any of that. What I did see was the space between them, and the angry waves rolling in that space.

But first, the show. KROQ was, at the time, a new FM station. They wanted to make a splash in the L.A. market, so they were putting on a big event at the Coliseum to support free clinics, packed with all the top acts they could find: Stevie Wonder, Chuck Berry, the Bee Gees, Sha Na Na, Mott the Hoople, the Raspberries, the Four Seasons, the Eagles. "Ultimate ROQ," they called it.

The show was bigger than big. It was too big. For starters,

KROQ had overbooked talent and couldn't fully pay bands. (Ken fronted our expenses in exchange for an ownership stake in the station. It started a relationship that got bigger and bigger for him and eventually brought him millions. But that wasn't happening yet.) Kids broke onto the field before Stevie Wonder even started his set. Yoko Ono phoned in to apologize for John Lennon's absence and they put her voice on the PA system. There was a midnight curfew but midnight came and went before many of the acts even got a chance to play, including us.

When we finally got out there, I had to fight the Coliseum staff over lights that were too bright, and something was messed up with the equipment. Nothing worked or sounded right: not the organ, not the monitors. I couldn't get what I needed out of any of it, so I played a song or two and shut it down.

Tired, demoralized, the band and crew went back to the Hotel Cavalier in Hollywood, where we were staying. Joe Hicks was there with us being his usual laughy self, always with the ha ha. Talk turned to the show and then to the organ. I got more and more angry and finally decided to do something about it. Moose, who ran the equipment, was sleeping upstairs. I went to his room and woke him up. I yelled and screamed and yelled and screamed some more, and then I told Eddie Chin to take care of it.

Meanwhile, the tension kept tightening. There were rumors flying everywhere that night. That threatening calls had been made. That people had looked into putting contracts out on each other, maybe someone from Larry's camp putting one out on me, maybe someone from my camp putting one out on Larry in return. That because of all that, Larry had to check underneath his car before he drove it. I didn't know anything about that at the time and I feel bad that anyone ever had to think about things like that. At the hotel, Larry was upstairs with his guys and Patryce when we got word they were planning on coming down and causing trouble. Bubba and Eddie had no problem with trouble. They went into the stairwell to make sure that nothing happened. But something did happen: Larry's guys came down, saw Eddie and Bubba, and then it all erupted. Bubba went after Larry's guys, cracked a hand on a head. Larry's guys fought back even though they were getting the worst of it. In the middle of the mayhem, Larry somehow slipped away. Pat Rizzo says that he got a call from Larry, panicked, at the Cavalier. Pat went over and drove Larry and Patryce away. Pat says that Larry shoved some tapes in a bag and went: songs that he and Patryce were working on for their new project. And that was that for Larry in the band. I don't blame him for leaving either. You don't know everything about a person's attitudes and aspects. Just because someone has been in the same place for a long time doesn't mean that they should be there longer. There are times to stay and times to move.

The group didn't break up when Larry went but we broke down some. How could we go forward without a bassist? Freddie had his eye on Rustee Allen, a young player who was working with Little Sister, a cool cat, afro and sunglasses. I met a white guy in New York who had style. And then one night I was out with Bubba to see Eddie Kendricks sing at a club somewhere in San Francisco. We went in and saw Larry. He was sitting down with a girl. That's not the end of the story, us seeing Larry. Larry turned and saw us. That's not the end of the story either. He took her hand and hit the door quick.

Bubba and I stayed and saw Eddie's show. His bass player was named Wornell Jones. He was from D.C., had been in the Young Senators, had joined up with Eddie for a record, the one that included the hit "Girl You Need a Change of Mind." He could really play. "That's him," I said to Bubba. "That's the one."

Bubba couldn't connect with Wornell that night but he drove

out to Las Vegas, to their next show, and approached him at the break. Before the show was over the two of them were in the car coming back to California. Wornell went into the running to replace Larry. As it turned out he sounded too similar and I couldn't hear the sense in that. The white kid didn't work out. Rustee ended up being the guy. We were making our next record, *Fresh*—like fresh fruit, something new for the shelves. Larry was already on a song or two, but we freshened up with Rustee and went forward.

# 10
# ✳

## In Time
### (1972–1973)

**B**ack up for love.

Jerry Brandt, who had started the Electric Circus, closed it down it 1971 and became known for throwing the best parties. He hosted the best faces in the best places.

In Los Angeles, in spring, at a Jerry Brandt party, I saw Kathy Silva for the first time. She was the most beautiful girl in the room, perfect face, long black hair like vinyl. I singled her out. She was going to be my girlfriend. I was sure of it. I walked a little toward her and then pointed my finger at her. That was a signal: come over by me.

She did. We talked for a little while. A little while after that, I left the party and she left with me. We went back to my house. Kathy went into a room and relaxed, then went to sleep, while I went into the studio and worked. Eventually I went to find Kathy. We did what people do.

Kathy and I started seeing each other. She was a mix of Mexican, Hawaiian, and Filipina. I liked women that were a mix of things. It gave them more dimensions in how they looked and in how people looked at them and in how they could move through the world. She was around all the time, and then her sister April came to stay with us. I was with April too for a little while, but that ended and I was still with Kathy.

One day, Kathy told me we needed to talk. Was it trouble? Did she want our relationship to end? It was neither of those things. It was news: She was pregnant. That changed everything. My mama told me I had to marry her, and I had nothing to say except that I agreed. It was the right thing to do. It was the only thing to do.

*Fresh* came out at the start of summer. If *Riot* was dark, this album was light, almost blindingly so. I had started feeling rich, and not just in the bank account. It was in my frame of mind. The success of *Riot* meant that people were happy listening to my music, that they were rewarded by it, and that was the richest feeling I could imagine.

Richard Avedon took the cover photo. I was used to working with Steve Paley, who was simpler and got to the overall concept quickly. Avedon was more artistic, more European. This would be a portrait. But I liked him and the way he worked. For the photo, I put on a leather and rhinestone outfit, jumped in the air and kicked out a leg. He knew I was going to do it. It wasn't like I surprised him. It was my idea, to see how high I could get off the ground—not Superman or Super Fly but Super Sly—and for him to capture it. I had to get a little bit of a running start, four or five steps. I had to jump ten times. I stopped because I got tired but by then he had the photo that he needed.

The music on the album was also about staying up. The band was still mostly there, the original Family Stone, but it was shifting. I was still working the way I had worked on *Riot*, building the songs up from my demos and then adding in other musicians as needed. The credits say I did "organ, guitar, bass, piano, harmonica, and more." Rustee had stepped in for Larry. And we had a new drummer again. One day I was sleeping at home, then half-sleeping, and I noticed a young white guy in my bedroom. He wasn't a prowler, because Big Daddy and Bubba were standing nearby looking calm. "Who are you?" I said.

"Andy," he said. "Andy Newmark. Pat Rizzo told me that you needed a drummer."

I was in a leather suit on a black-fur bed. I don't know how it looked to him. He looked like it looked surprising. "Are you funky?" I said. He said he was, but not in a convincing voice. "Play," I said, pointing at a little drum kit I kept in the room, almost a toy set. He did, and that convinced us both. He could really play. He wasn't a straight rock drummer or even a straight funk drummer. "Who do you listen to?" I said. He told me he had been listening to Tony Williams, who had played with Miles Davis and in his own band, Lifetime. Andy had studied him, especially how he extended the drum fill past the one into the bar. That was Tony's trick and it was Andy's trick too.

It got me up on my elbows, dancing there in the bed. "You're my new drummer," I said. I asked him if he wanted to stay, but he told me that he was playing with Carly Simon at the Troubadour. "When?" I said. "Right now," he said. He had driven up to see me between sets. Of all the drummers I had, Andy was the best. Bubba and I sometimes made fun of the way he talked—suburban voice, suburban accent—but he could keep a motherfucking beat.

And that motherfucking album had no shortage of them. I recorded it at the Record Plant in Sausalito, in my home studio at the Bel Air house, even in New York, where I had an apartment at the Century, Central Park West between Sixty-second and

Sixty-third. Wherever I went, ideas for songs followed, and that meant engineers had to follow, too. Sometimes I would bring Tom Flye in on a plane: Superflying.

*Fresh* started off with "In Time." It's one of my favorite songs. Funky as hell. I got the organ part in my mind, then the guitar part. I was working with the Rhythm King still, and I programmed beats. Other groups might do that as a guide for the live drummer. But I added Andy right on over the top of the programmed beats, split time into both mechanical and human versions. I sat with him, taught him the part like I heard it, and then let him loose to play it.

The lyrics were a match for the music. They were written in pieces, sometimes on a legal pad, sometimes on the backs of envelopes. They came into my mind in the car or in the house. Some were improvised. "There's a mickie in the tasting of disaster / In time, you get faster" is how it starts. Fame speeds everything up and you have to speed yourself too or you get left behind. That's in the next line, too. "Switched from Coke to Pep, now I'm a connoisseur." Those products were their own kinds of drugs and their own kind of drag. I still remembered the pressure of being asked to deliver the record, and the record before it, so I built in a joke that played off Epic's old ad campaign: "Two years, too long to wait / Two words, get it straight."

The song went on. There were lines about getting in your own way and the intoxication of fame ("I felt so good I told the leader how to follow"). There were lines about the difficulty of seeking wisdom and one about the weight of waiting on yourself ("Harry Hippie is a waste as if he hasta / procrastinating"). "Harry Hippie" was the name of a Bobby Womack song that Jimmy Ford had written for him. The way I sang "procrastinating," I held off on the "-ating," delaying a word about delay. "Dance to the Music" hadn't meant much except itself. Five years on, here was a song that maybe meant too much. It was a question of where the meaning stopped.

The other songs were simpler than "In Time." They had to be. But not by much. "If You Want Me to Stay," made live in the room with me singing and playing organ, was straightforward in some ways. If you want me to stay, tell me. Otherwise, I'm gone. But people couldn't decide how wide a lens to view it through. Was it a love song? Was I singing it to my audience?

Every song stood up for itself. "Frisky" was a picture of my room, the way I kept instruments all around the bed. A guitar, a keyboard, something to blow. An alto sax, I mean, not cocaine. I learned to play a little. I played what I could. "Thankful N' Thoughtful" was what it said, a philosophy of gratitude. "Babies Makin' Babies" was another one of those slogans that I either pulled out of the air or put there.

"Qué Sera, Sera" was a gift to Doris Day, Terry Melcher's mother. For years people spread rumors that I dated her. I would never have done a thing like that. She was a nice lady, polite to me whenever I saw her, and a good singer. Terry played her original version for me one day, and right away I could hear how it could sound. It was like the covers we did back at Winchester Cathedral. Take something old, make it new. We made it new. We slowed it down. We thickened it up. We stayed loose. Rose messed up in the second verse. So what? An error is only something you do that others don't. I have no idea what Doris thought about it. I never played it for her.

But we played the album for almost everyone else. At the height of that summer we headlined a big show in Central Park. One of the networks, ABC, I think, was showing it on TV, prime time.

Miles Davis came to watch us. He loved "In Time." The rumor is that he played it over and over again for his band, trying to work out the rhythms of it, failing. In Central Park, he stood around in the backstage area with Morgana King, a jazz singer who had just played Don Corleone's wife in the *Godfather* movies.

Later that summer Miles and I went to see Morgana sing at a club. I remember I told him I wasn't gonna wear socks and he said then he wasn't gonna wear them neither. We walked out of his place on the Upper West Side, walked down Central Park West, saw Morgana sing—she was a bad motherfucker—and then parted ways. Another night he came to the window of my place and knocked. I saw his face, eyes white in the dark, and asked him what he wanted. "Let me get in the house so I can eat some of that white girl pussy." I laughed but didn't let him in.

*Fresh* was released during strange days for the label. That year, Columbia dropped a number of major jazz artists: Charles Mingus, Bill Evans, Keith Jarrett, Ornette Coleman. The fault went to Miles, maybe, and then maybe to me. It was the "In Time" problem. Miles had been turned around by the kind of music we were making, and the musicians who went in the same direction as him used us as a compass also. Herbie Hancock named a song for me on his *Headhunters* album that year. Anything else got tossed like old food.

Clive Davis got tossed from Columbia at the same time. They alleged that he had liberated a hundred thousand dollars from the company, claiming it was for expenses when it was going to other things: renovating his Manhattan pad, renting a summer place in Beverly Hills, paying for his son's bar mitzvah (I didn't attend).

I was buying shit left and right myself, including too many cars. At one point there were thirteen, a lucky number as far as I was concerned, all carrying insurance so I could take them out on the road. I loved them all. You could look at a car and get a feeling. I had a special place in my heart for my Jaguar, and more places for my Cord and my Mercedes 600 limo with three doors that I sat in while Teru drove me around. They were garaged, kept safe and sound.

Cars weren't just for me. I bought my dad a Cadillac every year, or every other year at least. It went on like that for a while, maybe ten years. The reason I bought him one was simple: He didn't need two.

One afternoon Etta James came over. She would drop by now and then to sing and hang. This time she had to go to Texas, and she wanted to borrow some money for a plane ticket. "Fuck that," I said, and gave her a car. I had a Cadillac that felt too new somehow, like next year's model but back then. That went to Etta. She and a guy named E, I guess her boyfriend, set off for Texas.

Three or four days later I got a call from the Texas cops that the car had been stopped and flagged as stolen. That made sense to me because I had bought it stolen. I could get it cheap that way, and I didn't think I'd get busted for it. But on the phone I said I didn't understand why the cops were calling or what they wanted from me. "Can I help you, officers?" I had done all the right things to move the car over to Etta, all the right paperwork, transferring title. I don't think she got in too much trouble.

It wasn't my only interaction with the law that year. In February cops came to the Bel Air house and found weed, coke, Placidyl, and angel dust. The angel dust was tapering off by that point. The guy who sold it to me went to jail and I didn't look hard for a new supplier. I just used it less. But what was found led to an arrest, which led to a year of probation.

Another time I was out riding in my Winnebago, cruising up and down Santa Monica Boulevard. The cops stopped us and searched the vehicle. They were looking for drugs, obviously—this was follow-up from February—but they didn't find them. I maintained respect and politeness throughout. Can I help you, officers?

Those were big years, star years. I would fly east in a Lear Jet, take Bubba with me or Freddie or Pat. My dad never went with me in those small planes. He didn't trust them for shit. I would play guitar at fifty thousand feet, talk to the pilots, maybe joke with them about the plane getting into trouble. I thought about getting a pilot's license myself but never got around to it. Stars in the sky.

Kathy was pregnant and then the family was increased by one. I wanted my name to be on the baby and it was: Sylvester Stewart, Jr. Muhammad Ali was his godfather, which is why his middle names were Bubba Ali—I wanted to pay tribute to both of them. I remember the first time seeing my first child. How did it feel? How can you ever feel about a thing like that or how can you describe it? I was a new father which meant that there was a new being looking up to me as I looked down into his light. A star is born.

Life was good. I was hanging at the house, out at shows, riding bikes with Bubba. He and Rose were together solid now, heading toward marriage. I saw movies when I could, loved *The Sting*, still do. One afternoon, I was coming into San Francisco in a limo. It was a stretch and then some. Bubba joked that it was so long that the other end was still in Oakland. Sergio, one of the bodyguards, tilted up his chin enough to agree. "Livin' while we're livin'," he said. Stars in our eyes.

I remember going to a studio to rehearse and there was a big touring bus outside. I walked in the back door and immediately someone called my name. "Sly! Sly!" It was Stevie Wonder. I don't know if someone tipped him off or if he heard my feet and knew that it was me. We joked around, played a little bit, hung a little bit. It was cool, just a nice warm time. Even now I get a smile coming back onto my face thinking about that bus. A star vehicle.

Larry had stirred himself into Hot Chocolate and renamed it Graham Central Station. Their first album, same name, was out. Freddie was credited with co-writing one of the songs, "People," but I think it was left over from earlier. Larry wanted success with his new group and got it with a song called "Can You Handle It?" Shooting for the stars.

In October we were booked for a tour with Bob Marley and the Wailers opening. Seventeen dates total, their first major American exposure. They played the first four shows with us, Tampa, Lexington, Denver, Annapolis, and then we took them off the tour. People said that they were upstaging us, but that wasn't true. They just weren't a good match for our audience. They played slow. They had accents. Bunny Wailer, one of the original members of the band, wasn't even with them anymore. There was no offense intended on our part but we shipped them off. Black Star Line.

At one show, I was standing in the middle of the arena before a show, talking to Jerry Brown. I don't think he was governor of California yet. A little person came up to us and asked me if I knew what their song was. "*Your* song?" I said. He explained that they had an anthem in the little people community. Could I guess what it was? I made some kind of joke: "Is it a short song?" He had a confused look on his face, not really hurt, but not happy. "No," he said. "It's 'Stand!' Because of the 'midget standing tall / and a giant beside him about to fall' line." He didn't say anything about the joke I had made. He let me off the hook. Lucky stars.

# 11

\*

## Say You Will

### (1974)

I was sitting on a couch, watching TV and thinking on my situation with Kathy and Sylvester Jr. Getting married still seemed like the thing to do, and more and more it seemed like the thing to do soon. I called Steve Paley.

He answered and I proposed—not to him, but I proposed the plan. "A wedding?" he said. The idea filled the line. "Where are you thinking of doing it?" I said Hawaii, where Kathy was from. Then I said New York. I liked the city. I liked walking around. I loved sushi. I had my place at the Century. Either me or Steve said that it should happen at Madison Square Garden and the other one laughed. But the seed had been planted.

The next day I called Steve back. He wasn't there so his answering machine picked up. "This is Sly," I said, "and I need you to help me make this wedding the year's biggest deal." I told the machine to tell Steve to call me back. I may have even knocked out a rhythm on the rim of the receiver and said "What time is it?" I did that to Steve sometimes. I didn't want him to say noon or two thirty. I wanted him to say 3/4 or 4/4 or 7/8. He liked watching me listen to other people's music. He said I nodded in strange rhythms that were like previews of songs I'd soon be making.

He called me back later that day, and we grew the idea from a seed to a bud, from a bud to a flower. I could do a gig, get paid, and get married at the same time. "Go, go, go," I told him. He went and went fast. We set the date for June 5, a Wednesday. We'd have a ceremony just before the concert, right there on the stage. Then a concert, then a party afterward at the rooftop lounge of the Waldorf Astoria. Steve wanted everyone to wear gold to keep the shine high. Invitations went out:

> You are invited to a golden affair, the wedding of
> Kathy Silva
> and
> Sly Stone
> at Madison Square Garden
> on Wednesday night the fifth of June,
> followed by the concert of
> Sly and the Family Stone.
> And to the reception immediately following at
> the Starlight Roof of the Waldorf Astoria,
> 49th Street at Park Avenue.
> Kindly respond by Friday, May 31, 1974.
> Wear something gold.

I asked Steve to be my best man. I knew he would make the event easier, and figured he'd make it easiest if he was in it. Later I found out that Freddie wasn't sure why I didn't pick him. If Freddie had talked to me about it, I would have switched over. It was not a slight, just a sense of how Steve could help.

People held meetings. Meetings were held by people. I was unable to attend due to concert commitments (all of which I kept). Much of those meetings, I was told, involved ironing out details for the reception. What kind of food would be served? What kind of champagne would be poured? What kind of cake would be cut? Japanese and soul food, to pay off the Hawaiian bride and black groom. New York champagne, to pay off the city. A round cake with a gold record on top, to pay off the business I was in.

People made calls. Calls were made by people. I was not on the phone. Money was an issue—the boat needed to keep floating in the lead-up to the wedding—so Ken Roberts called in the rest of the advance for the new album, *Small Talk*, which was coming out in the summer. Or maybe Ken called Steve and Steve called the Record Plant and the tapes were released to Epic in exchange for a big check. The boat floated.

People hired designers. Designers were hired by people. I did not participate in the hiring. Steve took care of it, along with a guy named Joe Eula. Joe worked with Halston, the celebrity fashion designer, who had agreed to make clothes for everyone: me, Kathy, my parents, the entire wedding party. Steve and Joe started thinking of ideas to make everything bigger. Some of them were communicated to me: something about doves released to fly around the stage, something else about the wedding party marching down the Garden's main aisle.

Steve and Joe and the others made decisions. In some cases, decisions were made for them. The ASPCA wouldn't allow the doves. The wedding party couldn't march down the aisle without extra security, and extra security carried an extra cost. Improvisations followed. Steve found an artist to make projections that would take the place of the doves. The march down the aisle got scrapped.

When I got back from touring, I was told that I would be expected the following morning at Halston's studio for a fitting. Kathy and the bridesmaids had been already, more than once.

Steve and my friend Buddha, who worked as a kind of assistant, came up to escort me down. There was an article written about the wedding back then in *The New Yorker,* and even though I don't remember the reporter coming upstairs, he must have, because he got a good look at my apartment. He noticed the colors of the place (red, white, and black, like my redesigned American flag), the big stereo Epic had given me. He even wrote down the names of the magazines on my coffee table: *Fred Russell's Car Care, Gambling Quarterly, Texas Football, Basic Automotive Tools & How to Use Them, Popular Imported Cars, Action Black Belt.* No *New Yorker.* Some of them I still remember. I used *Basic Automotive Tools* to work on my cars or think about working on them. I used *Gambling Quarterly* mostly to satisfy my curiosity about poker or sports or horses. I got *Action Black Belt* because I was still learning karate, not just with Teru but at a kempo school in Los Angeles.

"Let's go," Steve said, tapping a watch. Time for Halston. But I couldn't just go over there in the first clothes of the day. I changed into a beige cowboy suit studded with red stones. It was a Nudie original. Nudie was a Russian Jewish designer who had a shop in North Hollywood, big with musicians (he made the gold suit Elvis wore on the cover of *50,000,000 Elvis Fans Can't Be Wrong*). He loved cars almost as much as I did. Did Halston know who Nudie was? I also had diamond pinkie rings that spelled out my name, first name on the right hand, last name on the left, and a bracelet that spelled out both first and last.

At Halston's place, a secretary brought us into a room of mirrors. Halston was in most of them, thin, dark hair, turtleneck. He didn't mention the Nudie suit, but he told me about what the bridesmaids would be wearing, and what he thought about those outfits. Then he sat at a desk while his assistants took my measurements. They had to do it all over again when an NBC crew showed up to help promote the concert.

The concert? Of course: The wedding was also a concert. A concert needed music and a wedding needed special music. I tried to get a recording down of a wedding march in the band's style, in my style. That meant lots of calls to Steve to help arrange a session of some kind. I asked for someone to come out to my house to record me there, which would have been better than nothing, but nothing doing. I got him to schedule time for me with John Hammond at Columbia, but I never made it there. The march fell apart but everything else was falling into place: people's hair and makeup and final fittings, rings for the ceremony to come, introductions between people who needed to be introduced. I took a car to the Garden and had a few minutes to rehearse some of our new songs.

And then it was show time. It had happened hundreds of times before, in little clubs in New York City, in front of a huge crowd at Woodstock. But it had never happened on a night when I was getting married. We had twenty thousand guests at least, with some of the estimates as high as twenty-five. Years later I saw a picture of a ticket someone kept: $8.50 for a wedding and a concert both. A bargain.

Eddie Kendricks opened for us, and then my mother came out to start things off. Her main point, expressed on the microphone, was that a wedding was a holy moment that should not blend so easily into the rest of the night's entertainment. My niece Lisa reminded everyone again by coming out and singing a spiritual, the same way I used to sing in Vallejo: "I don't worry about tomorrow for I know what my Jesus says."

Faith went out and fashion came in. Models appeared, carrying the gold palm leaves. Then Kathy came out. I had seen the dress in Halston's place but I had not seen her in the dress. Then it was me, sunglasses to block the glint from all the gold.

Bishop B. R. Stewart (no relation), flown in from San Francisco, described the evening's purpose: "We are gathered together here tonight in the sight of God and in the face of this company to join together this man and this woman in holy matrimony. Sly, would you repeat these words after me? Don't be nervous." I laughed, but I was, a little. When it was Kathy's turn, Bishop Stewart, adjusting the microphone for her, accidentally called her "Cynthia." A slip of the lip can sink a ship, but we went on. She reaffirmed the vows. As Bishop Stewart, with the power vested in him, got ready to pronounce us man and wife, he doubled up my name, "Sly Stone Sylvester Stewart," like he was afraid to leave anyone out. But this time he called Kathy Kathy. And then we were married. The crowd screamed. It didn't change much except in the eyes of the world, and the eyes of the world were on us.

The reception at the Waldorf had lines down the block of people trying to get in. A few were me, or people who claimed to be me, dressed up to pass, like I wouldn't have been inside already at my own wedding reception. A few claimed to be Sammy Davis Jr., too. The party was drinking and dancing and smoking and joking, until the late hours and then the early hours, the kind of thing you remember only from the pictures you see afterward.

The next day there was more news. Bishop Stewart wasn't registered in New York. He had to go down to the city clerk and ask to have his paperwork put through so that he could be official and our marriage could be counted. He did. He was. It was.

The story was perfect for magazines. In June, a new magazine named *People Weekly* covered the wedding by putting my name on the cover, even though I didn't get the photo—it was Henry Kissinger and his wife, Nancy, also newlyweds. The most famous *People* cover that summer had a shirtless Telly Savalas, chains dripping down his chest. I watched *Kojak* sometimes. "Who loves ya, baby?" he would say, but what he meant was that you should love him. Telly Savalas was a singer, too, and a few years later he turned "Who Loves Ya, Baby" into a song, working with the arranger Gene Page, who gave the song a little funk. If you were a big enough TV star, you could go anywhere you wanted.

Was I a big enough TV star? I seemed to be. In those years. Geraldo Rivera hosted a show called *Good Night America*. It was mostly a newsmagazine, with one episode about kids dodging the draft and another about the Zapruder film. Geraldo and I knew each other that year, more acquaintances than friends. He had been at the wedding, in it as an usher even, because he maneuvered his way up onstage. Two weeks after the wedding he booked me and Kathy on his show. We went out in matching outfits, black pants, silver sequined tops. I added a hat. Geraldo opened with a joke. "This is the most conservative I've ever seen you dressed," he said.

"Street clothes," I said.

"They said Sinatra coming out of retirement would be the biggest thing in showbiz this year. Your wedding just eclipsed it." Sinatra had said that he was retiring a few years before but then reversed course. *Ol' Blue Eyes Is Back* was the album, and it was all over the airwaves.

Geraldo asked how we had planned it. How in the *world* we had planned it. I gave credit to Steve and Joe. "We just kind of enjoyed it and shared it with lots of friends," I said. "Sometimes people are not aware of the friends they really have."

"Everybody was just so happy that it was a warm feeling," Kathy said. "It was just a happy event. Beautiful."

Geraldo leaned forward. But *why* had we gotten married? "Mainly the society in which we live and the people that are affected by that," I said.

"Are you talking about little Sylvester?" he said.

"Mainly," I said. "But a number of other people think that if you don't get married you're not really serious. They come down on the lady involved and the young man. They try to make you feel like you are kind of kidding around. With the baby, I want to let him know that I ain't kidding around."

We talked about whether Kathy's parents had been shocked by the spectacle. She explained that she came from an artistic family. "Her mother played in *Planet of the Apes*," I said. "She was an ape."

"Is that a mother-in-law joke?" Geraldo said. It was not. "And you were a piece of furniture in *Soylent Green*?" he said to Kathy. "You really have a distinguished acting background in your family."

Interviews had obvious beats. Interviewers hit those beats obviously. Geraldo asked about my reputation for missing gigs but he stood up for me at the same time. "In the two years that I've known you, you never missed one," Geraldo said. He commended me on being the "most together cat" in the record business and asked if Kathy had helped to set me on the straight and narrow path. "I don't know how straight and narrow in relation to last year or the year before," I said.

He clarified: Would I be a traditional husband, he wanted to know? Would I, "within the limits of my business," be faithful? "Within the limits of my own frame of mind and my own conscience," I said, "but not within the limits of things that I read about traditional husbands." He didn't know what I meant. "Like a Dick Van Dyke–style husband," I said. "I don't mean Dick Van Dyke. I don't know the man. He seems very nice. But I don't know if I like that."

Geraldo showed film of the reception, him dancing with his wife, others dancing too. He named some of the guests: Andy Warhol, Penelope Tree, Lorna Luft, Diane von Furstenberg, Donyale Luna. Underneath the footage, a line from "Family Affair" played: "Newlyweds a year ago / Still checking each other out," like it had played at the party. The night went on and on. "I was starting to get a little weathered," Geraldo said. But then he had noticed me up in the balcony, taking a break, watching the festivities.

"I didn't know how long it would go on," I said, "so I thought I would just cool it."

"Did you ever get your second wind?" he asked.

"I hope so," I said.

The show ended with a question about my music. Ken Roberts had told Geraldo that I mostly listened only to Ray Charles and wrote my own stuff. How did I manage to innovate, and how did I keep audiences connected to what I was doing?

"Well, I think the words and the music are almost all the time—and maybe all the time—indicative of the life that I live . . . They relate to the way that I lived, the way that I live now, and the way that I plan to live in the future." Geraldo predicted that the wedding was going to help people see me in a new light. "Good," I said. "That's good. You get tired of being accused of being late, man, and lots of other things. It's good that new things take place and new people have new ideas and find out new things about you."

# 12
✳

## Small Talk
### (1974)

uhammad Ali," Mike Douglas said, but he was talking to me. (This was May of 1974, filming episodes before the wedding that would be shown after it. Mike Douglas was on during the day, while Dick Cavett had been on at night. The title cards for the show had six-petal flowers that looked like the stickers that kept you from slipping in the bathtub. I might not have seen them back then. I was on the air, not on the other side of the air.)

"Yes!" I said, happy to be there, happy to show it. The "Yes!" wasn't a reaction to Ali. It came earlier in the show, right near the beginning. (For the week, I was not just a guest but a co-host. It was Mike's trademark. He would tap a celebrity to sit in all week, allow them to set the tone, have some guests already booked but invite the guest host to bring along some host guests of his own. The guests during my week included Mama Cass; the child actor Rodney Allen Rippy; Michu, the world's shortest man; and table-tennis champions.)

"A hundred thousand," I said, "maybe two hundred thousand." (I was speaking to Mike's shocked face, to his question about how much I spent per year on my clothes. "It's better than buying a place in San Gabriel," I said. I don't remember who I was thinking about when I said that. It fell into a hole somewhere along the nearly fifty years. But the clothes justified the expense, a jumpsuit with gold-glitter suns, moons, and stars, and a belt-buckle that said "SLY" in giant bejeweled letters.)

Mike and I cycled through what were by then the standard questions. The beats. Was I friends with Doris Day and how had I met her? (Yes, and through her son, Terry, and she was a nice lady, and no I had never . . . taken her out. But she had given me a car, a Mercedes. He wanted to know why. "Maybe I'm nice also," I said.) Was it true that I had been a DJ back in San Francisco? (It was, and to prove it I ran through Lord Buckley's Nazz routine. Nearly fifty years later, watching it, I launched into the routine again. Addictive thing, that monologue, at least to me. Hard to hear even a piece of it and not do the whole thing.) I had said something about feeling nervous before the show, but that was impossible, right? (It wasn't.) Was that a star around my neck? (Yes, I said. It was six-pointed, like the flowers on Mike's title card. "Star of David," I said, "maybe David Kapralik." I tugged on my ring. "But I have one with five points also, like Muhammad." I meant the five-pointed Islamic star, but Mike took it as a transition. "Muhammad is with us today," he said, meaning Ali.)

We went to commercial, came back, speculated whether a karate champion would beat a boxer or the other way around, and then I brought out the honored guest. "I *love* Muhammad Ali," I said. He wore a dark suit, light blue shirt, patterned tie. We hugged. I moved down a seat for him.

"You never walk out with a smile," Mike told him.

"I am troubled," Ali said. "We have so many problems in the world. These shows are so phony."

"That's right," I said. A good host is hospitable to his guests. But something about the way I said it brought chuckles from the audience.

"Everybody's laughing," Ali said. "Kikikiki." He showed shiny teeth to demonstrate how fake his laugh was.

"You too," I said. "Kikikikiki."

"Is there an echo in here?" Mike said.

Ali dug in. "To get attention, I play, I clown," he said. "It ain't always good-time Negroes." He matched his fake laugh with a fake smile. "Everything is so good." He gestured toward me but wouldn't look at me. "He makes a little money, I make a little money. But his brothers and uncles and mine are catching hell and hungry. I can't go on pretending things are rosy."

"Muhammad," I said. My tone must have been too sharp, because when he turned to look at me there was no smile left on his face, fake or otherwise. "The only thing we can do for brothers is to do what we're doing," I said. "Be examples. And to be hee hee hee happy and to be intelligent like you are and like you always say."

I was lowering a line, but Ali didn't take the bait. "I'm too intelligent to debate with the brother on television or even clown with him on television," he said. "Behind the doors we can have a good time, but not with all the people watching."

Ali was performing just as much as I was, and I thought I had to say so. "We'd be phony if we didn't do the same thing out here," I said. "We're going to clown around. If you don't like it, I'm going to whup you."

This, I knew, would break the ice. Ali relaxed. We discussed Ali's training camp up in Deer Lake, Pennsylvania, where he was housing and feeding older fighters like Kid Gavilan and Johnny Bratton. We talked about Ali going over to Zaire for the Rumble in the Jungle to fight George Foreman. Even though Foreman had a reputation for being a big brute, Ali said, he didn't punch that hard. "Muhammad hits so hard it's ridiculous," I said.

"Has he hit you?" Mike said.

"I had a pea coat on," I said. "He hit every button on my pea coat without hitting me. I mean I'm talking about speed buddy. Speed. B-r-r-r—r-r-r-rrrr."

Ali was not the day's only guest. Other chairs were filled. The singer and actor Theodore Bikel came out to discuss *Fiddler on the Roof* and how Tevye was a true man of the people. Wayne Hays, a congressman from Ohio, came out to discuss the importance of honest government in the days of Watergate. When Mike asked Ali if he ever thought about going into politics, it was like a bell announcing the next round of fighting.

"No, sir," Ali said. "When you people discuss things, they're not our problems. I am looking at black people as a nation. All of our problems, you all don't have nothing to solve them." He couldn't be a politician, he said. "Because I got to have the white man's flag."

"No, you don't," I said. I began to describe the red, white, and black option.

"I'm talking to them," Ali said. "Take your hand out of my face."

"I want to change the color of the flag," I said. "I'm serious about that."

Ali sighed. "We're going to change the color of the flag? That's a heck of a job. Now we're talking about all kinds of stuff that makes no sense." He leaned forward and talked past me about how other communities had advocates. "My program is only worried about my people first," he said.

"And where do you live, my brother?" I meant Cherry Hill, rich and mostly white. Ali did not like that. A stare froze the space between us.

We went to break, were back in a flash. Wayne Hays extended an olive branch in the form of praise for Barbara Jordan, a black congresswoman from Texas. I extended an olive branch by taking up Ali's point regarding black representation but also Mike's point about entertainment. "What Mike's saying," I said, "is that there's a way to say all of this without having any animosity." Bikel called my idea simplistic. "It's not simplistic," I said. "It's simple." The difference between the two, a complicated matter, was not explored.

Hays reiterated that he only wanted peace. That word struck Ali as ugly. "You kill off all the Indians," Ali said, "you kill off all the blacks, and you get everything for yourself, and now you say that you want peace?" He talked about the Vietcong and how even they could move freely when they came to America. So could the Japanese and the Chinese and the Germans. The only people without this privilege, he said, were black people.

"Where can't you go, Muhammad?" said Wayne Hays.

"Okay," Ali said. "I'm one big nigger, I'm a nigger, got ten million dollars, I'm a great fighter, so I can go. But I'm not talking about me. I'm talking about the brother who can't pay his rent, ain't got nothing."

"What is the answer?" Mike said.

At that, I burst out laughing. It was at the idea that we could find a real answer sitting in chairs on syndicated TV. But Ali thought I was laughing at him. He turned toward me, on me. "People want the truth," he said. "All this laughing and giggling."

"You're laughing and giggling, too," I said, "just like everybody else." But he wasn't.

Mike made a final plea for entertainment as a unifying force, but Ali blocked it. "My brothers are catching hell and catching hell and catching hell," he said.

I put up my arms like a referee trying to end a bout. "Let's be happy," I said. "Time for livin'." I was preaching calm and also advertising our new single.

✳ ✳ ✳

After the commercial, I wasn't with Mike anymore. I was across the stage, with the band, to play a version of "Stand!" that started dreamy and a little hazy. It picked up speed and energy. The front rows of the audience came to their feet. White women, black men, old, young. Our crowd. I went and stood among them.

We also played "I Want to Take You Higher," and stayed up there the rest of the week. My mother was in the audience one day and Mike asked her if she was proud of me. She surely was. Mike talked about my wedding. I tried on some clothes. We discussed my car collection, which included my Cord, a Model A I got from Joe Hicks, a Rolls, and a George Barris Titan built on a Thunderbird chassis. "Soon," I said, "I'm going to race Tommy Smothers's brother." The next day, unless it was the day before, David Steinberg asked me if I had ever been offered any movie roles. Some, I said. What kind of character did I see myself playing the first time out? "The star," I said.

I sat Mr. Froehlich in the audience as a guest of honor. I had flown him out from Vallejo. He came back to the hotel after the taping and was surprised by what he saw, ten guys, a dozen, not the band but other people hanging on. He was hungry, so I told him he could call down to room service and charge it to the room. The second it was clear that he was ordering, everyone else started piping up, too, asking for their own steaks, drinks, shrimp cocktails. By the time the food came all the other guys were gone and it was just Mr. Froehlich.

On the final show of the week, Sylvester Jr. was carried out to sit with the band. As we were introduced, Mike held him up to the audience. But Sylvester Jr. wasn't out there just for show. We performed "Small Talk," the title song from our new record. He cried his vocals on the track. Two years later, Stevie Wonder put the noise of a crying baby on "Isn't She Lovely." I don't know if he got the idea from me and I don't mind if he did. A good idea should travel around the world. Sylvester Jr. couldn't cry on command, so for the TV performance, I put my fingers over his lips and he kazooed happily.

**✳ ✳ ✳**

Sylvester Jr. wasn't just on the title song of *Small Talk*. He was on the cover, too. It was a photo of me, him, and Kathy, everyone smiling. Family fare. Norman Seeff took it—he had taken a similar photo for a Bobby Womack album a few years before. The back cover of *Small Talk* showed me in bed, just waking up or just going to sleep, hanging in the middle between the two, and also hanging in the middle of the bed. That was my spot, where I felt comfortable. You can say tranquil or you can say tranquilized.

People said both. *Small Talk* was a gentle record, with swing and sway and strings to show the way. The first single was "Time for Livin'," the one I had quoted at Ali. It was a song about coming together to put away fear. Another song we played during the week on Mike Douglas, "Mother Beautiful," had a simple message: listen to Mother, whether it's Mother Earth or the mother of your children or the mother who sits in the crowd and tells the world she's proud of you.

I was still reaching out into the world for ideas. There was a song called "Livin' While I'm Livin'" that reached back to what Sergio had said in the limo a year before. Bubba told another story about playing in Queens right after *Fresh* came out. As I was walking toward the stage a voice from the crowd yelled out at me. "Sly," he said. "Sly! Don't take no wooden nickels." I went through the barrier to find the guy. I had never heard of wooden nickels before. Was it an insult? A slur? Bubba calmed me down by explaining that a wooden nickel meant something that didn't mean much. "You got to get that chip off your shoulder," he said. According to him, that incident, and the phrase "wooden nickel," got loaded right into the lyrics of "Say You Will." Good story. Never happened.

Some of the songs were short. "Mother Beautiful" was two minutes and then it hit the road, Jack. "Livin' While I'm Livin'" and "This Is Love," a doo-wop ballad with strings, were under three. Even the ones that stretched out went to four minutes, not six (like "In Time") or eight ("Africa Talks to You").

Take "Loose Booty." Funkadelic—the Detroit funk-rock band led by George Clinton—had a different song with the same name a few years before. Mine was built on top of the story of Shadrach, Meshach, and Abednego. It was a Bible story: Three men refused to worship King Nebuchadnezzar and were thrown in a fiery pit. But they didn't die. They came out, with a fourth figure leading them, the prophet Daniel. Shadrach, Meshach, and Abednego were figures of resistance. Louis Armstrong had a song about them. Martin Luther King, Jr., mentioned them when he wrote from the Birmingham Jail. I didn't retell the whole story but I wanted a taste of it in there. Music could help you resist everyday problems. Music could keep you out of the fire.

Side one ended with "Can't Strain My Brain," another song whose title rhymed with something Funkadelic did—they had put out a song called "Can't Stand the Strain" the year before. My song came clean about worry and anxiety. The lyrics weren't abstract. They were concrete enough to weigh me down—like I had told Geraldo, indicative of the life that I was living. I was worrying in those days, maybe not all the time but plenty of it.

Some of it had to do with drugs. They hadn't gone away. They had come to stay. Some people were scientific in the matter of drugs. They approached it like they were their own doctor, read medical books to get a sense of how much coke to take and when, and how long before or after the coke you should take a barbiturate so you didn't bounce too high. I was interested in the science but mostly it was about the music.

Some of it had to do with money. For years I had been generous with everything. What Mr. Froehlich had seen in the hotel happened in every hotel. It wasn't just food and drink. It was drugs, too. I would ask if anyone wanted to share in my stash, not just drop-bys but bellboys, maids, anyone. They would usually decline at first but the second day I would come into the room and see them doing a line.

Some of it had to do with the marriage. The picture on the cover of *Small Talk* was just a picture, and just a cover. Like I had told Geraldo, I wasn't Dick Van Dyke. The start of things was full of starts and stops. Kathy and I loved being parents. There was not a single negative in or around the baby. But it was hard to share your life with another person when you weren't around much, and a common wavelength came and went.

Some of it had to do with the band. Rose was starting down a new road with Bubba, on the edge of marriage, and there was an overall sense of fatigue. We were still family but we were family at the end of a long day.

Though "Can't Strain My Brain" put caution tape around everything—it was about a brain that wasn't just feeling strain, but feeling pain—I kept working. I played with REO Speedwagon (another Epic group) on a song called "You Can Fly" and for Elvin Bishop (another California artist) on a song called "Ground Hog." (Mixed messages.) I sang with Kathi McDonald, who had started singing backup for Ike and Tina Turner, on the title track of her solo record *Insane Asylum*. I worked on the Temptations' *Wings of Love*, which Jeffrey Bowen produced. Jimmy Ford wrote most of that record, but I did three songs with him, including "Up the Creek (Without a Paddle)," the lead single. They got credited to Truman Thomas, somehow—he was an organ player, from Texas too, played on the record.

In a year of other people's music, we still had our own. We were playing everywhere—Cincinnati, Grand Rapids, Lawrence. Everywhere included the TV. You could find us many nights on *Soul Train* or *Midnight Special* or *Don Kirschner's Rock Concert*. I didn't like those shows so much. Don Cornelius on *Soul Train* was cool enough to talk to. But shows like that . . . you couldn't get a true flow going. The cameras were on you from all angles. Some programs, like *Midnight Special*, got too frantic, with people in your sight line scurrying and pointing. Were they pointing at me? And if not, was I supposed to look? It was hard to concentrate on anything and I was required to get into the music correctly.

The year wound down with another *Mike Douglas* appearance, not co-hosting this time, just guesting, Richard Pryor the other guest, some joking, some jawing, Pryor sitting like a child on the floor in front of my chair, then standing when I stood, playful shoving between us, and then a dare. Could I get Richard to play drums? I was the only one who could, and I told Mike Douglas that. "You gonna play drums?" I asked Richard, who went all fake-serious with his answer ("When we here are striving for a better future for our people").

I changed clothes behind a screen ("I ain't gonna change *with* you," Richard said), came out all silver, walked over to where the instruments were set up, picked up a guitar, strummed, stopped.

"You didn't tune it," I said. I sat down at the piano. Richard sat down at the drums. We rolled through the opening of "If You Want Me to Stay." Richard kept the beat or tried to. "Come on, Richard," I said. Then I walked off like I was disgusted. He made like he was hurt. "How you gonna fire me on national TV, chump?"

The wind-up for 1975 was a weeklong January stand at Radio City, Kool and the Gang opening. The first show was on January 16, and it looked like there were as many people on the stage as in the audience. The newspaper clocked the crowd at a thousand. They also clocked us on the fade. Our set was short. The *Times* complained that we were only playing hits instead of new material, and that energy was wanting. That may be true. I don't remember much about that show because I don't want to remember. After those gigs, there were crossed wires, pointed fingers. No one could agree on anything except that we couldn't agree on anything. When people flew back west, it really felt like they were leaving.

There were already some songs for a new album, and others were making the rounds in my mind. One of them, "I Get High on You," sounded like a hit. Another one, "Crossword Puzzle," sounded like it could be even bigger. I started to get new blood for (and from) the Family Stone. A teenage bassist named Bobby Vega came on, as did my cousin Little Moses Tyson, at the time just fourteen in Vallejo, who played organ. Gail Muldrow, a guitarist whom I had known since high school in Vallejo, started playing with me. For backup vocals, I got Rudy Love, a soul singer from Kansas. I liked the name of Rudy's group, Rudy Love and the Love Family. Sounded familiar. And I sent the word out for more. During a session at the Record Plant, in the Pit, a singer named Dawn Silva showed up and sang backup. She was able to get the songs right away, half-hour tops, and afterward I sent for someone to bring her in. I was back in the lips bed with Kathy and some others, and Dawn came back and I said hello, shook her hand, and welcomed her aboard.

Along with reloading, I relocated, up to Novato in Marin County, to a big house on forty acres at the end of a road up a hill, Cabro Court, lots of greenery and water, big driveway for the cars (by this point a Mercedes or two, a Rolls-Royce, a Maserati, an old Ford truck). A pair of peacocks roamed the grounds. We set up shop there, me and Kathy and Mook—that's what I called Sylvester Jr. sometimes because it's what we would call each other sometimes, a nickname we borrowed from a friend of Bubba's. Bubba was there, too, and Buddy Miles, and Cynthia, and the violinist Vicki Blackwell. Who exactly depended on what day exactly. But some of those who exactlys were running up my long-distance bill, so I had the phone company come out and install a real coin-operated phone, to make everyone aware that calls cost money.

In February 1975, Ken Roberts got me a gig cohosting the American Music Awards with the pop singer Helen Reddy and the country singer Roy Clark. We flew down to Hollywood, checked into the hotel, and then went over to the Shrine Auditorium for the awards. Everyone was there that year: Al Green, the O'Jays, Karen Carpenter, Stevie Wonder, Tom Jones. Michael Jackson came by my dressing room before the show to shake my hand and say hello.

The idea of the cohosting was that we were all artists melting in the same pot, which we illustrated by singing parts of one another's songs. Helen did "Everyday People," Roy did Helen's "Leave Me Alone," I did Roy's "The Lawrence Welk Hee-Haw Counter Revolution Polka"—and then the three of us lined up to perform the show's theme song, which was about how American music brought together rock and pop and soul and country.

I was wearing the moon, star, and sun bodysuit I had worn on *The Mike Douglas Show* with Ali, smiling the same smile from the *Small Talk* cover photo. Freddie and Rustee came to play the awards, but additional reinforcements were needed. I put together a band quick for that show. Rose didn't make the trip, so I had Dawn Silva back to sing her parts.

At one point during the performance I lifted my guitar and the strap snapped. I set the guitar down but I was setting down more than that. There had been plenty of times when the band had changed. It changed when I moved down to L.A. It changed when Larry left. But in those early months of 1975, the Family Stone, at least the way I thought of it—the group that had come together in my parents' basement on Urbano, graduated to Winchester Cathedral, signed to Epic, danced to the music, stood, taken the stage at Woodstock, reached number 1 three times, helped make a new sound out of old ones—was over.

**PART THREE**

# Remember Who You Are

# 13
✳

## Crossword Puzzle
### (1975–1979)

One afternoon I was rehearsing the singers up at the ranch. Rudy Love was there and my dad was there, too, walking out in front of the place. A guy I didn't know very well, someone connected to Bubba, got up on a bike and started driving right at my dad. He looked like he was going to bump into him or run him over. We were all frozen watching it unfold.

That was also the year I got a briefcase phone. Bubba and I were in the Las Vegas airport one afternoon when I saw a guy with a black leather briefcase standing near a counter. The case was open and a wire ran from it to what looked like a brick at his ear. "Come on, man," I said to him. "Are you really talking to someone?" He showed me. I got briefcase phones for myself and Bubba. I remember my number still. The last digits were 262. I'm not going to give out the whole number.

Back to my dad and the bike. The bike got closer. Rudy Love, in one quick motion, grabbed my briefcase phone and threw it at the guy. It hit him and stopped him. He never hit my dad. The phone worked perfectly to send a message. And it kept working as a phone, too.

The phone was working and we were working too, on the new record. Sometimes we were at home. Sometimes we were in Sausalito at the Record Plant. Working on music was the only thing that truly settled my mind. When I got deep into the new songs, I didn't need anything else. That included drugs. Some weeks I would quit completely. I'd be seven days clean, ten days clean, only into the music.

It never lasted.

Someone would come around with coke or angel dust and I would use one night and then the next night and on the third that was mostly what was filling the house and on the fourth I would realize that I had forgotten to sleep since the night before the first night.

That snowballed into episodes where I'd end up laid out on the floor of a bedroom or a bathroom, waiting for someone to pick me up. Someone always picked me up. But when that happened, it could be hard for me to pick up the thread and keep working.

It wasn't just drugs. There were other distractions. In October I had to go back down to Bel Air to work out some tax shit. It was on me suddenly. Someone once told me a theory that it was a direct result of *The Mike Douglas Show* the year before. It wasn't Mike's fault, but a condition of existence, which was that the IRS had agents watching when celebrities appeared on TV, keeping track of what they claimed to own. I had mentioned my car collection and some people thought that it had put a burr under their saddle. I can't prove that but I can prove that suddenly it felt like there were lots of questions about taxes. I asked Dawn Silva to manage the ranch while I was gone.

The momentum of work was hard to get back. I tried. I didn't want to get into the situation I had been in with *Riot*: years going by, record label asking questions. And it wasn't just records. We had music to play, much of it on TV: Helen Reddy's show, Tony Orlando's show, Tom Jones's show.

One day I was sitting in my RV, looking out the window, and I spotted two figures about a hundred yards away. It looked like Bubba and someone else, maybe his man Black.

One figure started moving faster. He was fifty yards away, then thirty, ten, and then Black was inside the RV, holding a rifle. Bubba had the idea that it was his job to force me to record. I might have been the source of that idea: make sure I get this record done, man. This was his interpretation: send Black up into the RV with a rifle to push me along. But I had stopped for the day and didn't give a fuck.

Black got up on me. Bubba should have stopped it but he wasn't in the RV at first, and even when he showed he just stood back. I went outside and Black followed me. Then I was running and he was running too, and when I turned to confront him he hit me in the eye with his fist.

That was enough. "Get the fuck out of here," I said to Black, but also to Bubba. It was almost like he was waiting to hear me say it. For all Bubba's criticism of Larry—that he was grabbing the spotlight, growing his presence at the expense of the group—he was doing some of that himself, not for his own benefit, but for Rose's. He was her husband and her manager now, and he thought that it was her time. He had started looking into a solo career for her, especially with the Family Stone winding down. So he got the fuck out of there, too.

People moving out, people moving in. I had space up in Novato so I gave one of the spare rooms to Dawn Silva and her son, also named Bubba, who was about the same age as Sylvester Jr. They played together. One morning, too early, Bubba started beating on a drum set. "Shh," Dawn told him. She thought I would be mad. Instead I gave him some drum lessons and sticks of his own. A few days later crying came loud through the house, both baby boys at once. I investigated. It turned out that Bubba and Mook had fought. Bubba had been drumming, and Sylvester Jr. had broken one of his sticks and thrown it at him. Bubba came back with a punch in the nose. Bubba won. Kathy wanted me to give out punishment to Bubba but I was fine with what had happened. Bubba learned to protect his things and Sylvester Jr. learned not to mess with other people's things. Lessons all around. I gave Bubba two new sticks, gave Sylvester Jr. a hug, and got back to business.

Business was the new record, *High on You*. The cover photo tried to recover some of the energy of *Fresh*—it was another shot of me jumping up in the air, taken not by Avedon but by Herb Greene, showing me not in a leather suit but in patchwork jeans.

The album was a patchwork, too. "I Get High on You" was a hit, like I thought. The rest of *High on You* was mostly me, laying down instrument after instrument except for the horns and the backup vocals. That meant the songs were funky. "Crossword Puzzle" picked up where "Babies Makin' Babies" had left off, telling a story about an unmarried mother and asking questions about how our society valued women and children. As the song went on, it reached back even further, to "Everyday People" or even "Underdog." One person had no right to low-rate another just because different choices had been made: "How can you wish her pain / 'Cause she has a maiden name?"

Songs separated good behaviors from bad ones. "Who Do You Love?" wondered what was right and wrong in matters of the heart. "Organize" talked about getting your shit together no matter what shit you might be doing ("a drug is a drag if you're dragging"). "Le Lo Li" played off "different strokes for different

folks" to tell a story about coming apart more than coming together: "Different pills for different thrills / Different days for
different ways / Different freaks for different weeks."

✳ ✳ ✳

One afternoon the phone rang. It was Dawn Silva. She was at her
sister's house, she said. "Fine," I said. That didn't sound like big
news. Then she explained the rest, which did.

She had been seeing a lawyer who had done some work with
the Black Panthers, and he asked her if she wanted to meet Huey
Newton. By then, the Panthers had been infiltrated by
COINTELPRO—the FBI's program for disrupting so-called
subversive political groups. They weren't at full power anymore,
but they were still doing their free breakfast program and community organizing in Oakland. Dawn went to their penthouse
headquarters at the Lakeshore Apartments. When she got there,
Huey had an audience with five or six other women and told
them they would all be expected to do their duty. "Which is?"
one of the women asked. He explained: They needed the women
to help breed supersoldiers.

Dawn wasn't interested, but Huey wasn't interested that she
wasn't interested. He made her take her clothes off, then he told
his lieutenants to hide them and lock her in the apartment naked.
She got food and water left by the door but nothing else: no
phones, no way of contacting the outside world. A day passed.
Another day.

The third day or so, Huey came home with a woman. They
went into the bedroom to breed some supersoldiers and Dawn
grabbed a towel and made a run for it. She made it down the hall,
down the stairs, and to the front desk, where the doorman hid
her in a closet and got her a raincoat. She took a cab to her sister's house in San Francisco, changed out of the raincoat into

some clothes, and called me. "I'm at my sister's house," she said again. Now I understood.

I picked her up in my Rolls-Royce and we went to the CBS studios on Folsom. That's where we were going most of the time to work. The Record Plant was in financial trouble and the bank shut it down sometimes. I used the phone there to call Huey. "Bring Dawn's clothes over here," I said. He started explaining but I cut him off. "You can't have this one," I said. "She's mine."

I rescued Dawn, but I couldn't rescue everyone. Dave Kapralik was in a bad space. He felt separate from the scene at Bel Air—when he would come around he wouldn't know where to look—and like everyone else, he was losing control of the drugs he was taking. He sank, or forgot how to swim, and when he saw more water than sky above him, he went to the Beverly Hills Hotel and poured a bottle of pills down his throat. He meant to die, but he ordered up a big last meal from room service, ate too much of it, and threw up the pills.

That was it for him. He moved to Boston, where he started over singing songs for kids. The last time I saw him it was in the office of a lawyer we both knew. When we ran into each other, we had no angry words, but I knew things were different.

Dave had a different memory of our last meeting. He said that he came back a few years later to L.A. on a visit (could be), went to a motel to see me (could be), found me with a girl in a room (could be). He sat on a chair, he said, and sang me a song about how he had a spiritual reawakening when he went to a zoo and a hippo kissed him. That seems like the kind of thing I would remember hearing.

✳ ✳ ✳

There were girls coming in and out of the Novato house all the time. Maybe three, maybe four, maybe more. If a new girl came

London, 1973 (Michael Putland / Getty Images)

What a fine young man. (Family photograph)

FACING PAGE: Hard at work as a DJ at KSOL, San Francisco
(Michael Ochs Archives / Getty Images)

Plus "C'mon and Swim" by Bobby Freeman, cowritten and produced
by one Sylvester Stewart

AUTUMN

BOBBY FREEMAN

Record No.
2
Time 2:43

Taracrest Music
(BMI)

C'MON AND SWIM
(Stewart – Coman)

A COUGAR PRODUCTION

Live at the Fillmore East, 1968 (Michael Ochs Archives / Getty Images)

ABOVE: At Woodstock (Michael Wadleigh, courtesy kpa Publicity Stills / United Archives / Alamy)

BELOW: At the Harlem Cultural Festival, 1969 (Alamy)

Sly and the Family Stone, 1969: (clockwise from bottom left) Rose Stone,
Cynthia Robinson, Jerry Martini (with glasses), Larry Graham,
Freddie Stone, Gregg Errico, Sly Stone (Stephen Paley)

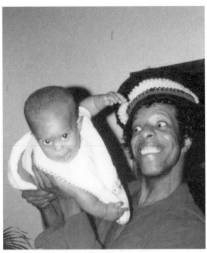

With the babies!

(Family photographs)

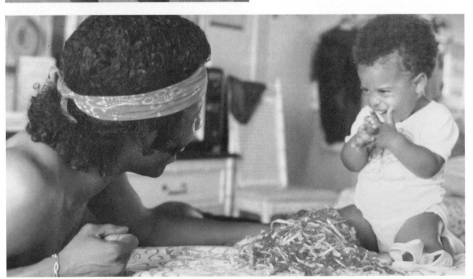

Live fast!
(Motorcycle photograph by
Stephen Paley)

ABOVE: With Clive Davis, 1972 (Photograph by Stephen Paley, Michael Ochs Archives / Getty Images)

BELOW: With George Clinton, Los Angeles, 2009 (Amanda Edwards / Getty Images Entertainment)

Reclining at the Warner Brothers lot, Los Angeles, 1970

(Photograph by Stephen Paley, Michael Ochs Archives / Getty Images)

A more casual day with Kathy
and Freddie (in the middle)
(Family photograph)

At the Halston studio
looking at a dress for
the wedding
(Photograph by Stephen
Paley, Michael Ochs
Archives / Getty Images)

Wedding at Madison Square Garden

(TOP: WWD / Penske Media / Getty Images; BOTTOM: Everett Collection Inc. / Alamy)

A family affair. CLOCKWISE, FROM ABOVE: With Sylvester Jr.; with Sylvester Jr. and Phunne; with Cynthia and Phunne; with best friend Arlene, then and now; with all the kids; and with Nove. Los Angeles (Family photographs)

ABOVE: (from left) Freddie Stewart; Sylvester Stewart, Jr.;
Nove Carmel; Vet Stone (above Nove); Rose Stone; Sly; and Phunne (Family photograph)
BELOW: (from left) Freddie's wife, Melody; Phunne; Freddie; Arlene;
Sylvester Jr.; and Sylvester Jr.'s wife, Jessica (Family photograph)

Thank you. (Family photograph)

to the door and I liked the looks of her, I'd ask her to come upstairs with me. But I was still with Kathy, too. We had Sylvester Jr. We were a family, even if I wasn't Dick Van Dyke.

One day rehearsal at the house was done, and I went upstairs to a room while Dawn went to the pay phone to call her mother. Over the intercom system I heard a noise from a bedroom. It was Kathy. That was fine because she lived there, too, but the bedroom noise was her and a guy named Michael, a drummer who had played with us. I bolted from one room to the other, caught them in the act. It threw me off.

I ran out of the room, grabbed a hammer, and ran back in. He jumped out of the bed, swept up his clothes in a ball, and ran down the stairs. I went after him, hammer held up. He went out the front door and I followed. He started down the hill and I followed. I chased him all the way down until he found another gear and a burst of speed. I didn't hear anything else about Michael after he ran down the hill. He may be running still.

When I got back, I went to the garage, got something heavy, and went after Kathy's Mercedes. I smashed the windshield and put dents into the body. Kathy was still naked, still in the bedroom, shivering and crying. I avoided looking at her like people avoid looking at the sun but I saw the shadows she cast. She had an excuse, which was that she thought Michael was me. But if she could make that mistake, it was still goodbye. I called her father. "Come get her," I said.

"Don't hurt her," he said.

"I ain't gonna hurt her," I said. But she had to leave. She came back, but nothing was the same after that.

The bad feeling with Kathy hung around and joined other bad feelings that were hanging around, too. I hadn't solved the tax issue when I had gone down to L.A. The IRS took the Bel Air house and then they came up to Novato and drove away some of my cars. They also went to the Record Plant to take some of my instruments, but by that point I was a step ahead. I had moved operations over to CBS Records, and was hard at work on new music for as long as it took to get it right: ten hours straight, twelve, twenty.

During one of those hours, Kathy and Sylvester Jr. came back from the store to the house. She put the baby down and Gun, my pit bull, attacked him. Gun got Sylvester Jr.'s entire head in his mouth. Teeth went down one side of his face and took off part of his ear. Kathy screamed, rushed to separate them, drove Sylvester Jr. to the hospital so he could be patched up, called me.

As soon as I heard, I rushed home. I hugged Sylvester Jr. and then took Gun upstairs for a talk. People tried to stop me from having the talk. Cynthia did. Dawn did. But the talk needed to be had. Gun was my best friend. I understood him. "Let's go," I told him. We went up to the bedroom and then out on the balcony. I got out a rifle and pointed it at him to make him apologize. You can get a motherfucker to be good. But he didn't apologize. He made a noise that told me he was never going to be sorry. I shot him and then threw the body down into the canyon. It was the hardest thing I had ever done. He was my best friend. It tore through me. After that it was even hard for me to look at certain places in the house because they made me think about him.

The episode with Gun made bad things worse. Work was coming in, but I couldn't focus on it. Jeffrey Bowen had me come over to one of Berry Gordy's mansions to help with some songs for Diana Ross. Berry was there, running his mouth in a good way. He had money and that seemed to move his mouth forward. I liked him. But I was liking Jeffrey less and less, though I still admired the way he hustled. It seemed like his gig was to be around me. Anything I did he'd want to do it. He'd want a deal or a hookup. He was like that with everyone. At Berry's place I saw him driving one of Berry's Rolls-Royces, a look on his face like it was his own.

I worked for a few days on songs for Diana but the vocal arrangements didn't fit with the sound she had in mind. I don't remember exactly why but I do remember that she was musty. I think she had been napping and someone woke her up to sing. I also wrote a song or two for Rose. Bubba had connected with Jeffrey, too, and set up a solo record for Rose at Motown that included a version of "I Get High on You" and another one called "A Whole New Thing." I didn't work on that for very long, and when I stopped, Bubba wrote some new songs in imitation of the Family Stone and even brought some of the band over to play.

In a hard time, you try to make things easier, keep energy up, get further from what feels bad. Partly that came through drugs. Now some of it was freebase, which was cocaine turned pure with ether and then smoked. Partly that came through people. There was a woman in Novato named Olenka Wallach. She lived down the hill. Her family had livestock: cows, maybe sheep. They would wander onto the road and make their way up to my property. She would come after them with a stick and try to guide them back onto her property. I think I first saw her from my balcony. As soon as I saw her, I wanted to meet her. I gestured for her to come up to the house, and she did. She was quiet. I liked that about her. She was part Brazilian, mixed background like most of the other women I liked. When she came up to the house, she also came upstairs.

The new group had its ups and downs. We brought on more singers, including Lynn Mabry, whose mother was cousins with my mother, and Lady Bianca, who also played keyboards. Everyone got fired for one reason or another at one time or another.

Maybe someone would make a comment about how I was going to fuck everything up with angel dust. Gone! Maybe someone would sing their parts too loud. Gone! But it all settled, and we made it to stages, usually not late, alongside Barry White, the Dramatics, Rufus with Chaka Khan.

In the midst of it all, Cynthia had a daughter. Her daughter and my daughter, too. Cynthia and I had been together on the road off and on over the years, and definitely on earlier that year. Count the months backwards.

The first time I saw Cynthia's daughter—my daughter, too—she was in an incubator, with tubes in her nose and poke holes in her fingers and toes. There had been complications that meant the doctors couldn't send her home right away. She had started breathing before she came out, so she was taking in fluid. There were worries that she would be slowed down because of it, that she would struggle in her life. That all turned out to be wrong, but doctors couldn't see the future any more clearly than anyone else. I didn't try to see the future. I tried to see the baby, tried to get a real look at her through the tubes and the poke holes. She was beautiful.

We named her Sylvette Phunne Robinson. I picked the name because I liked the word and the concept. She was just born but it was fun to be born.

Kathy and I were trying to get back together, or maybe I was trying to see if I believed that she was trying. When Kathy found out about Phunne, she went to Cynthia and asked her if it was true. "Come in and sit down," Cynthia said. Kathy wasn't happy but what can you do? A baby can't be unborn.

When Cynthia got back from the hospital, she started to come over to the Novato house, sometimes with the baby. Musicians were also coming by, including a bunch that belonged to a Sacramento group called the Chocolate Chips: a guitarist named Joe

Baker, a bassist named Dwight Hogan. The Chocolate Chips had put out a single called "There You Are (I See You)" where they were trying to sound just like me. I turned the factual into actual and made them my new band.

I had new songs for the new band, though they were coming out into a less brave new world. When I first heard disco, I tolerated it. But I knew it was a formula: four on the floor, same more and more. Rose Royce had a top soundtrack with *Car Wash*. Wild Cherry played that funky music white boy all summer long. I was going in the other direction, more toward composition, more complex arrangements, more subtle sounds.

The record that came out of those sessions, *Heard Ya Missed Me, Well I'm Back*, had another Herb Greene cover photo, this one showing me as a one-man band, an accordion on a shoulder strap, a drum and cymbal on my back, a kazoo wedged into a harmonica holder, a top hat in my free hand. I was smiling wide. I wanted to remind everyone that music could be good for everything and that I was not good for nothing.

The lead-off track, also the title track, was a love letter to the audience, a confession that I couldn't stay away from making songs for them. The rest of the songs were about lessons learned or not yet learned. "What Was I Thinking in My Head?" was about how people (me?) had a habit of getting in their own way, sometimes because they had a habit. "That Thing" tried to teach people (me?) the importance of commitment, and "Everything in You" tried to teach people (me?) to let their full selves emerge without shame or worry.

I remember talking to a reporter and he said something about how the new record was "dangerous." I think what he meant was that I had new ideas that pushed against the ideas that were already there. But I didn't like the sound of it. "I ain't dangerous," I said. "I love, man. I love. I love. I love. That's what's wrong.

People are afraid of my love. I love, man. I just love I love I love. I love, I love, love, love, love, love, love, love. People are afraid of my love. They tighten up."

Epic wasn't being straight about the record. They kept moving the release date and they weren't delivering on promotion—I saw one magazine ad, but nothing beyond that.

We brought in a teenager named Neal Austinson, who was friends at school with Jerry Martini's daughter. Neal was a huge fan of the band, eager to get into the outer circle and then the inner one.

One day Neal knocked on my bedroom door. I came out and stared at him. I don't think either of us said a word for a minute. Then he told me that he knew John Farey, who played keyboards with me. "John's in there," I said, pointing with my chin downstairs to where the band was rehearsing. He didn't move. "John's in there," I said.

He caught my drift and drifted downstairs. I stayed up in my room. I had only one rule, which was that I didn't want noise. But noise kept coming. Freddie's daughter bumped into a drum set. Someone pinged a high note on a piano. Each time I ran downstairs and got louder and louder about the quiet.

Eventually they cleared out. Neal stayed in the room. He was looking at a movie poster, *Blazing Saddles*, I think. I came up behind him. He turned around and saw me but before he could say anything I turned off the lights. In the pitch-black room he bumped into two, three things before I turned the lights back on.

But I liked Neal. He kept coming around. In school, bored like I had been twenty years before, he was making flyers for imaginary concerts. I put some of them up in my bedroom and had him start to do grassroots promotion for the record, which meant calling radio stations and requesting all the songs all the time.

Soon enough I went back on the road. Usually I was accustomed to being in the driver's seat. This time I was the passenger. George Clinton and P-Funk took the wheel.

George was my boy. I called him "the funk baby" because that's how he was born, or reborn. He had started singing doo-wop, written songs in Detroit, had some soul hits, and then had his head turned by rock and roll and the psychedelic sixties. He ran Parliament and Funkadelic, two bands that used many of the same musicians. Funkadelic was extreme, with loud guitars, more out there than the most psychedelic Temptations records. Parliament made funk that popped.

Funkadelic had opened for us years before but grown into an enterprise. As George played to bigger and bigger crowds, he preached the gospel of funk in interview after interview. He gave credit to James Brown and Dyke and the Blazers and Wilson Pickett, of course. He gave credit to Richard Pryor, for his bit about *The Exorcist* ("What the fuck is that funky smell and all that racket upstairs?"). He gave credit to Jimi Hendrix, especially late projects like Band of Gypsys. And he gave credit to us. Early songs of ours like "I Cannot Make It" and "Trip to Your Heart," he said, felt foundational to him, and on top of them he built a funhouse.

If P-Funk's albums were a funhouse, they were the whole amusement park onstage. There could be a dozen people up there in crazy wigs and crazier costumes, each doing their own thing. They called it the Earth Tour but it was from another planet. And by the time each night's show ended, a real spaceship had landed onstage—the Mothership, which George had built so that he could come out of it like an astronaut of funk.

I joined the tour in Houston in October. It was Halloween, but with George every night was. Bootsy Collins and his Rubber Band went out first, did his best to pay off history, and then I had my set. The songs sounded good, but I also started to see that it was history for most of the kids in the crowd. It was the past as far as they were concerned, no matter how well we played. We went on for more shows in Texas, a few in Oklahoma and Louisiana, and then east to Maryland, but by Thanksgiving I came off the tour.

\* \* \*

They say nothing is certain except death and taxes. I heard it loud and clear from 1978.

"I have a question." Bobby Womack was calling me.

"Okay," I said.

"It's about my son."

"Son?" I said. I wasn't aware of one.

He explained that he and his wife, Regina, had a baby on the way. I wondered if he wanted me to be the godfather. "No," Bobby said. "I want you to help name him."

"I got it," I said.

"Good," he said. "I'll give you time to think about it."

"No," I said. "I mean I got it now. You've got to name him Truth."

"Why?"

"Because you lie so goddamn much." Bobby laughed. He knew I had him. That was the name he went with, Truth Bobby. A few months later he came in late from a gig. He and Regina were talking out in the living room. One of them went to the bedroom to check on the baby and saw that he had fallen into a space between the mattress and the wall. He suffocated in there, not even five months old. They kept him alive in other ways. Bobby named his production company Truth and then the next year he and Regina had another baby, another boy, and named him Bobby Truth. I took every chance I had to look at my own kids and make sure they were safe at home.

Safe, home: By then I had left Novato for a place in Mandeville Canyon. I was just down the way from Ken Roberts, though he had acreage. One day, one of my bodyguards came upon a young guy standing out in the street in front of my house. He wanted to get inside and couldn't explain why. He tried to push his way onto the property and got shot. He was rushed to UCLA Medical Center but they couldn't save him. I heard about it later, but I didn't hear it at the time. I was in the back in my bedroom. My bodyguard was cleared and no charges were filed.

Charges, filing: The IRS issues hadn't gone away. I couldn't get my head around them, so I put them in Ken Roberts's hands. Ken arranged a payment schedule or a settlement, but when the day came for the hearing I didn't show up. Ken didn't seem happy about that at all. He said it would only make things harder. But how had they gotten so hard in the first place? It made no sense to me. Maybe they had seen me on TV and thought that I owned too many cars, but what of it? Work it out. I figured that there was still money because there were still papers to sign. Maybe I'd be walking into a hotel and someone would push a paper in my face. "Sly, Sly," they were saying, but really they were saying "sign, sign." There was always an assurance that came along with it—it was someone who had been friends with Dave Kapralik in the old days or Ken in the new ones. Sometimes they mentioned my parents' names to prove that I was right to trust them.

I must have signed too many of those papers, or failed to sign a different kind, because the bill came. I did what I could. I tried to live a slimmer life, traded down from a Mark IV to a Mustang. I got rid of any property I didn't need. The bill didn't seem to be coming down fast enough. When there was nothing more I could do, I couldn't do anything else, and I sat on the stairs at the

Mandeville house and watched them take my things from me. They meaning the government. Me meaning me.

The year could feel relentless, unless you were in the middle of it, in which case it just felt like days turning to weeks turning to months, some of them good, some bad. I didn't really keep score except when it came to scoring. Getting high and making music pushed time forward. But there were some moments that stood out sharply. Late in the year, Epic dropped me. I had been there more than ten years. It was more than a second home. It was a first home. Millions of records had been sold. But the recent albums had fallen off and fewer and fewer true believers remained at the label.

I went looking for another home. Warner Bros. came in with a strong offer and Ken Roberts recommended giving it a serious look. I wanted to stay with people who knew me. After Clive Davis had left Columbia, he had founded Arista Records. Clive and I met at the Beverly Hills Hotel. We had a long meeting and a good one. I told him I had songs already written and that they added up to most of a record. He listened to me carefully and listened to some of the songs. Clive was never less than careful. But he didn't bring me over to Arista.

We got back to Warner, accepted their offer, and completed the record. Freddie, Rose, and Cynthia were on some tracks. Pat Rizzo was back. Joe Baker from the Chocolate Chips was back. I borrowed some musicians from Billy Preston to round out the group and brought on my niece Lisa, Rose's daughter, as a vocalist.

When I delivered the record, Warner assigned it to a guy named Mark Davis, who had worked with bands like Rose Royce and Stargard. He was entrusted with final production. Mark was moving up at the label and could sometimes have a high opinion of himself. But he wasn't the whole problem. The problem was the idea that it was a problem for me to produce the record myself. I had always done it, on my biggest hits. Why not now?

The album came out: *Back on the Right Track*. The cover photo was of me in a brown vest. I had a new and improved smile of new and improved teeth, and the whole album went with that same angle. The publicists lined up articles that were mainly or only about how I was mature and clean, newly willing to walk the straight and narrow. "Sly Stone Emerges Cheerful and Charming," said one headline. There was so much talk of being back that it was almost an affront.

The songs on the album played to this message of positivity and persistence, how to do it by sticking to it: "Remember Who You Are," "Back on the Right Track," "Shine It On," "Sheer Energy." I borrowed from the title of an old Ray Charles song for "The Same Thing (Makes You Laugh, Makes You Cry)" and borrowed from the ideas of "Everyday People" and "Everybody Is a Star" for "It Takes All Kinds."

When Warner pushed the album out, Epic pushed back. A month after *Back on the Right Track* they released a record called *Ten Years Too Soon*, which had disco versions of old hits, remixes designed for the dance floor. Disco was bigger than ever that year, which took some of the air out of the sails (and sales) of the new record.

Again, the year ended, and again the decade. Around Christmas I was driving to see Sylvester Jr. I had thousands of dollars with me to buy him whatever presents he wanted, cowboy shit, anything. But the closer I got to him, the less money I had. I stopped once and copped once, stopped a second time and same. By the time I got there it was all gone. I felt terrible. But I was straight with him. Tell the truth to the youth. "Man," I said, "I have nothing left for you. I spent it on dope." He wasn't mad and if he was sad he hid it. He just looked at me clear-eyed and told me we would get it the next year.

I was at home with drugs. I was comfortable with them but I also mean that one day I was in my house with them, home base, freebase. When you light up you have to be careful of the fire and the ether and that day I was not careful of either. There was a loud noise. I knew it in my mind and then I heard it outside my mind. The bathroom blew up completely. Noise, light, fire, everything. Time stopped for a second. Then the place was choked up with smoke, except for one spot over me that was clear, like a halo. I just stared up at it. Was I being saved? Singled out? I took a breath and looked around. I couldn't see how to get to the door. "Hey," I hollered. "Hey!" A voice came back: "Come through here." I ran toward the voice as fast as I could. As I got to the door, I hit my head so hard on the corner of the frame that I still have a knot. I was glad that was all I got.

# 14

✳

## Funk Gets Stronger
### (1980–1983)

**S**ly! Sly! Sly!" I turned around at the third one. I was in New York for a party at someone's apartment, and George Clinton was there too. I hadn't seen George for a little while. Since we had toured, Parliament had put out some bigger albums, and then Funkadelic had, and George had started a thousand offshoot bands, too. But he was starting to burn out from juggling it all: acts, labels, tours, money, drugs.

We talked for a long time at that party, more than we had talked before. He told me that he was heading up to his farm in Michigan, about an hour from Detroit, and that I could visit anytime. "Maybe I will," I said.

I did. Country living was clean air and a lack of distraction. We went fishing, made music, and got high, not always in that order.

George was a trip. I always thought of him as a human cartoon. If there was a way to make an experience more fun, he would find it. He was funny on his own, and together we were even funnier. If I wanted money to score I didn't have to lie and say that I was buying equipment or giving a girlfriend money for clothes. I would just come right out and ask: "Can I star?" But in this case, the headliner got attention first.

Sometimes George and I went to Detroit. Sometimes we went to New York or Los Angeles. Even though George and I used together, we didn't use in similar ways. He would go to sleep earlier and I would stay up later. He would stop and I was just getting started. Sometimes after he was in bed, I needed more drugs. I would write dope notes and slide them under his door. There was one he liked to bring up: "Knock knock. Put a rock in a sock and send it over to me, doc. Signed, a co-junkie for the funk." By now the drugs were in rock form, made with baking soda and called crack because of the crackling noise it made when it was heated up.

One night George and I drove to meet a dealer in a parking lot next to a restaurant, a Denny's or a Howard Johnson. I got all the shit ready so that we could smoke when the drugs came. That was right around the time that Richard Pryor burned himself up with the freebase. When I heard about it, I worried about him, for sure. I might have even worried about him while we waited for the dealer.

Finally he showed. We cooked and got down to business. Someone in the restaurant had been watching the whole time. It was obvious what was happening even before the car filled up with smoke. As we drove out of the lot, the cops were waiting for us. When we rolled down the window, the cop looked straight at us. "Sly," he said to me. And to George: "Dr. Funkenstein." He touched a finger to the brim of his hat. In the trunk they found a broken piece of pipe and brought us in with that, though they only kept us overnight.

Another time we met a dealer who was a big fan of mine. He knew every song from every Family Stone record, even *A Whole*

*New Thing.* We had to wait for the drugs while he asked detailed questions. Was it a harmonium on that song? What was the gear we used for the other one? One afternoon on the way over there George and I turned out our pockets and realized that we didn't have money for dope. When we got there I didn't wait for the dealer to start talking about my music. I went in on it myself. And then I hit him with a bonus. "We're light," I said, "but I'll give you a copy of the album I'm working on as collateral. You can't listen to it, but you can keep it safe for me." I went out to the car and came back with a tape. I think his hand was shaking when he gave us the drugs, he was so excited.

On our way home, George congratulated me on thinking fast. "Good idea to give him a copy of the record."

"What record?" I said.

He was staring at me like I forgot something that had just happened.

"You know," he said. "The tape. The music."

"There's no music on there," he said. "There's nothing. It's empty."

I don't know how long George laughed, but it seemed like it was the whole ride home. He eventually told the dealer, who wasn't even mad. "You have to respect that," the dealer said.

Not every tape was blank. We were making new music. Dawn Silva and Lynn Mabry, who had sung with me, had gone over to P-Funk and gotten set up in a group called the Brides of Funkenstein. When I started coming around, they were starting on the third Brides record. I helped write a song called "Catch a Keeper," but the album stalled and the track was shelved. We had more luck with a Funkadelic album called *Electric Spanking of War Babies*, where I wrote and sang on a song called "Funk Gets Stronger."

I hung with George's group. Bootsy Collins and I connected especially well. He had taken my style and kept going with it, the suits, the hats, the rhinestones, the glasses. He was the chief car-toon in those days and a solo star still rising. Sometimes when I was out walking people would call to me, "Bootsy! Bootsy!" I didn't mind it so much.

During that time, George was being courted by Capitol as a solo artist. I remember riding in a limo with him and a Capitol A&R guy who kept saying how great everyone was, George, me, all of us, right to our faces. We were geniuses, legends, the best in every way.

I could take some of that but not too much. I closed my eyes and leaned against the inside of the car door. If the A&R guy thought I was nodding out, he would stop talking to me. But he didn't stop talking in general. When he finally got out of the car, I told George I thought that he was the emptiest-suit mother-fucker I had ever met. George signed with Capitol anyway and had a huge hit with "Atomic Dog," which doesn't disprove a thing about the suit.

I went back on the road with P-Funk and a bunch of funk acts: Bootsy, Roger Troutman and Zapp, Bernie Worrell, Junie Morri-son, Maceo Parker, me. Sometimes I had a short set of my own.

The tour was so crowded that it was sometimes a fight for the spotlight. One night Roger said something that hit Bootsy side-ways and Bootsy took off for the hotel. About a half-hour before he was scheduled to go onstage, he still wasn't back. George sent me to go get him. I went to his room and started pounding on the door. "Come on," I said. "You made me promise I'd be good but you're not being good. Teach me. Teach me." I could hear him laughing. He came back to the arena late, his point made.

One afternoon we were all at an airport when I heard a voice calling my name, my real name. "Sylvester? Sylvester Stewart?" I looked around, saw nothing, and then looked down and saw a lady in a wheelchair. "You were real good last night onstage," she said. Usually I would just nod but I felt proud. I bent down to give her a kiss on her cheek but she had something else to say. "About time you got your shit together."

It was like she slapped me. I flinched. "Fuck off, you wheel-kneed bitch," I said. All around me people were starting to laugh. I might have laughed too but hollowly.

Another night I felt lots of positive energy coming back from the audience. I was getting a good response from them when I sang, and when I waved it got even louder. I felt like I was that kid up in front of the congregation again, sending out the spirit through song. What I didn't know was that George was right behind me, naked. The crowd wasn't cheering for my ass. They were cheering for his. I got a little mad at him for that.

But I liked working with George. Cynthia said something about how it was hard for me to play with Bobby Womack or Billy Preston for too long because we were all chiefs, and you needed some Indians. George was something else. He wasn't a musician in quite the same way. He was more like a comedian and a philosopher and a ringmaster all rolled into one. He asked me once if he should take formal music lessons. Never, I said. That would interfere with what he had. He was funky all on his own and he could give you a hundred verses to illustrate it.

George also was smart about never throwing anything away. "Catch a Keeper," the song I wrote with him for the Brides album that never happened, was still hanging around, and there was another called "Hydraulic Pump" that I helped him finish. Other people came in: musicians like Bootsy and Bobby and Maceo and Junie and Gary "Mudbone" Cooper and Blackbyrd McKnight, singers like Philippé Wynne and David Ruffin, Lynn Mabry and Jeanette McGruder and Sheila Horne. We cut more tracks, including a James Brown cover, and the tracks were packed, to the point where George built a new album from them called *Urban Dancefloor Guerillas*. He also had a solo record, *You Shouldn't-Nuf Bit Fish*, whose title also talked about what to keep and what to throw back but illustrated another idea, too—you had to know your way around a hook.

I caught a keeper myself in 1982, when Olenka gave birth to a daughter, my third child. I thought of her name myself. My favorite number was still nine, which is *nove* in Portuguese, so I named her Novena. In those days, I was mostly on the move, staying with friends. Each time I moved to a new place, I brought equipment, a keyboard, a microphone, set it up in the biggest room I could have, and got to writing and recording.

I did a show with Bobby Womack at the Roxy. Mostly I played keyboards. There was a break for "I Want to Take You Higher." Bobby pointed at me. "Give a very good friend of mine a round of applause," he said. "We wouldn't be standing up here if you weren't sitting down there." I played some of my own shows, too, in Canada and the States. Barrymore's in Ottawa, backed by a band named Jamport. Jonathan Swift's in Boston, two dozen tickets sold. Cabo's in Chico, California. Flat Street nightclub in Brattleboro, Vermont. "Where am I, man?" I started asking. Good question.

"I'm very excited about my first guest," the man said. "One of the most controversial figures in the world of entertainment." This time, I knew where I was: New York City, Rockefeller Center, for *Late Night with David Letterman*. I came out wearing a sweatsuit, sneakers, and sunglasses. Not very controversial, and I even took the sunglasses off. David Letterman started the interview by asking me why I hadn't been much in the public eye in recent years.

"I got tired," I said, "so I retired. Then I got tired of being retired, so I'm working." I was back, I said, for many reasons. "I needed attention and money and I have new songs. I was encouraged by my mom, mainly. If I wasn't making music, it felt like a lack of contribution to society."

"You're going to make some new music?" Letterman asked.

"I'm going to make some hit records," I said.

"Those are the kinds to make," he said.

Before we got any further, I had an announcement. "I've got some guys in Chicago that I'm calling the One-Eyed Jacks," I said. "Mainly because that's what they called themselves before I met them. Jack wanted me to give his phone number out." Letterman didn't want me to do it. He worried that Jack might get lots of prank calls. "That's okay," I said. "Jack's prepared for that." Jack was Jack Sweeney, the group's keyboard player. I had been staying with him in Chicago, in Marquette Park, sometimes gigging a few hours south in Decatur. I gave out the number: A minute later, I gave it out again. "These guys want work," I said.

The conversation turned to my reputation for missing shows. Every interview still had beats. I told Letterman how promoters had double-booked me, triple-booked me, set up guarantee bonds for these impossible situations and then split the forfeiture money behind my back. "They tricked me," I said. "I was kind of high-strung." When they threatened me, my main response— "from impetuous youthfulness," I said—was to tell them to fuck off. (I didn't say that, but my gesture did.) "I don't blame them. I have a reputation for not showing up but that reputation will be over as soon as this next record comes out." (Next record? That was *Ain't but the One Way*, a new Sly and the Family Stone album put together at Warner Bros.)

"You were not only here," Letterman said, "but you were here early, well dressed, and courteous."

We moved on to the second predictable beat, troubles with the law (there had been an arrest earlier that month in Illinois that had amounted to nothing, charges dropped almost immediately), and the third and final predictable beat: Doris Day. "I know the lady," I said. "She's a great lady. I met her through her son. I wouldn't date that lady. I'm too afraid. Black folks gotta be cool." I played a medley of "If You Want Me to Stay" and "Stand!" and went up into the crowd.

Back in Chicago, I hooked up with the Jacks for a few weeks of performances at a small club called the Prime and Tender. *Ain't but the One Way* came out on the heels of that, with a cover photo that went airborne again, like on *Fresh*, like on *High on You*.

Some of the record was old material made new. A song called "Hobo Ken" was an old song I had written and produced for Bonnie Pointer, "Ah Shoot," with new lyrics about Ken Roberts. "Ha Ha, Hee Hee" updated a song that Pat Rizzo had started years before. I had been playing around with covering the Kinks' "You Really Got Me" for decades, done a draggy version in the sixties, and finally got it right. There were two up-tempo songs, "Who in the Funk Do You Think You Are" and the title track. Then there was "Sylvester," the shortest song on the album, forty seconds of me accompanied by my electric piano, tucked into the middle of side two. It started off talking about messing around, about wrestling (still happening, more than a decade after I was wrestling with the devil on *There's a Riot Goin' On*), about strangers and family, about mirrors and identity. What was it, exactly? A fragment? A figment? A piece of tape that was also peace of mind? There's no point in blaming the mirror if your face looks strange.

* * *

That spring in a Florida bar I met a guy who was booking small clubs. He lined up a few gigs for me, including a pair of summer shows in Fort Lauderdale billed as Sly and the Family Stone, though I wasn't with any of the original band members. It went well enough that I was scheduled to play the next night in Fort Myers, at a bar and restaurant called Harry's. I flew down there in a private plane owned by a man and woman I had met at my Fort Lauderdale gig. I don't remember much about the Fort Myers show except that it wasn't memorable. I may have been a little late and a little out of date.

Afterward, I went back to the Ramada Inn with the girl from the plane. The guy from the plane was treating her bad, beating on her. She peeled off and came with me. We went up to my room and drew the curtains. The next morning I called down for some food. The room service people came up but when they knocked on the door I didn't answer. When they knocked on it again I didn't answer again.

They got a key and entered, expecting . . . I don't know? The worst? That's not what they got. They got me on one bed and the girl on another bed, both of us asleep. Next to her on the bed was a razor and a torch. On the table were bottles of butane.

The cops called the paramedics. The paramedics asked me if I wanted to go to the hospital. I didn't. Back came the cops, who arrested me and brought me to the jail. The charge was cocaine plus something ridiculous, like not paying off a restaurant bill. There were four other guys in the cell that night, picked up for who knows what. I kept to myself and slept to myself, staying in there for a day and a half or so until I was bonded out. Later I heard that a kid who worked in the public defender's office had been at the show and got himself a copy of my booking sheet as a souvenir.

The lawyer I was assigned did a good job. First, he obtained a delay when a prosecution witness couldn't be located. Then he arranged for a no-contest plea, which meant acceptance of punishment without the crime going on my record. At sentencing, the judge told everyone at court that he was worried I wouldn't show up. But there I was, getting a $2,500 fine and six months of rehab.

The rehab was at the Lee Mental Health Clinic in Fort Myers. Olenka brought Nove to see me there. She was real little, not even two. James Brown called me when I was there. Michael Jackson did, too. Michael was respectful, always that way and extremely so, to the point where I would sometimes wonder if he was for real. I wanted to know about *his* shit. The Moonwalk was everywhere that year. But he only wanted to talk about my music.

At Lee, I had a keyboard that I got on a shopping trip with a nurse there who was a fan. It went in my room. I didn't write any new songs but I played the old ones every once in a while, mostly for myself, pass the time, keep the music in my mind.

Rehab had a goal, which was to get me off drugs, but there were different ideas about how to get there. Dr. Richard Sapp, who ran the place, was one of the people who thought that I was two people, Sylvester and Sly. Dr. Sapp said that he wouldn't accept Sly in his sessions, that it had to be just Sylvester who attended. I don't know where he got the idea. It could have been from reading old interviews with David Kapralik. (My dad said something similar to a magazine—that he and my mother could tell right away on the telephone whether they were talking to Sylvester or Sly. "If he tries to tell a ten-minute story in ten seconds," he said, "then it's been a Sly Stone kinda day.")

I still had it as bullshit. In my mind I was responsible whether I was Sly or Sylvester or anyone else. That's what I tried to tell Dr. Sapp. He didn't hear me as clearly as his wife, Charlotte, who was my counselor at Lee. She was willing to think about other parts of the problem. Maybe, she said, there had been kindness and goodwill flowing freely through my life when I was young that had been blocked by other forces like fame and money. Maybe I reacted by withdrawing, developing unproductive behaviors that would keep me from feeling bad that there wasn't as much kindness and goodwill flowing anymore. Once I knew that there were parts of my personality that were negative, that made them less negative.

I was cool with Lee in general, which surprised me. People had tried to get me to deal with the drugs over the years. In New York in the seventies, Steve Paley had introduced me to his psychologist, Mildred Newman, who was famous for teaching self-help, but it didn't take. At Lee, I got clean and found that I liked the feeling.

After a few months, I started to go out on the road with Bobby. I was still in treatment, but I'd get loaned out for a weekend to perform. I got to the shows on time and then did cup tests before I came back into the center to prove I wasn't using. The tests were always clean, even though at some point I wasn't.

I had an inside connection helping me, the nurse who got me the keyboard. The cup tests were supposed to be random but she told me when they were coming so I could pass them, either by adding something to the sample or arranging to have someone else produce it for me. Rehab had worked at Lee but it hadn't worked permanently.

# 15

**✳**

## Crazay

### (1984–1986)

**S**an Diego summer, Jack Murphy Stadium, Kool Jazz Festival. Bobby Womack was there, playing the second night, had played already in fact, which was why he was backstage and I was going to see him there.

Bobby was cooling out, talking to a young woman. She had long dark hair and was wearing a pink T-shirt dress that was buttoned and belted. "Arlene," she said, introducing herself. She had auditioned to be a background singer with Bobby the year before, left for an opportunity that didn't pan out, and was coming back to see if she could go out with him again on the road.

"I'm sorry," he said. "All the spots are filled."

"You should have asked me," I said. I was joking, trying to get her attention.

"Who are you?" she said.

"I'm Sly," I said. She didn't know what that meant. Was I describing myself or naming myself? I started running through a list of songs. "Family Affair"? Shake of the head. "Everyday People"? Shake of the head. "I Want to Take You Higher"? Now a squint and a tilt of her head before she shook it. Then I got to "Hot Fun in the Summertime."

"Oh," she said. "I know that song. They played it at the end of the year when we got out of school."

"Well, that's me!"

We talked a little longer and then I went into the bathroom to get high. When I came out Bobby pulled me over. "You like that girl?"

I nodded.

"She's been with me."

The way he said it sounded like bullshit. I walked back into the room and asked her outright. "Not true," she said. "He has been trying, but nothing happened." I pressed her on it. After a couple minutes she was getting angry. "Bring him in here and I'll ask him to say it to my face."

I knew then—Bobby was my boy, but he lied and lied.

"Let's get some food," I said to Arlene. The first place we went was a diner or a Denny's, nothing fancy, but nothing wrong with it either. There was a long line of people waiting to sit. I started for the front of the line but the other people recognized me about as well as Arlene had at first, and started booing. Instead we went to a 7-Eleven, picked up some sandwiches, and took them back to my hotel.

I didn't hit on her that night. Instead we talked. She was twenty years old, from New York, half Jewish, half Dominican, had danced on *Soul Train*. I invited her to come see me and Bobby play the next night in Oakland. "I don't have any way of getting there," she said.

You could fly on someone else's ticket back then, so I gave her a plane ticket up to the Bay Area. The next day, Freddie picked her up at the airport and brought her to the Urbano house, where she met Big Mama and Big Daddy, and then Freddie put her back in the car and brought her to my show.

I had to fly back to rehab in Florida between performances, and there were some other things I had to do on judge's orders—Bobby and I went on the *Today* show to discuss the dangers of drugs—but I started calling Arlene as often as I could, which turned out to be almost every day for two and a half months. She was easy to talk to and it was easy for me to talk. I took to calling her R-nine—my favorite number, again.

Rehab ended right around her birthday, August 3. She was turning twenty-one and having a party. "I'll be there," I said. She laughed. But when the night came, I walked right in the door. She was celebrating along with a friend of hers named Gina, who had danced with her on *Soul Train*, dated Richard Pryor, and worked for the Jackson family.

When I came in, I could tell the eyes of the crowd were on me. I walked past the cake ("Gina 23, Arlene 21"), found Arlene, and took her hand. "You're with me from now on," I said. Arlene was smiling but some of the eyes in the crowd narrowed, Gina's especially. She wanted half the attention and for a minute there she had closer to none. Arlene went out with me after the party, and when we came back Gina had put all our stuff out in the hall.

I didn't have a home anymore, not really—the tax debt was still hanging over me. Sometimes the amount was two million, sometimes three, sometimes more. Whatever it was, it didn't seem real, and it seemed like someone at the IRS was just waiting for me to make a deal. Until we got to that point, I needed to find a place to stay. At first Arlene and I went out to the Valley, to the house of a drug dealer. You wouldn't have known that he was a dealer from the looks of his place—he seemed like a regular suburban dad, wife, newborn baby, car and lawnmower in the garage. We went from there to another dealer's house, and another's. Some of them were fans and tried to connect me with other singers who were using, like they were producers.

After a little while of bouncing from place to place, I got hold of Ken Roberts and explained my situation to him—had girlfriend, needed place to stay. Ken put us up in a bungalow at the Beverly Hills Hotel. We were there for a month, maybe more. One afternoon, Rick James called. He wanted to come over and party. At the time he was one of the hottest stars around, and I didn't like the idea of him meeting Arlene. I was worried that he would see her and like her and try to take her away. I told her I needed her to run an errand, to pick up a jacket in a distant part of the city that I knew would take hours to do. She looked at me a little weird but I looked back at her normal. "Okay," she said.

Rick came by, hung, partied. He left and soon enough Arlene came back with the jacket. About an hour later, the phone rang. Arlene answered. "Who is it?" she said. She handed me the phone. "It's Denise," she said. I knew a girl named Denise, but it turned out it wasn't that girl. The voice on the phone said her name was Vanity and that Rick had noticed that I was all alone and wondered if I needed company. Did I want her to come over and hang with me? "If I need anything I'll call you back," I said. I turned to Arlene. "I don't know who Denise is," I said, "but that girl said her name was Vanity." Arlene was shocked. She told me that Vanity was the hottest girl around, a singer with Prince who had been on the cover of *Rolling Stone*. I shrugged. That made Arlene happy, that I wasn't interested in giving the hottest girl around the time of day.

The Beverly Hills Hotel lasted for a bit and then Ken moved us to the Oakwood. The Oakwood was an apartment complex in Toluca Lake, a series of blocky beige buildings with balconies. Ken found a two-bedroom on the third floor, facing the parking lot. It was a thousand square feet or so, fully furnished, even with pots and pans. That made things easy, though it also made them anonymous—no more coordinated red, black, and white furniture. In the apartment just beneath us there was a *Playboy* Playmate named Donna Smith who was on that month's cover, posing with her sister Natalie.

Ken not only paid the rent but set me up with an allowance, $500 a week or so. He used to tell people that he never saw me doing drugs, and that may have been true. I wouldn't use in front of him. But that doesn't mean that his money didn't go in that direction. I would beep the dealers and they would call me back. Sometimes I had to go out to meet them at a spot but more often they would come to the Oakwood. T (my bodyguard ) and Mario Errico (Greg's older brother) kept security going for me. While I was waiting for the coke or the crack, I would smoke weed. I never laughed so hard. One of the girls who was calling for the dope couldn't stop laughing. "You're funnier than Richard Pryor," she said. Of course I was funnier. I was waiting for the drugs.

Drugs stayed in the picture. I would either buy the coke already in crack rock form or buy powder cocaine, shake it up in a little bottle with baking soda, add 151 proof rum, and cook until it turned to rock. Even then, I wasn't strung out with the blinds drawn. I didn't like that kind of user, and I didn't want to be one of them. I wanted to do something, to stay productive. I would get high and record. I turned Arlene into an engineer. I taught her to plug in the equipment, mix the master reel down to a slave reel, synchronize. She didn't understand everything at first but I taught and she learned.

I liked to show her off. She was also my walking telephone book. One time I had a group of people over and she was asleep in the back. I went in and woke her up. "What's happening?" she said, still half asleep. "Is something wrong?"

"Jimmy Ford," I said. "Telephone number." I didn't want to call him but I wanted the number. Arlene, still half of half asleep, recited it like a computer. Everyone laughed.

Oakwood wasn't the kind of party that Novato or Bel Air had been. I didn't have the space or the money. Some people came around to see me. Mark Davis, from Warner, drove his big Mercedes over. He was still flashy and loud. Lou Gordon was there, reminiscing, telling stories.

Other times people came to stay. Rose was between relationships—Bubba was long gone from her life by now—and needed a place for herself and her daughter Lisa. "I got an extra room," I said. Rose and I understood each other. She didn't intrude into my world and I didn't intrude into hers. I made sure to go behind closed doors to use. There was a kid around.

The biggest difference with Rose there was that we could suddenly eat well. Before she showed up, we were living on Top Ramen with chicken franks and onions added in. If we had cash left over after a score, Arlene and I would go to a place on Santa Monica and Highland that had great roasted chicken. After Rose arrived, we had real food, including oxtail stew. She could cook.

Cynthia and Phunne came to live with us for a few months, too, when Cynthia was trying to save money for her own place. Right after they arrived, a belt that Arlene had bought in the Dominican Republic somehow made its way into the hall closet. Arlene asked me what she could do about it. Should she say something to Phunne or Cynthia? She didn't know what had happened, but she didn't want to make waves. "You don't have to say anything," I said. "Get the belt and wear it in front of everyone. When they see it on you like that, they'll understand."

Phunne was also the door—when anyone rang or knocked, she would check who it was. I usually already knew. I had cameras and microphones set up. But she liked answering and telling me. One day, Ike Turner came by. A few weeks before that, Cynthia had been talking to Phunne about music. Phunne liked Tina Turner, who was big again because of her *Private Dancer* record. Cynthia had told Phunne how Ike had treated Tina when they were together. Ike knocked. Phunne was the door. When she opened it, Ike was all sweetness. "Oh, you must be Phunne. It's so nice to meet you. I have heard so much about you."

Phunne sent back an icy stare. "Don't talk to me," she said. "My mama told me about you."

"Let's go," I would say to Arlene. Sometimes I still called her "R-nine," other times "Arlo," like Arlo Guthrie. "Let's go out." Out could mean Santa Monica and Highland for food or to the liquor store for drink—once a drunk bumped me and before anyone had time to breathe I went for my .22. Arlene got between me and the guy. "Don't shoot," she said. I got pissed at her but I was pleased at the same time. It took lots of heart to jump in front of a pistol—I could have shot her by accident. Going out could also mean going to the store for clothes or electronics or wigs, though once I saw that Arlene knew how to shop at the wig store I would send her to Hollywood Boulevard by herself.

Another time we were driving to a motel in Hollywood so I could buy dope. As I pulled the Lincoln into the parking lot, I saw people sitting on the curb, lined up like in school. I didn't think much of it, or didn't think fast enough, or I would have realized that it was a bust. All of a sudden cops came out of the bushes, guns drawn.

They took us out of the car and searched it. "I found dope in the back seat," one officer said, holding up a bag. Arlene started talking to another officer, explaining how that was impossible. We had searched the car before we came out and knew there weren't drugs there. "Are you saying my partner's a liar?" said one cop. Arlene wasn't. She was just saying. I told her to be quiet.

After I got charged, Bobby Womack lined me up with an attorney. When we showed up in court, the assistant district attorney saw Arlene and started asking questions: Who are you and what do you know about this situation? Because the ID Arlene had given them at the motel had her parents' address when they booked us, they thought she was just some girl from somewhere else, not a real girlfriend. Arlene explained that she was in the car with me and lived with me and was there to testify. The ADA was flustered, shuffling papers around. "I don't see how that's possible," she said. But it was possible, and when Arlene got up on the stand, she explained what had happened at the arrest, how drugs in the car made no sense when it was a car going to buy drugs. The case was dismissed, and I was very happy that it was.

Going out could also mean a party at someone else's house. I remember a party with Herman Rarebell, the drummer for the Scorpions. Grace Jones was there with her boyfriend Hans, who turned out later to be her boyfriend Dolph. I was on Grace to smoke some crack. She got royal about it. "No, thank you," she said in her slippery Grace Jones accent. I kept making the case. Eventually she came around. "I'll try it," she said. "I don't like it," she said. I couldn't believe it. Who did it once and stopped?

Another night, another party, Ike Turner put his shadow into the room. Since he had arranged for the drug dealer, we decided he could have his pick of the girls. I told Arlene to take everyone in the back room so Ike could make his choice. Next thing I know she came running back into the room. "What's the matter?" I said.

"I did what you said," she said. "He looked them all over, one by one, and then he turned and pointed at me. There's no way in hell. If I have to walk down the street in the middle of the night to get out of here, I will."

"Calm down," I told her. But she was wound up completely. I had to say it more than twice for it to take effect. "Calm down, calm down."

I went to handle it. Ike didn't want to listen at first. Eventually I got him level and off the idea of her, but it wasn't easy. Arlene wasn't the only one who felt her skin crawl around him. He made everything crawl. He made people want to sleep with one eye open. He was bad vibes all the way down.

Even so I partied with him. He had connections I could use. And Arlene and I weren't always getting along. She would step on my last bit of patience and I would tell her to go. "Where?" she'd say. Fuck if I cared. She would stay with a friend or another friend and be back in a day or two. Things would sail smoothly for a while and then another land mine. Go. Again, where. Again, fuck if I cared. Once she just got her bag and walked out without a word. A few days later she hadn't come back. She called. "Where'd you go?" I said.

"My apartment." She told me that she had gotten her own place in West Hollywood, on El Cerrito. I didn't like the sound of that. Ike Turner and I went over and tried to break in but Arlene caught us. Another time, I went over there, made friends with the starstruck neighbors, and jumped from their balcony to hers. When she came home, I was in her apartment, grinning like a cat and smoking with Ike. Arlene put up a fight that time. She didn't want him in her house. Eventually I promised I would never kick her out again and we gave that apartment over to some dealers we knew, Mexican Mike and Lil Mama.

One night, I got tired of whatever party I was at. The faces around me were suddenly inhospitable to my mind. I decided to leave, and I left Arlene with an assignment: "Find me the prettiest girl and bring her back," I said. Arlene was home about an hour later, empty-handed. "I couldn't find anyone pretty enough," she said nervously.

"I knew you wouldn't." I watched her face, especially her anxious eyes. She was trying to measure my tone. "Because you're the prettiest girl." Now I could see the relief flood in.

Ken Roberts engineered the sale of my catalog to Michael Jackson. The rest of my catalog: Michael had bought up some of it a few years earlier. Ken added up all the cash he had put out for me over the years and decided that this was a good way to recoup. Some people said we were letting it go for too cheap, but it made sense to me, because I didn't understand how old songs could make money. As far as I was concerned, it would have to be new songs doing the earning, getting back on the charts, or nothing.

I was closer to Michael's brother Jermaine, who was married to Hazel Gordy, Berry's daughter. They had a big house with a big lawn, and during summers they would host parties there. The kids would swim and play and dance and eat. Phunne, who was about the same age as Jermaine's son, went over there for one of those parties. The whole time, Jermaine kept mentioning to people that I was going to come by. "Sly's coming," he said. "Sly will be here in a little while. If you stick around, you can meet Sly."

When I finally arrived, it was late afternoon. Phunne saw my car pull up, ran over, hugged me hello. She told me about the day she had been having, the swimming and playing and dancing.

The kids had all been practicing their break-dancing moves, and Jermaine filmed with his video camera. Then she got on to the eating. The barbecued shrimp, she said, were better than good, the best she ever had. "Bring me some," I said. She ran off and came back with a plate piled high with shrimp. I ate them in the car and then drove off. Too bougie for me.

During that period, Jermaine was spending time with other people and didn't want his wife to know. He would tell Hazel that he was going to work in the studio with me. He would make a point of coming by Oakwood for a minute, maybe even coming into the bedroom and touching a keyboard or two. Working in the studio with me. Then he would look at his watch. "I'm going to take off," he would say. If Hazel called, I would tell her—or have Arlene tell her—that Jermaine was in the studio.

Jermaine was grateful. He would bring me gifts as reward and encouragement. I got a nice mixing board that way. Once the arrangement was in place, he wouldn't even come by Oakwood, just call me before and tell me that he was interested in a studio session. That was my cue to know what to do when Hazel called.

One night I was in the bedroom working on a song and I heard Arlene calling me. I turned down the music. "What?" I said.

"It's Jermaine Jackson," she said. "He's calling from London."

"What about?" I said.

"He wants to give you a gift," she said, coming into the room with the phone. She pushed it toward me.

"I'm not talking to him. Hang up the goddamned phone."

"But he wants to give you . . ."

"Forget it. Hang up." She did. I could tell that it hurt her to hang up on Jermaine Jackson with his voice still coming through the line. But I had to set a limit, and it worked. He stopped asking me to cover for him after that. It wasn't the only time I turned away a phone call. Once Jack Nicholson called and I told Arlene I didn't want to talk to him either. She had to politely explain to him that Sly couldn't come to the phone. He took it in stride.

I would say that drugs didn't affect me too much, but I didn't have to be around me. Other people did. And they said that my mood changed from cocaine, that I would start a fight based off something someone had said a day ago or rush out of a back room with a dark look on my face like I needed the rest of the place to be silent or else. It kept my energy up, kept me intense, kept me thin, kept me in constant motion, shark-style.

What was certain was that if I wasn't straight, I didn't have much interest in being straightforward. When Arlene would come back from errands, I would greet her at the door with a note that listed what I wanted: to eat, to work on a song, to go to bed. Sometimes I would tell her to go get a pen and paper and when she brought them to me I would write out a note and then hand it to her. "Why are you writing these notes?" she said.

"To be clear," I wrote.

Eventually I got tired of writing. I would still tell Arlene to get pen and paper, but then I would start to dictate. "Listen," I would say. "I'm going to tell you right now the three people that I love the most, and I want you to make a list." She'd nod. "My three kids." She would write that down. "Now I'm going to tell you who my best friends are." She'd nod again. "My best friends are Freddie and you."

One day my best friend told me that a man was sitting in his car out in front of our place, day after day. I thought I should send T out to talk to him. "I'll go if you want, Mook," he said. But a guy in a car didn't sound like anything to worry about. More information came in a day or so later. The guy was a writer for *Spin* magazine, and he wanted to do a piece on me. "He can just go on home," I said.

"Why don't you want to talk to him?" Arlene said.

I explained. I had done so many interviews. Reporters listened, or pretended to listen, and then they twisted your words into different shapes before they reached the page. What would be different this time?

But Arlene felt bad seeing this guy out there day after day. He seemed nice. Why wouldn't I give him a chance? "Okay, okay," I finally said. "Bring him up."

He spent a few days with me in the Oakwood. I drove him around town. I told him about the music I was working on. I even played him some songs. He listened and nodded and wrote in his notebook and went away. The next I heard from him was when the article came out. It hurt. It had its ideas about me already in place before the first word even hit the page. "Sly Stone's Heart of Darkness," was the title, and it went on from there.

In one of the early scenes, my mother was in church praying for me. There had already been a spiritual turn for Freddie, who had cleaned up earlier that year and was heading back into the church. She was worried that I needed more prayer to get me out of the darkness. Someone said that drugs hurt me but that the real demon was ego, implying that even if I got clean I would still be doomed.

It went on in that spirit for thousands of words. That's all the writer was looking for, darkness and defects, failings and flaws. When I gave people nicknames, it was part of my "habitual wordplays," because he had to keep reminding people that I had a habit. When I laughed it was "devilish," because he had to remind people that there were goods and evils and I didn't have the goods anymore. He said that I got Arlene excited by flashing cash at her. I hadn't flashed a fucking thing. It was the normal allowance from Ken Roberts. She saw it every week. On top of that, why would I show off something that made me feel dependent? It's true that I had allowed the situation to get that way, rent and expenses covered, but it wasn't a source of pride. Not the way music was.

I read on, my sinking feeling sinking even lower, past the part where my place was dreary, past the part where my "mindfucking continues, with a vengeance," past the part where I was despondent and the part where I was convoluted and the part where he refused to believe even my most honest answers. When I was done reading, I closed the magazine and then my eyes. "Now you know why I don't do interviews," I said.

The article did get a few things right. Two. The first was that I wasn't sure of any relationship because I wasn't sure that anyone saw me as I really was. "I really believe because I play rock 'n' roll, there's a certain image of me that makes it harder for anyone to imagine how I'm really a down-home person," I said.

The second was that I was working. My Oakwood bedroom setup wasn't the Record Plant, but it included a TEAC reel-to-reel, an E-mu Drumulator, a Yamaha DX-7, Linn and Roland drum machines. I would program the drums. I would play the guitar and bass on keyboards. Then I would add vocals.

I was making things all the time. I had new ideas that needed expression through new melodies and new lyrics. I knew that if I could just get the songs done and get them out, I could get people listening to them. Sometimes I would bring my tapes to Silvery Moon in West Hollywood, Gary Stern's place, to get them pushed further along. I used to call Gary "Manson," because he looked a little like him, but that wasn't fair. He was a nice guy.

By the time the article came out, there were at least a half-dozen songs making the trip with me to Silvery Moon. There was a ballad called "Eye to Eye" with lyrics about time served in a relationship. The song was partly about me and women, but also about me and me, I to I with you. I wonder what Dr. Sapp would have thought.

There was an up-tempo funk song called "Day Ain't Got No Business in the Night." That one I made with George Johnson. The Brothers Johnson, George (the guitarist, nicknamed "Lightnin' Licks") and Louis (bass: "Thunder Thumbs"), had been around the scene for years, playing with Billy and Bobby and others. After they stopped working together as a duo, Quincy Jones put Louis to work on a bunch of records, including Michael Jackson's solo albums, and George was left to his own devices. The song we did was one of those devices.

One of my favorites was "Coming Back for More," another ballad, this one about never getting down and never giving up. It started with a verse about reaching your potential ("Been so high I touched the sky / And the sky said, 'Sly, why you just trying to get by?'") and went on to deal with accountability ("Finally grown to size . . . I apologize") and the power of art to heal society ("Writing songs and righting wrongs"). The last verse was full of help and hope and teaching the self to cope: "I be I, you be you / We'll get back and see this through." As the song faded, a female voice sang, "It's a family affair," and I answered with the same. I wasn't just name-checking the old song but trying to summon its spirit. I couldn't leave because my heart was there.

One afternoon, another knock at the Oakwood door. It was Kathy Silva. I hadn't seen her in a while. She still had the same long hair and a long story about our past together for whoever would listen. She liked to remind Arlene that she was the one from Madison Square Garden.

Kathy was bringing Sylvester Jr. around. She wanted him to see me, and I wanted to see him, but the goal was also to let him spend some time with Phunne. They were brother and sister but hadn't met much. By this point, he was twelve or so and she was ten. They got along great, which I liked to see.

One night Cynthia was out at a job or a gig, and I was the parent on duty. The second the kids caught me snoring they decided to sneak out to a nearby pool to swim. The first I heard of it was the knock of return: They had come home from swimming to find the place locked. I opened my eyes at the first knock, stood at the second, checked the kids' room (empty) on the third, and opened it on the fourth to see the two of them, still wet from the pool. And they saw me. Phunne said I was so pissed off that my eyebrows were all the way up to the ceiling.

They hurried inside and tried to make it to the bedroom, but I caught up with them. I took Sylvester Jr. into the bathroom. I made like I was going to whip his ass but mostly I scared him. Scaring was a noisy business, which I wanted: Phunne was out in the living room listening to the whole thing.

When I was done with Sylvester Jr., I went back out and took a step toward Phunne. She dropped to her knees. "Don't whup me, Daddy," she said. "I'll do anything." I walked away. I wasn't about to discipline her like that, anyway. I mentioned it to Cynthia when she got home. "Hours have passed," she said. "What do you want me to do about it now?"

"Talk to your daughter," I said. She went into the room with Phunne. I think I heard them laughing.

Kathy wasn't just reuniting the family. She also had some professional ideas. "I can help you get a deal with A&M Records," she said. Her father had been a producer and she knew John

McClain, the exec who was running the label. John had grown up around the music business, gone to school with the Jacksons, worked with the Sylvers, written for Lionel Richie. A&M was riding high at the time with acts like Janet Jackson. Kathy thought I would be a good addition to their roster and told John, who told her to see if she could arrange something.

I had a song in my mind, not one of the ones I had already finished, but a new one I was calling "Eek-a-Bo Static Automatic." George Clinton has a story about the title, that I was in the studio and heard a voice coming in on the headphones, figured it was the engineer, talked back, heard no answer. A few minutes later the voice came in again. I started freaking out but then I figured it out. There was a piece of equipment, a keyboard with a sampler, and I had accidentally recorded a few seconds of my own voice that was coming back to me on a loop. George says that I called that "Eek-a-Boo"—the ghost in the place. That's not my memory. I just remember hearing the title in my head, thinking it sounded cool, weaving a song from there.

George and his crew came to Silvery Moon when I was making it, and they all fell out over how funky it was. They weren't the only ones. When John McClain heard it, he offered me a deal for a single, which I knew could lead to more. We met in Herb Alpert's office—Herb was the A in A&M, the guy who had founded the label with Jerry Moss—and he went absolutely nuts over it, too. "This is big," John said. But John wouldn't leave big alone. The needles were in the red on my version, like they should have been. The distortion was what made it sound nasty and funky. John gave it to engineers who smoothed the edges, fucked it up. The label's version appeared, along with a duet with Martha Davis on Joan Armatrading's "Love and Affection," on the soundtrack of a new movie, *Soul Man*.

John McClain set up another song. Jesse Johnson, the Time's lead guitarist, had a song on his new solo album, "Crazay," that

John thought would work as a duet with me. Jesse and I got to-gether to record. I played him some of my new songs, which he loved. He started telling reporters about them, and even said that he was going to produce my next record for me.

When it was clear that "Crazay" would be a hit, A&M made a video for it. It was mostly a performance video but there was a small subplot with cars, including one of my own, a Lincoln Continental. I didn't want a stranger driving my car so I asked the director to pull one of the girls out and put Arlene in instead. That didn't solve anything. She banged the car into a gate. John McClain told her not to worry about it, and he fixed the car up without me ever knowing about the damage. Those scenes got cut from the video anyway.

# 16

\*

## Time to Modulate

### (1987–2001)

**S**omething was shaking in my dreams. I opened my eyes and something was still shaking outside of them. Something? Everything. The bed, the chair, the keyboards on the floor. A record fell off a shelf.

Earthquakes get names. This one was Whittier Narrows, October 1987. When the room stopped moving there was a knock on the door and a voice outside it: "Sly, Sly." We opened the door. It was Verdine White from Earth, Wind and Fire, who lived right next door. "Are you okay?" he said.

Was and wasn't.

We weren't at the Oakwood anymore. Ken Roberts had called to say that we needed to get gone from the place. Even after he explained, I couldn't quite understand the reason. Was it drugs? Nothing had changed on that front. Was it rent? I thought he was taking care of it. Was it noise? Music required a certain amount of noise, but much of mine was made in the studio. I had recorded the theme song for *Burglar*, a movie starring Whoopi

Goldberg. I almost never went out—to restaurants, to movies, to anywhere—but when *Burglar* was released, I went with Arlene and Cynthia and Phunne to Grauman's Chinese Theater to see it. I was dressed down, inconspicuous hair, tracksuit. I didn't stand out. But any time the song played we all giggled and laughed.

I didn't giggle at all when I did a morning show on KTLA, our local Channel 5. I went in with one rule: I would only talk about my music. "Whatever you do don't ask me about drugs," I said. I had my reasons. What was I going to tell them, the truth? If they asked me if I was using and I said no, I'd be lying, and I didn't like to lie. But if I told them I was using, what was the point of that? Kids bought records. I didn't want to turn kids on to drugs. The best thing I could do—the only thing I could do— was to keep away from that conversation, and the only way to do that was to keep it away from me. They asked me a question about music, and then another question, also about music. The third question was about drugs. I got up and walked out.

Where did I walk, with no Oakwood waiting? I walked to the hotel. Until a new apartment turned up, John McClain had put me and Arlene up at the Sunset Hyatt House—called the Riot House because lots of bands stayed there when they came to town, and lots of bands meant lots of parties. Staying there was fun until it wasn't. One morning, two detectives knocked on our door. They had cuffs and then they had me. I figured it was a drug arrest, but it was for nonpayment of child support. Kathy was seeking something like $5,000 for her and Sylvester Jr.

Someone could have paid the money: John, Ken. No one did. That led to a restriction of my freedom: L.A. County Jail, cell block 1750, which was called "high power." Sounds like a song title. Prominent inmates went in there, whether they were famous on the inside or out, whether other prisoners needed protection from them or they needed protection from other prisoners. You could have been looking at a murderer doing life or a singer doing less.

They didn't take your memory away when they locked you up. From the sixty-square-foot cell—bed, toilet, nothing else—I could remember the Oakwood, a thousand square feet, and I could remember Bel Air, six thousand. In my blue prison uniform, I could remember black leather suits and red wide-brimmed hats. Alone, I could remember packed houses, those where I lived and those where I played. In silence, I could remember the music I wasn't able to make.

I was in jail for weeks going to months. When Arlene visited—it was one of the only bright spots—she wanted to know if I was scared. I shook my head. "They don't fuck with me," I said, which was true. But I didn't fuck with them either. One day I heard screaming. A guy had killed another one, right there in the jail. Another day Arlene had a strange look on her face. "What?" I said. She told me she was coming down the hall and saw, on the other side of the glass, with shackled hands and feet, Richard Ramirez, the Night Stalker. He had killed something like twenty people and was waiting for his trial. She said she could feel that motherfucker's evil right through the glass.

Jail was a problem, but it was also a solution. I could just take a break, be away from it all. The restriction of freedom meant that I wasn't able to use while I was in there. I got healthier. Visitors started remarking on better skin, brighter eyes, sharper memory.

When I got out, Ken moved us into another apartment, different complex, same kind of place. The Oakwood had sold off some of my old stuff to collect back rent, so I had to start over buying clothes and equipment. I also had to start over with a record label: work with A&M, from new songs to Jesse's production, dried up during the time I was in jail. What hadn't dried up was drugs. People were putting them in my face and that put them back in my mind. The restoration of freedom? Then the earthquake happened. Then it kept happening.

✻ ✻ ✻

In November I was booked for a series of shows at Las Palmas Theater off Hollywood Boulevard. I assembled a band together with Billy Preston and started getting ready.

Rehearsals were rocky. The smaller venue meant less money, and less money meant that I couldn't hire the people I wanted, and not being able to hire the people I wanted meant that all I could do when someone wasn't up to snuff was hope that they'd get better fast. The drummer wasn't up to snuff. I didn't want to deal with it so I handed the task off to someone else and went backstage to be alone.

There was no alone. I had a group of people with me, including Arlene, Buddha, Freddie's ex Marisa. Lou Gordon was there, true believing as usual. Reporters waited with them. They wanted to talk about the show. Was it a comeback? Did it remind me of shows from the past? "Things are different now," I said, looking around. "My circumstance has changed." (It had.)

Would I be playing only old hits? "I've got some new stuff that's real good," I said. (I had. It was.)

A third reporter wanted to know my age, and when I didn't answer right away, people started guessing: Forty-five? Forty-three? "Forty-two sounds about right," I said. (It wasn't.)

A fourth reporter asked about drugs. He knew there had been issues in past years, busts, rehabs. Would any of that be a factor in the performances at Las Palmas? "I'm clean," I said. (I wasn't.)

That was it for the press conference. One of the club managers came by to walk me back to the stage. The drummer was still there but a guitarist had dropped out. The sound system was even less up to snuff than the musicians. The early show started late, and the late show ended early. At some point I came out with a drum machine and re-created "Dance to the Music" all by myself.

The second night I decided to walk into Las Palmas through the back of the theater, come up the aisle to the stage. I never made it inside. Cops were waiting for me. I heard later that Marisa ran back screaming, "They took him, they took him!" She collected herself enough to speak to the crowd. "Sly was arrested ten minutes ago outside the theater," she said. "He was clean and they picked him up for parking tickets. Some people have a hard time forgetting about other people's mistakes."

The crowd was told I'd be back in an hour. Billy stalled with some of his hits and some jamming. The hour passed and then another. An announcement was made: "Sly is in for the night." They did not specify where "in" was.

Arlene was in as much of a panic as Marisa. She hadn't had a chance to speak to me before I was hauled off, and she needed to. I had given our apartment key to a drug dealer named Bear—the same one we were going to see at the Hollywood motel the night the cops searched the back seat of our car. I owed him and the key was collateral. She was worried that he was going to come in without warning and take something or worse. If she heard a noise at night, would she be able to climb out the back window fast enough? She went to Billy, who went to Bear, who surrendered the key.

Parking tickets, Marisa had said, but that wasn't true. It was child support again. They took me down to the jail but couldn't book me for medical reasons, and instead took me to the jail's medical ward at County-USC Medical Center. They said I couldn't stand up and when they sat me on a bench I slid down off that, too. They found crack cocaine paraphernalia to explain the behavior. Those drug charges got added on top of the child support. I spent the weekend in the medical ward and was released into the new week.

A month later, I failed to show for a court hearing. Two months after that, I failed to show for another one. Warrants went out. People made jokes. Arrest records were my new records, and I was hitting the charts. Court dates were my new concerts, and I was still just as good about arriving on time.

I heard them all at my back because I was gone. I went to the East Coast, stayed with friends in Virginia, friends in New York. Arlene was with me for part of it, including time in New Jersey with James Mtume, who had played percussion with Miles Davis and had a big hit, "Juicy Fruit," with his own band.

Mtume set us up in his basement and I worked on a song called "Time to Modulate," funky as hell, a David and Goliath story rewritten for Popeye and Bluto. The rest of the song was about regrets and resets, how you could feel like you were "still making payments on something you shouldn't have bought." The chorus came in big: "When you wind up making your mind up / That's when you find up instead of down." That's how the year was, working in the basement, finding up instead of down.

We left Mtume's for a week in Virginia, a week in Pennsylvania. Then it was back to New Jersey, to New Brunswick, to stay with a woman named Ruby Jones. She had been on the scene in San Francisco in the early days, and in New Jersey in the late days she ran a boardinghouse. She gave me and Arlene a pair of rooms. We slept in one and loaded up the other with equipment, some of which I brought, some of which Ruby bought for me.

Ruby would tell anyone who listened that she was against drugs. She was always talking about bad behavior in the news, from robbery to child abuse, and wondering if drugs had played a part. But like Ken Roberts, she gave me money, and drugs were one of the things that I bought with it. Arlene couldn't come around to the scene in New Brunswick. She thought Ruby was moving on me. When Ruby put up a big picture of me and her from the past, looking like a couple, Arlene took it down. Arlene also was tired of the drugs and didn't trust that I'd get my shit together. At some point in the summer of 1988, she said good-bye. It wasn't dramatic. There weren't angry words. She just packed her things and left.

I stayed in New Jersey, kept working, kept recording. I called Steve Topley, who had worked back at Stone Flower, and played some of the new songs for him, including "Just Like a Teeter-Totter." It was about finding the proper path and holding yourself to the truth. Again, my main audience might have been myself. Steve liked what he heard and called a friend of his named Jerry Goldstein, and they came out to meet with me.

Jerry had started out writing songs for other artists in New York and then formed a group called the Strangeloves, which pretended to be Australian and had a hit with "I Want Candy" (it was on the charts at the exact same time as the Beau Brummels' "Just a Little"). He had gone on to create the L.A. funk band War, to set up the first version of Eric Burdon's group after the Animals and stay with them through the seventies and eighties. Pat Rizzo had played with a version of the group in the late seventies, which created some overlap.

Jerry seemed nice, had a friendly face, plenty of knowledge. He and I talked about music and money. He explained one in terms of the other, and I entered into a management contract with him. It was all kinds of papers folded up on one another. Jerry drew up a contract that would pay me a salary, starting high fives, moving to low sixes. Ken Roberts had given me $500 a week. This was a major raise. Jerry and his lawyer, Glenn Stone, set up companies that were partly in my name, and reiterated the relationship between music and money again: if I concentrated on making the first, they would work hard to get me the second.

When Jerry showed up in New Jersey, it was with three big guys who I think were ex-cops now working in security. Their new assignment was me. The next stop was a house in upstate New York, a nice big place with all the music equipment I already owned and some new shit too. The ex-cops split the day into shifts and took turns watching over me. I kept working and I kept using and everyone seemed fine with that.

It was a week before I even thought to leave. When I went to the door, that thought was replaced by another one: that I couldn't get out. The handle was wrapped up in rope, not string, not thick, sort of a middle weight between a wire and a jump rope, wrapped four times around. I pushed and pulled but the door wouldn't give. I couldn't think of anything except leaving through that door. That's when it came to me: a torch. I had been smoking, so I had one, and I knew right where it was. I fired it up and burned the first rope. I started in on the second. There were more, but not for long.

Getting out of that house didn't mean getting free, exactly. I moved around in New York and Connecticut, bankrolled by Jerry, trying to move songs forward. One day I was in Wilton, Connecticut, when a knock came on the door. It was past the point where a knock could be good news. This was the FBI. They asked me who I was and this time I gave my real name. They took out papers and read from them: "fugitive from justice" was one of the things I heard. They sent me back to California to face the music. And there was plenty of music to face. There were old drug charges, and the child-support arrest at Las Palmas now had layers and layers on top of it, including the court dates I had missed. Overdubs. I got fifty-five days in county jail and nine to fourteen months of rehab for the rest.

I went to rehab at CRI-Help, a kind of halfway house that worked all the way. I got clean. I started to spend time with family again, normal time, going to eat, going to the movies. Arlene and I started to talk again, not about getting back together, but about rebuilding our friendship. We went to an industry dinner, me and her and her sister, and sat at a table with David Crosby and Steve Perry. Everyone was straight and the conversation was cool. She drove me to an electronics store, a Good Guys, where one of the salesmen recognized me and rushed over to help. I told him what I needed. He asked a few questions. That was all, but that was something. Arlene drove me back to the halfway house, each time prouder than the last. I even promised her mama that I was going to stay straight for as long as I could, and I meant it.

One evening I was driving on Hollywood Boulevard in a Ferrari when I came to a red light. There was another car stopped, too. I looked over to see Bobby Womack behind the wheel. I kept looking in his direction and eventually he turned his head. "Sly," he said. "Hey."

"Hey," I said back. The light changed. I pulled away. When I saw Bobby's car in my rearview mirror, I had second thoughts. I backed up. "Man," I said. "How are you? Call me. I'll call you back."

I don't know if he called me. If he did, I didn't call him back. It wouldn't have been the only promise that I broke that year. I was clean for a while, but at some point I was using again. I can't say exactly why. It might have had something to do with familiar faces that popped back up, and familiar behaviors that popped up too. It might have had something to do with frustrations with getting my music out: I had songs but no record deal. And it might have had something to do with a lawsuit that Ruby had filed. She claimed that I had been "surreptitiously removed" from her home back in 1989, along with the equipment she had bought me, and that I had not followed through on a promise to write songs with her. Jerry Goldstein was named in Ruby's suit, too, along with Glenn Stone and Steve Topley and some of the companies set up in my name. (One was called IBIUBU, lyrics from "Coming Back for More.") Glenn defended me in the suit, arguing that my drug use back in 1989 meant that I did not have the capacity to enter into an agreement with Ruby.

I was backstage at the hotel, dressed in a shocking blue jumpsuit. "Backstage" might be an exaggeration. I was somewhere behind the stage, sometimes in the kitchen, sometimes just outside it in the hall.

The call had come in a few months before. "The Family Stone has been voted into the Rock and Roll Hall of Fame for the Class of 1993," said the voice. There was no Hall of Fame building yet, just a committee picking artists. But they had picked us.

We were in good company. In the first years of the Hall, they had inducted the artists who had made me want to sing in the first place: Little Richard, Ray Charles, James Brown, Sam Cooke, Jackie Wilson. The next years added in artists who came up in the early sixties: Aretha Franklin, Marvin Gaye, Smokey Robinson, the Beatles, Bob Dylan, Jimi, Ike and Tina.

Now it was our turn. Other inductees our year included two other big California bands of the sixties, Creedence Clearwater Revival and the Doors, and some major R&B singers, from Ruth Brown to Etta James to Dinah Washington. Frankie Lymon was in the class. Van Morrison was in the class. Dick Clark, Cream. A good class.

George Clinton had been selected to introduce the Family Stone. He and I hadn't been in close contact over the years, but the Hall saw him as the right man for the job. They might have also figured that putting him up on the stage was the best chance of getting me to the ceremony. It was in Los Angeles that year, at the Century Plaza Hotel, instead of at the usual spot at the Waldorf Astoria in New York City. Maybe that was also an accommodation.

I got to the hotel early the day of the ceremony and set up back in the kitchen and the hall beside it. The people out in the ballroom were going through the run of show, loud enough for me to hear. Who knew I was there? My parents, who were in the crowd, knew. George knew. But what about the rest of the band? I had talked with George about maybe coming out after everyone else had spoken. Had he told them? I was dressed for the occasion but not sure of the equation.

George came onstage, long rainbow braids, a shirt of the flags of the world. I found a spot where I could hear him without being seen. "Wow," he said. "What's happening? I had a lot planned to say when I first got here. I thought I was going to be real cool, I was going to be clever, going to be deep, and I was going to be real effective. I walked in and the first thing I saw was Larry Graham, Freddie, Jerry, Rose, Cynthia, Greg." He didn't mention me. "I forgot every damn thing I was going to say. The one thing I always wanted to see, like some people wanted to see the Beatles back together, is to see Sly and the Family Stone back together."

He went on talking while I went on listening. He called us "the greatest funk band that ever was." He told a story about how Dave Kapralik had first turned him on to our music. "We went on to be in the shadow of Sly for some years," he said. "Finally we met him and it was a love affair from then on."

He introduced the group to applause and out they came, the

six of them, to gather in a half-circle while the house band vamped. They sang a little of "Thank You (Falettinme Be Mice Elf Agin)," a little of "Dance to the Music." Larry added some bottom.

For speeches, each of them took a turn at the microphone. Once a band that traded off vocals, always a band that traded off vocals.

Freddie stepped up first. "I know I'm not supposed to lean on the podium," he said. His voice was gentle. By then he had rejoined the church fully, had been ordained and was on his way to being named pastor at Evangelist Temple Fellowship Center in Vallejo. "This is truly a great honor," he said. "When I heard about this, I didn't believe it. I am so grateful that you remembered us. We didn't know. Personally I didn't know the impact the group had in the music industry. We couldn't really tell. We would just go from place to place—that is when we did go from place to place." Then he went from face to face, naming each of the people in the group, saving me for last. He didn't say my name with any special spin, didn't let on whether he knew I was there.

Cynthia was next. It was her birthday, which she mentioned. "Thank you from the bottomless part of my heart," she said. "And to all the squares, you don't have to go home."

Then Jerry, who was brief, and Greg, who was slightly less so. They thanked their families. I wasn't mentioned, much or at all. Did that mean they knew I was waiting backstage?

Larry was dressed in white like a pastor or waiter. "My name is Larry Graham," he said, booming that bass again. "As I was sitting over there watching the whole program, something very special happened to me, which may have happened to you." When Larry got a chance, he would talk. I found a comfortable space to lean and settled in for a duration. "Stand!" had been only three minutes long but I knew I'd have to stand longer. He went on, explaining how he had a deeper appreciation of the gift of life after losing elderly relatives, how he was touched to the point of tears by music and spirit, how he had tried to live a positive life.

Finally, he got around to the question of my location. "The thing that really got me," Larry said, "is that some of the group members, band members, could not be here to appreciate this once-in-a-lifetime privilege." Now there were a few scattered laughs. Was he taking a swipe at me? Or was he rolling out the red carpet for my surprise appearance? "The fact," he said, "that each and every member of Sly and the Family Stone is alive. You know what I mean? Do you know what I'm saying? It's good to be alive. It's still possible for something else to happen."

Rose was last. Last, that is, if I wasn't there, though now it felt more and more like the band was prepping the crowd for me. "Good evening, everybody," she said. "It's time to go home now, so it's good night, almost." She thanked my mother and father, gesturing toward them in the crowd. She thanked her daughter Lisa. She thanked Ken Roberts. "Oh, wait a minute," she said. "There's something else. I almost forgot. What was it?" If I was going to go onstage, it was now or never. I started to move toward the stairs. "Oh, I know what it is," Rose said. "As usual, it's just us."

I came out on cue. Larry had talked a blue streak but I was one, entering from stage right in my jumpsuit. The band started talking right at me. "There he is." "You showed up." "It's this guy, here."

They began to clap as the house band returned to "Thank You (Falettinme Be Mice Elf Agin)." When the music ended, that's how I started my speech: "Thank you." I spoke clearly and slowly, head bowed slightly. "I believe everything's been said, probably. I don't want to forget anyone in saying thanks, you know, so thank you all very much. I love you personally very much. See you soon."

And I was gone. Groups being inducted are asked to pose for pictures afterward. I didn't pose, wasn't pictured.

I turned on the radio and heard a familiar song. A second later I realized that it sounded familiar because it was mine. But it wasn't. Old songs were being made new again by hip-hop. LL Cool J used "Trip to Your Heart" for "Mama Said Knock You Out." Public Enemy used the start of "Let's Be Together" for "Power to the People." There was a Beastie Boys song that took parts of "Loose Booty" and an Arrested Development song called "People Everyday" that took parts of guess what.

Sampling didn't bother me. I liked it. I was flattered. Music was a universal donor. It was for everyone. Let them spread it wide. I had an idea that one day I would just sample back the songs they made using samples of my songs. I also liked that hip-hop artists used real language. They would cuss, come right out and say "fuck you" if that's what they meant. They would say "muthafucka" and "nigga" the way that real people said it.

Those were only some of the new songs that I heard on the radio. I heard Prince. People said that he was the new version of me, though they also said he was the new version of Little Richard and of Jimi Hendrix. Some days I understood what they meant and other days I didn't see it. One night Arlene was at the Roxbury on Sunset and met him. He only spoke to her through his bodyguard the way he liked to do. She mentioned that she knew me. He said that he wanted to meet me. She said she thought she could help set something up. Prince, in a weird whisper, asked his bodyguard to ask her who she was and what she was to me. "Engineer," she said. I liked that answer.

Prince must have, too. He spoke to her directly, in his normal voice. "Well," he said, "I would like to work with Sly." They arranged for her to talk to me and pave the way. She called me to tell me about the meeting. I wasn't always on Prince but that day I was. I told her that I was excited about the idea and I meant it. But he never called.

I was seeing a woman at the time. We were together for a little while, but we fought often as not. Once we were in a motel and she lost her temper, pulled a gun, and fired it, toward me if not at me. Another time we were arguing about something and she put my car into gear and pushed it toward and then over an embankment. Down it went, all the way to the bottom. I was not in it, though she was so mad that it seemed like she wished I was.

L.A. had all the news in the world in those days—the Rodney King beating had been back in 1991, followed by the riots. I watched them, feeling helpless. It was a different feel from the unrest of the sixties, less anguish, more anger. Then came the Northridge Earthquake, a big one, though for some reason it made less of an impression than Whittier Narrows. And then Nicole Brown Simpson and Ronald Goldman were stabbed to death on South Bundy Drive and O. J. Simpson was driven down the 405, slow, a black man in a white Bronco. I watched the whole trial and when he was acquitted, I was happy about it. I didn't think that he had done it, though I think so now.

I watched those things on TV, different ones at different houses and apartments around the city. Jerry Goldstein got me into some of them, which was partly his job. He was responsible for taking care of me. At the same time, I was frustrated that everything I was doing—the gigs I was playing, the old records that were still selling—didn't seem to be bringing in enough money. I asked Jerry questions but I didn't feel like I was getting straight answers. Did he think I was too high and too dumb? At times, that was my strategy, to seem less aware than I was. Was it backfiring?

I stayed with Sylvester Jr. in a mansion in Beverly Hills, where I taught him how to record and use equipment. The landlord, a lawyer, said that I ripped up his place, put gold paint on the walls and black paint on the floors. I didn't disagree. We did paint the floors, and the whole bathroom too. Things should look the way you want them to look. But he also said we were having parties without permission, which made no sense to me. Why would I have to seek permission?

For a while I was up near Wilshire and Comstock. For another while I was in Eagle Rock. I finally settled into a house on Summitridge Drive in Beverly Hills, high up with a view over Beverly Park. By then I had a new girlfriend, Shay. She was part-Cuban, with the finest body I'd ever seen. She liked to ride motorcycles with me. I bought her one. We got along more often than not. She and her twin sister, Lasha, stayed with me, helped manage the house, ran errands for me: Go out and get more incense, buy me bidis, I need lightbulbs, whatever.

One day, Arlene came by with a friend. Shay and Lasha went out to meet them. "Sly will be with you in a minute," Shay said. "He's currently occupied." I was in the back. How did I know what they were saying if I was in the back? Because I had set up microphones. I liked to listen to conversations, and sometimes there were cameras, too.

Arlene sat at the table talking to her friend about nothing special for twenty minutes, thirty, more. At around forty-five she stood up. "Sylvester," she said. "It's not nice to make us wait that way. I know what you're doing." She was speaking to the air but she was speaking to me. She had set up the microphones and cameras for me at Oakwood back when we were together. She knew the game.

I took visitors for various reasons. Arlene turned me on to a young fan named Jon Dakss, a college student in New York who had built a website to honor the band's music. A website? I didn't know what that was. She printed out some pages from it: It was lists of my records, some interviews with band members and people from the group's circle: Dave Kapralik, Bubba, Steve Paley. Arlene had been talking to him and thought that he might be able to explain computers to me, maybe even come out to help set up some equipment. "You should call him," she said.

One night I did. I didn't dial. I had Shay and Lasha call Jon and talk to him for a while to make sure he seemed to have the right attitude and approach. Then I got on the phone and screened him some more. How did a person that young know about my music? His dad had been a fan. Was his dad a musician? Not a professional, but yes. What instrument? The accordion. That made me laugh. I also wanted to know more about the Internet. Could I release music through it? Could I do it anonymously to test out new songs? At the end of the call, I gave him my phone number. "I better not hear from anyone who's not you," I said. I didn't. He was good with the number and we started calling each other.

A few months later, we flew him out. Arlene picked him up from the airport and took him to lunch at Jerry's Famous Deli. She called me from there. "I'm here with Jon," she said.

"Good," I said. "You're bringing him over?"

"I wanted him to stop by and look at my computer for a minute before."

"Fuck that," I said. "He's here for me."

"It's right on the way."

"You didn't hear me?" We went back and forth for a little. "Fine," I said, and told her that she could just drop him at his motel. Time passed and I got madder and then less mad. "Lasha," I said. "Here's the address of the motel. Go get him." Once he was in the car with her, I called her and had her run through all the questions again, how he knew my music, what instrument his dad played. It was like an early version of cybersecurity. "Bring him over," I said, and went into the back room with my music equipment. I heard them pull up to the house then I heard the dog barking, or at least the sound of the dog barking through a speaker hung just inside the front door.

Lasha and Shay showed Jon to the couch, brought him a drink. I found out later that he thought that would be his final stop, sitting him on the couch until someone came out and told him that I wasn't going to meet with him. He waited and waited for a while longer. Then I called for him. The second he came through into the room, it was cool. I shook his hand, showed him all the equipment, and we got down to business. While he set up the computers, we talked about my music, about the machines I had used to make it—he was interested in the Rhythm King and how it worked—about old concerts and TV shows. I asked him who he had made contact with from the old days, and he mentioned Steve Paley. I hadn't talked to Steve in twenty years. "Tell him I'm getting married again," I said. "I'm not but maybe it'll get him to come see me. Maybe I'll even marry him."

The next day Jon called me. "Guess who I'm with," he said. There was bumping on the line as the phone was passed from hand to hand and then I heard Steve Paley. "I got married already," I said. "Now it's a divorce." He laughed. It was good to hear his voice. Jon met me at the studio and I showed him how I was making music in those days, taking a loop of bass, drums, and keyboards, running it over and over again, and listening for the song inside the loop to make itself known. Before Jon left, he told me about the Family Stone music he had collected, some studio sessions, some live gigs, many of which I didn't even have myself. I told Jerry to set him up with whatever he needed to make me copies. You try to keep the past when possible.

**✳ ✳ ✳**

On the morning of September 11, 2001, someone from New York called to tell me to turn on the TV. I did. My first thought was what the fuck? It was my second thought too. I didn't know what I was seeing. I thought it was a war. I wanted to be prepared, so I bought camouflage clothes, more guns, gas masks.

The days afterward were quiet. All the planes were out of the sky. But the damage had been done. People applauded bin Laden because they hated the United States. A few years later, people applauded the capture of Saddam Hussein because they hated bin Laden. They weren't the same people but they were doing the same thing. And if there was no applauding on your side, you could be sure that there was applauding on the other side. None of it made sense. Why did people feel such excitement at the idea that we weren't all on the same side? I was never going to be at peace with that.

# 17
*

## Coming Back for More
### (2001–2011)

**T**he group stood close together. Tears welled in the corners
of their eyes but there was love coming through the tears. Someone mentioned Big Daddy, but Big Daddy wasn't there. We were
at Evangelist Temple Fellowship Center in Vallejo for his funeral.
Evangelist Temple Fellowship was Freddie's church. He was the
pastor now. I shook hands, accepted condolences. John Turk, my
friend from way back, was there to pay his respects. Toddy, Vet's
daughter, sang. Though I still wasn't God-fearing, I felt the spirit.

I was proud of Freddie, not only for reconnecting with his
faith but for reconnecting with his music. He had finally made his
own solo album, about a year or so before Big Daddy passed, a
gospel-soul record called *Everywhere You Are*. It was funky,
faithful, and familiar—Rose sang on it, along with her daughter
Lisa and Freddie's kids Casey, Joy, and Kristi. I thought about
that record, and other records, at the funeral. Big Daddy was one
of the two people who made Freddie and made me, so in a sense
he had made all the music that we had made, plus the music that

Rose had made and Vet had made and Lisa and Casey and Joy and Kristi and Toddy had made. He had made music of his own before we were even born, but we were his music, too. I tried to keep the tradition going—we all did—by giving out whatever we could to the kids, from instruction to instruments to inspiration.

Two years later, my mother joined my father. I didn't go to her funeral. I couldn't. Someone said that losing a mother was like walking through a window that you didn't know was there. The glass was all around you and you didn't know whether to check yourself for bleeding or start picking up shards. Someone else said that losing a mother was like not being able to find the sky. Back on *Small Talk* in 1974, I had written a song called "Mother Beautiful." It was about Kathy as a mother to Sylvester Jr., but it was also about my mother as a mother to me. The last line of the song celebrated the connection: "Sometimes I call my mama—yeah, she's here." But then one day she wasn't. Losing her was beyond anything I could stand or understand, so I stayed at home and wondered where she had gone.

There was a line in "Time," from *There's a Riot Goin' On*, "Take your time / But you've got a limit." As the new century started up, it became more and more true. Soon after my parents passed, Ray Charles died. Terry Melcher went a few months later. Billy Preston followed, and Mike Douglas, and James Brown.

I was almost on the same bill.

One day I was out riding in Beverly Hills, thinking about the afternoon weather, which was nice, and the bike, which was nicer. It was a Harley custom four-wheeler that was basically a California Highway Patrol Road King set into a two-wheel frame in back. It could really move. You could see how those mother-fuckers got up on you so fast. I liked taking it around. A few

months before, Vet had put together a group called the Phunk
Phamily Affair to play a charity show for the Braille Institute at
the Knitting Factory in L.A. I took the Harley there, parked it in
front, went inside. I kept my motorcycle helmet on the whole
night, so it was hard for people to recognize me.

As powerful as the bike was, it had a problem. The way it was
customized, it was too rigid to turn well. You had to lean as hard
as you could to bring it around a curve. That day I leaned as
hard as I could, but it wasn't good enough. I smacked into a mail-
box and went along the road, dragged by the weight of the bike
until it came to a stop.

In a daze, I felt up to my helmet. It was cracked, but at least it
wasn't my head. I was bleeding pretty bad but I didn't know from
where. Then I saw: It was my right hand. One of my fingers was
hanging by a tendon. I stumbled to a house, blood spurting with
each beat of my heart. I was worried that I would lose conscious-
ness and that would be it. I knocked on a window to get help. I
saw an older white man in there. He came to the door and opened
it a crack. "Help," I said. "I'm hurt bad." He closed the door and
then the curtains.

I started to think about the quickest way to get help, and that
was to break something. The white man would call the police,
and when they came they could get me to the hospital. I got a
rock up in the only good hand I had.

Right at that moment, Shay showed. She had been waiting for
me longer than felt right so she came down the hill to find me.
Her brother-in-law drove me to the hospital, where the doctors
reattached my finger. They told me I was unlikely to ever get full
motion or sensation in it again. I tried my own kind of physical
therapy, which was at the keyboard.

It wasn't the only time that gravity had it in for me that year.
I was walking near home with Shay, eating some Mexican food
from a bowl. I was trying to impress her, a little move, a hop to

one side. I was smooth. I could glide. But I lost my footing and slipped down off the side of a cliff. The second I went over I remember thinking that it was going to be bad. Five or six times on the way down I had the thought that I would just stop myself from falling. It was almost a calm thought but it wasn't true.

Eventually I hit the ground at the base of the cliff. I could barely move. I looked over and saw that I was still holding the bowl of food. Not a single bean had spilled. Shay called down to me, called for help, and it took about an hour and a half to get me back up from there. That time I didn't go to the doctor. I just took care of it myself, took to the bed to recover.

Recover, covers: Jerry had arranged for an album with Starbucks that had contemporary acts doing versions of our songs. It got some traction and some action. Sony was due to rerelease it and there was a Grammy tribute planned for that year's ceremony at the Staples Center. Nile Rodgers was the musical director for the segment, which started with the other singers and ended with the Family Stone.

The night of the ceremony, Dave Chappelle made introductory remarks. "The only thing harder than leaving show business is coming back," he said. People laughed, not because he was talking about me, but because he was talking about himself. He had just walked away from his TV show, left a pile of money on the table.

The tribute included Joss Stone (no relation), John Legend, and Van Hunt singing "Family Affair," Maroon 5 singing "Everyday People," and Will.i.am singing "Dance to the Music." Then Steven Tyler gripped the mic and screamed, "Hey, Sly—let's do it like we used to do it." I wasn't sure who "we" was, but "it" was "I Want to Take You Higher."

I came out in a big metallic silver robe, platform boots, Sly belt buckle. I also had a blond mohawk. It felt too long and I wasn't sure about the color. But it got people's attention, which was a mixed blessing, because they also noticed that my right hand was still wrapped and I was hunched over. While I was healing up from the cliff, I had fallen out of the bed and hit my head so hard that it folded up my neck.

I went behind the keyboards. Thirty seconds or so into it I realized that my mic was off. Were they angry that I hadn't been there for rehearsal? Were they paranoid about what I might say? Whatever it was, it hurt me. I came out from behind the keyboard, threw my right arm up into the air, and walked offstage.

If the evening didn't include the performance I would have wanted, it included something that was much more important. Phunne was there. We hadn't seen each other in years. She had been through some things in her twenties, and I had a period where I was angry with her, which led to a period where we were angry with each other.

Cynthia brought Phunne to the tribute. Before the show, she was in the hall, or so I heard later. I didn't see her. She was upset, ran outside, called a friend. When she calmed down she came back inside. Now the hall was even busier, more crowded, but somehow I saw her. "Phunne?" I said. She couldn't hear me over the noise but she saw my mouth moving in her direction and ran up to me. We hugged so hard that I thought we would squeeze the breath out of each other. Tears were everywhere. "Don't go anywhere," I told her, and went to play the show. But when I came back, Phunne had gone back to her hotel.

I sent Mario over to her. "Come downstairs with me," he told her when he got up to her room. "I have a gift for you from your dad." She asked what it was. Mario wouldn't say. I told him not to say. She went down and saw a BMW convertible parked outside the hotel. She came to the after-party but didn't stay long. Later she told me that she jumped in that motherfucker and went home before I changed my mind.

At the Grammys the next year, the "Family Affair" version

from the tribute album, the one with John Legend, Joss Stone, and Van Hunt, won an award for Best R&B Performance by a Duo or Group with Vocals. Something we never did.

A few months after the Grammy tribute, I moved from Summitridge up to Northern California. My first stop was with Vet in Vallejo. While I was there, Neal Austinson reappeared. He still lived in the area and had driven by a yard with an Austin Princess that reminded him of a picture of me stepping out of one in London in the old days. He asked if the car was for sale. They told him that if he could get it out of there, it was his. He called Mario and they arranged to bring it up to me. The day it came, I was hiding in Vet's house, watching the flatbed pull up with the Austin on top of it. When the truck stopped, both of the car's doors, which were held on only by leather straps, fell off. I appreciated the gesture, though.

I brought that car when I moved out of Vet's place to a house in Napa County. Napa was beautiful, filled with hills and winding roads, and the property itself was a match: a large main building with a pool, a guesthouse, and a garage to store the cars and bikes. Shay and I had a nice life up there. Even in times when we fought she could cool out in the guesthouse for a few days.

Napa was close to everyone. Freddie and Vet were in Vallejo, half an hour away. Sylvester Jr. and Phunne and Cynthia were in Sacramento, an hour away. Jerry Martini was in Folsom, an hour and a half. Greg was in Petaluma, a half hour. Family again.

Other kinds of visitors came by, too. There was a pair of Dutch twins working on a biography of me, and another Dutch guy who was a filmmaker. An American writer was working on a book about the band, too. Visits went smoothest when people brought presents: a drum machine, for example. I was never into it for the money as much as I was for toys, instruments, vehicles.

The drugs were still around, but they didn't dominate. Some days I would light the torch and start a story: maybe I would tell Neal about Oakwood, assigning Arlene to bring home the prettiest girl, or remember all the way back to Urbano, Rose peeking her head around the door when she first heard the band. After a while Neal would point at the torch, which had gone out. "What's with that?" he'd say. I had never even made it to the pipe. I would light the torch again, but if the stories held my interest, that flame would go out, too, and I would pack up so I could do it all over again the next day.

I told the people who came out to the house that I was putting together an upcoming record. But what would that even look like anymore? The world had moved past vinyl, past cassettes, was starting to move past CDs into whatever was next: computers, Internet, music that rained down from the cloud. Based on what I had learned from Jon Dakss, I had been playing around with the Internet, and thought I might release music through a website I was starting called PhattaDatta. It was nothing like the past but the future was calling.

New music, and new stories, too. I heard that Carol Doda had opened a store in San Francisco selling lingerie, and I sent Neal down to meet her and ask her to call me. She kicked him out. Another time I had some dealings with the cops, maybe over a traffic accident, and when they asked who I was, I gave them Freddie's name. I don't remember what happened except that nothing happened. They let me go. And another time I had to get work done on my dentures. Mario had dropped his dentures and chipped them, and everyone told him they looked more real that way, so I had the dentist make me new teeth with a little chip. That set got left in a McDonald's one day. Neal was driving me back from Los Angeles, some record business, when I told him to turn around. "I threw away my mouth," I said. He had to jump in a dumpster to find it. A guy from the McDonald's came out and told Neal what a great job he had, working with a rock star, and it didn't seem like he was being sarcastic.

***

Nostalgia was a cycle—the safer kind—and it seemed to happen over shorter and shorter periods. There had been a series of reissues of our original albums in 1994 after we made the Hall of Fame, and it happened again in 2007 on the heels of the Grammy tribute. All the original Family Stone albums were rereleased in expanded form, with alternate versions and outtakes. The renewed interest in the band never seemed to bring me enough money to let me make my own choices. I had to stay tethered to Jerry, dependent for rent and everything else.

But it was about so much more than that. Once I was in a car with him, and he started telling me that I should take out a life insurance policy and make him the beneficiary. I was overcome with fatigue. I felt like every atom in my body had been dragged down into the earth. We pulled up at the house. I opened the car door. I went inside to my bedroom and went to sleep.

Another time the subject of mothers came up. I told him how sad I was to have lost mine, that I really missed her. He shrugged. "They get old," he said, "and they have to go sometime." I couldn't believe someone could be so dismissive.

But business was getting done, in some form. After the Grammys, interest had increased to the point where Jerry and Steve Green, our agent, were able to get us back on the road, for real, for the first time in decades, as a warm-up, and then we played the House of Blues in Anaheim. I was nervous before, to the point where I was sure that I would be nervous during. That meant throwing up obstacles in front of Neal and Mario that increased the difficulty of getting me there on time. Some happened at home, delays, distractions, couldn't find the right shirt, where are my shoes. Some happened as we drove down: unannounced stops, calls I had to take or make. And some happened in the club once we arrived, including my announcement that I was nervous. Neal got me a vodka and cranberry juice, which wasn't my usual thing but took the edge off.

The show was good enough that the bookings continued. I did a show with the comedian George Wallace (a longtime fan—he had been in the crowd for the wedding at Madison Square Garden) in Las Vegas, did another in San Jose, and then went to Europe for a few weeks to play a series of festivals: Montreux in Switzerland, Blue Note in Belgium, Pori in Norway, Jazzaldia in Spain, Lovebox in England. Our Paris show at the Olympia almost had old-days energy. The set lists were mostly greatest hits, though I let Vet step out front for "You're the One."

In the summer, *Vanity Fair* sent a reporter to discuss all developments. The writer and I couldn't connect at first, but eventually we met at a bike shop in Vallejo. He had lots of questions about old songs, which I indulged, and some questions about new songs, which I lunged at—those were the ones I really wanted to talk about. I recited the lyrics to one about humility, honesty, and accountability. "Ever get a chance to put your thanks on / Somebody you know you can bank on" was how it started, and it went on from that through grammar ("you can't face a noun so you're straight adverbing it") and clamor. I had another one called "We're Sick Like That" and another about how I wasn't a role model but a real model. I didn't want people to imitate the choices that I had made in my life. Sometimes I described the melodies and rhythms, sometimes I sang parts of them, sometimes I just thought about them. The interview didn't feel like a trick or a trap, and I sent the reporter a note afterward partly apologizing for dodging him and partly encouraging him to write fairly: "Just say the truth and hope he doesn't get pissed off at you," I wrote. "You don't need that. I'm invincible—'No Sly, you're washable and rinseable.'"

When the article came out, it was much better than the *Spin* piece from the eighties, from the headline on down: This time it was "Sly Stone's Higher Power" instead of "Sly Stone's Heart of Darkness." If I had any complaint, it was that it focused too much on my appearance: the neck brace I was wearing since my accident, mainly, but also my hair and my sunglasses. That was what the writer wanted, because he was building toward a scene at the end, when I took off my glasses to show him my eyes.

The year kept producing opportunities. Michael Jackson called. He had an offer for me, which was that he would sell me back my catalog with some conditions, one of them being that I got straight. I didn't like those terms, and when a meeting was set up, I was not in attendance. After that I wrote Michael a letter. I wanted to talk to him about working on a song together and even had one in mind for him. I gave it to a guy to pass it along to Michael. The guy never did. He sold it as memorabilia instead. That hurt my feelings. Michael wasn't the only one I wanted to work with. I wish that some of the rappers would have called me: Snoop, Mystikal, Ludacris. I could have made their music better, and if I didn't, they wouldn't have had to pay me. It would have been a guarantee.

During that time, there was even talk of the band playing the Super Bowl halftime show. The network people were in touch with Steve Green, and then they were out in Napa checking me out. Once we were out driving and saw a 1958 Studebaker Golden Hawk with a For Sale sign in the window. They bought that for me. They bought me a bull mastiff puppy, too, and also some equipment. Then one day I didn't see them around anymore.

In November, we went to New York for some concerts. On the way to the airport, Neal driving, Mario had an issue, or I had an issue with him, and I put him out of the car. He took his luggage with him, which meant that he also took a peanut butter jar that had drugs hidden in it, junk in the chunk. It took a few phone calls from New York back to Mario to untangle the mix-up.

New York during the holidays was familiar. But this time it wasn't the Garden. It was B.B. King's on Forty-second Street. The whole band was set to be there, but one by one the nos had it: no Freddie, no Rose, no Larry, no Greg. We had Cynthia and Jerry, though, and my niece Lisa singing Rose's parts. She could sing her ass off. "This is my family," I told the crowd. "You know when you have kids around the house and they're qualified?" Big laugh.

We played four shows over a few weeks. At one, I handed Neal some cards before we went onstage. "What's this?" he said.

"Those are questions I want you to ask me."

"Now?"

"In a minute. Onstage." He started to protest that he wasn't a performance guy. "You can be tonight," I said. "You will be."

The questions were jokes. I had him ask me, "Sly, what's the difference between this place and Madison Square Garden?"

I took a beat. "About twenty-three thousand people," I said. Bigger laugh. I also sent him to buy a big chrome vibrator and told him to walk it out to me just as we started "Sex Machine." It buzzed and whirred through the whole song, a new instrument.

I spent Super Bowl Sunday home in Napa, not playing the halftime show—Tom Petty did—but hanging with George Clinton. We cooked up some rocks and left a hill of baking soda on the kitchen counter. George passed out in a chair downstairs. I went upstairs to pass out in a chair in the bedroom.

April was Hollywood again. That show had a big publicity walk-up, articles in the paper that said I was coming out of hiding, Howard Hughes and the House of Blues. The spotlight brought celebrities, including Alec Baldwin, Rosie O'Donnell, and I think even Barack Obama, a senator still. We went to Japan for another jazz festival and then back to California, where Nove promoted a few shows around Los Angeles. I was back south again because Northern California had run its course. I had to leave the Napa house. Shay and I had split. Neal moved to L.A. for a minute but decided he couldn't stay, so George Clinton introduced me to a guy named BayBay to drive around, run errands, handle daily affairs.

Right around that time, I got back in touch with Arlene. She was married now, so it wasn't like that, but we had always been straight with each other, and I needed her to help manage things, especially when it came to breaking free of years of bad business.

I wrote her a long email. I asked for her help in holding on to my mobile studio, which had recently been towed. It was a white camper van with green stripes, a Pleasure Way that was everything to me: dressing room, hotel room, transportation, hideout, office. I could make music in it with Pro Tools. I could be on time to appointments. "I park it in different places for a change of scenery and write songs," I wrote. I needed to find someone to pay to get it out of impound. And it wouldn't just be good for me. It would be worth it to them: The van had low mileage and I'd let whoever paid hold the pink, the vehicle title. "It is the ideal investment," I wrote, "especially under these stressful economic circumstances that we are going through."

I reminded her of what she already knew, which was that I was more aware of what was going on around me than I let on. My method, I explained, was to watch them all along the way until I had enough evidence to make a move: "I've been on a verbal diet trying to organize certain info that I need to stay up on the facts of the matter and to not get thrown off by a sideshow of any kind."

I told her that what I needed most was her loyalty. "If you stay all the way down with me, regardless, I know how to see to it that it augments the value of Arlene," I wrote.

She agreed to come back. Her first order of business was what I said it should be, to get back my mobile studio. It cost cash to rescue, and it was cash I didn't have, but George Clinton came through with it. I was staying at a motel until I could get the camper back, and I waited there while she went with BayBay to the impound. Waited and waited.

She showed up in the late afternoon without the mobile studio but with an explanation about why. It was a mess of red tape, she said, with paperwork needed, including insurance, but they were going to go back in the morning. "Where's the money?" I said. "Let me hold on to it." I saw her expression change. She told me that she had it for safekeeping and was going back again in the morning. "Let me see it," I said. Again she said safekeeping, again she said morning, then she waved goodbye and was out the door.

I got up and went after her. She wasn't moving at normal speed, because she was already halfway down the stairs. I went quicker for catching. "Arlene," I said. "Come back. Bring me my motherfucking money!" She made it to her car before I made it to her, so I took off a shoe and threw it at her. That didn't slow her down. She was in the car and gone.

I started calling whoever I could, George, other P-Funk singers and musicians, telling them that she had run off with my money. I left Arlene message after message. "I don't know what's going on with you," I said. "You must have been hit over the head. Come back with my money."

What I didn't know was that Arlene had called George, too, to explain that she had held on to the money to retrieve the mobile studio rather than giving it up to me for drugs. George agreed with her. The next day, the mobile studio was back but I didn't thank Arlene. I didn't thank her the day after that either. It took three weeks for me to finally call her and act like things were normal again. In the meantime, the story had gotten around, and most everyone sided with her. When they found out that she had stood up to me even after the shoe came through the air, it put her in a better light.

So I was right. It augmented her.

Coachella was in Indio, a desert town about two hours east of Los Angeles that was a stopover for trains in the old days and for bands in the new days. Madonna had played the festival there in 2006 and Prince in 2008. When the poster for 2010 came out, on the final night, April 19, tucked between Spoon and De La Soul—two things I knew well—there we were, Sly and the Family Stone. And it was the real band, as many original members as we could collect. Larry would be with his band in the Netherlands.

We were scheduled for early Sunday evening. When the time came, I wasn't ready, mostly because I was still in Los Angeles. I wasn't Coachella's only problem. An Icelandic volcano—I forget the name—had erupted and filled the sky with ash, so much of it that many acts couldn't fly over from Europe. There was a British singer who was supposed to play after me, but they put her on before. Eyjafjallajökull. That was the volcano. The singer was Little Boots.

By the time I got out to Indio it was nine. By the time I got to the tent it was ten. I had rehearsed the band in L.A. but I gathered everyone around and explained that I was changing the set. Looks passed between the others. "I mean it," I said, but I didn't explain exactly what I meant. What I meant was that I had a plan.

The show started at eleven. Cynthia did her all-the-squares line from "Dance to the Music." After some jamming Val led the crowd in a chant: "Everybody say 'Sly Stone.'"

That's when I walked out, wearing a long blond wig that hid most of my face, a police hat that hid the rest, and a black sequined jacket. I stood behind the keyboard. I was dressed that way because I didn't want anyone to recognize me. I don't know if they did at first, but the longer I stood there, the more people figured it out.

I sat and played a few notes. But it wasn't right. The sound wasn't right and the spirit wasn't right either. I had another spirit in mind. "Okay, you guys," I said. "You guys just relax for a minute. Fuck rehearsal. Fuck it. I'm telling you. Check this out."

And then I came around to the front of the stage and told them exactly what to check out. "I got a lawsuit going on this year." I did have a lawsuit. I was trying to iron out my situation, where the money was going and why it didn't feel like enough of it was getting to me. How had it affected me? How hadn't it affected me? I told the crowd that I was living mostly in the mobile studio, in motels when possible. I also explained that I had enlisted some people, a lady and a man, who were seeking righteousness on my behalf and helping me get back to where I could buy my own shoes. People laughed at that last part. Laughter was a medicine. But I wasn't cured yet. I kept talking, head bowed, wig hanging down over the mic. I was fucked-up but the situation was more fucked-up. People up front were complaining loudly like they were in their living room. Others were calling out song titles. Why? They had come out to the desert expecting old hits done happily? I had just told them what was really happening.

"You say 'party' and everybody says 'party'?" I said. "Fuck

that. I got a computer. I'm going to play from the computer. I got my new songs in there." The crowd disapproved. "Wait, wait, wait," I said. "I swear to God I'll stay here for eighteen hours. Don't get mad at me, and in fact if you do, lie and say that you didn't."

The laptop laid down a beat. I recited the lyrics I had rapped for *Vanity Fair*: "Ever get a chance to put your thanks on . . ."

I sang along with a song called "If I Didn't Love You," which sketched out a bad relationship. Another one, maybe not finished, opened with a scene of a young soldier terrified in the bushes, trained in patriotism and warfare but not courage or conscience. I was on the edge of the stage on my back, then on my feet with my back to the crowd. The band didn't know what to do or how to do it. They tried to follow me but I hadn't led them to any of it. Fuck rehearsal.

Eventually I returned to the keyboard for a slow, jazzy version of "Stand!" The equipment was lousy with feedback and static. We did a piece of "If You Want Me to Stay" and a piece of "Hot Fun in the Summertime." Then the band tried for "I Want to Take You Higher," but I didn't want to take anyone anywhere except myself down into the audience, then backstage, then home.

\* \* \*

What I had said about the lawsuit, I had meant, and it was buzzing in my brain. I had found lawyers. They weren't exactly Shadrach, Meshach, and Abednego, but I figured they might have the same attitude when it came to refusing to worship the wrong king. I had filed a lawsuit to unravel the situation and figure out if I was rightfully owed money and how much.

I also had a new album, *I'm Back! Family & Friends*. It was billed as my first release in almost thirty years, but mostly it was old hits remade with guest stars: Ann Wilson on "Everyday

People," Bootsy on "Hot Fun in the Summertime." "Thank You (Falettinme Be Mice Elf Agin)" had a lead guitar part from Johnny Winter. What's up? Johnny is! A few new songs snuck on, "Plain Jane" and "His Eye Is on the Sparrow." The last one, "Get Away," was a love song both to a woman and to music. In the outro, backup vocalists kept singing about singing the melody, over and over again until it was the one true thing.

I didn't do much press for that record. Freddie gave an interview where he explained why it would be hard for me to come back into the light. "It wouldn't be worth it to me," he said. "Would you like someone to go on somebody's show and have somebody say some jokes about yourself that you know, or joke to you to your face, you know, when they don't know really what you've been through?" If reporters tried to reach me by phone, they got my machine's message: "You called, or did you?"

One day a British reporter called me—or did he?—and I hit him with my newest idea—a rock band made up of albino musicians. "My feeling about it is that it could neutralize all the different racial problems," I said. "To me, albinos are the most legitimate minority group of all. All races have albinos. If we all realize that we've all got albinos in our families, it's going to take away from the ridiculous racial tension." Was I serious? I was serious as a heart attack, and as funny as one too. Do Call Me Whitey, Whitey.

Even if I stayed out of the spotlight, people managed to locate me. Val Young, who had started out with George Clinton and had sung backup with everyone from the Gap Band to Bobby Brown, was friends with Eddie Murphy through Rick James. She sent word that Eddie was having a birthday party and wanted to meet me and George. We went to see Eddie at his house in Los Angeles. He had a video setup where he could watch old concerts, one after the other, and most of the ones he was watching were Family Stone shows. A few months later, he invited me back to watch a Floyd Mayweather fight. I showed up in boxing trunks, boxing gloves, boxing shoes: main event. I was brought back into a special VIP section where Eddie introduced me to Louis Farrakhan, who gave me a very dignified hello and handshake. "If you ever need anything," he said, "you be sure to let me know." Arlene and Phunne showed up a little later, Phunne on crutches for a busted leg, and met Samuel L. Jackson in the buffet line. The fight was projected on a screen outside, and Eddie offered me a blanket. "No thanks," I said, but it was a cold night and I had to leave the party early. It was also a cool night, partly because Eddie had a rule that no one could take pictures. If anyone got caught taking one, security would escort them to the door. Knowing that you could go about your business without worrying about that put everyone at ease.

When I left Eddie's, it was back to the Pleasure Way. I'd park in front of BayBay's parents' house, go inside to shower, charge my phone. When a newspaper report claimed I was homeless, I tried to explain the difference between living in a vehicle by choice and doing so because there were no other options available. I offered them a comment if they would pay to repaint my gold Studebaker. That seemed like it answered the question all on its own.

# 18

＊

## If This Room Could Talk

### (2012–Present)

**R**ead all about it: My Karl Kani shirt was decorated with newspaper headlines. Freddie and Greg both wore newsboy caps. Cynthia and Rose were behind us, Jerry and Vet off to the side. Sony had brought the crew together in a Los Angeles studio to listen to old masters. We were the old masters, and we were listening to the tapes that proved it. That room was like a time machine, able to take away all the other stresses of the world for as long as the songs lasted.

The engineers loaded up our three number 1 hits. First was "Everyday People." Freddie and I talked gear: what kind of bass Larry had been playing, how people tried to imitate Greg's drum sound by buying expensive new kits. "They never could find the style," Freddie said, "because it wasn't in money."

Next was "Thank You (Falettinme Be Mice Elf Agin)." We isolated the guitar and then brought back the full mix for the extended breakdown, never released, with different lyrics: "Gonna do what it do, every time."

Finally they cued up "Family Affair." The lyrics, especially those about leaving and staying, about going through the world and going back home, felt different at a distance. I heard something toward the end of the replay. "Go back," I told the engineer. "Loop that last part." They did, a bit of Billy Preston's electric piano splintering, the drum machines splattering. Freddie slapped the mixing board, keeping time with the flat of his palm. I joined him but with a single finger, like I was pointing up the board at the song.

Or was I pointing toward the future? How much future was left? I mostly measured the time remaining in terms of music. At a funk convention in San Diego, I met a guy named Sal Filipelli and ended up co-writing and singing on his record. We finished up my "Role Model" song and did two others. The record included an answering machine message from me: "Okay, Sal, there's something for you to hear and there's something for you to pick up, and it's here, so come get it."

George Clinton released a Funkadelic record called *First Ya Gotta Shake the Gate*. It included two songs I had tried out at Coachella and two new ones, "Yellow Light," hard funk with fuzzed-out vocals, and a for-old-time's-sake rerecording of Lord Buckley's "The Nazz" that I recited over a backing track. It was still cats and kitties whipping and wailing. It was still the strongest sweetest cat that ever stomped around on this sweet swinging sphere. It took me all the way back to KSOL. Half a century later, the rolling Stone was still with you to treat you right.

Others were not still with us. Ken Roberts died in 2014: heart attack, never recovered. Bobby Womack went the same year. He had beaten prostate cancer and colon cancer before he was taken by Alzheimer's. Johnny Winter, too, from pneumonia. Carol Doda, from kidney failure.

And then Cynthia passed from cancer. When I found out she was sick, it was so painful. *Damn*: That was all I could think. To me, she was the number one in the band, even over me. She held everything together. I didn't go to the funeral—again, too hard—but a group of us got together to remember her life. Larry and Freddie talked. It had been a while for them.

In early 2015 we got a jury verdict. According to the decision, I was awarded $5 million, which covered everything up until the date the lawsuit had been filed.

I didn't count my chickens, not even after it seemed like they were hatching. I knew how the system worked, meaning that I knew that often it didn't work. I was right: A few months later, the pendulum swung back the other way, and a judge blocked the award. "Mr. Stewart," he said, "entered into the agreement with the assistance of advisors and received a substantial benefit from entering into the agreement."

Sylvester Jr. talked to the newspapers about it. "Obviously, I'm kind of devastated," he said. That was how he felt. How did I feel? "He's really sick of this," he said, "of not having his money that he's deserved."

That was true. But he said the rest of what was true, too: "At the same time, he's not being a downer or an unpleasant person. He's still being as creative as he can be, given the circumstances." The circumstances were that I couldn't control the circumstances. I wasn't even mad at Jerry's lawyers. They were doing what lawyers did. If they hadn't taken the case, someone else would have.

To me, there was only one way to deal with any of it: keep singing that melody. A guy named Michael Ajakwe, Jr., had created a TV comedy about a pro athlete and his wife called *Beauty and the Baller.* I appeared in the pilot, at the end, playing myself, pretending I owned a fancy restaurant. I liked the part of acting where I got paid. The waiting around was hard. But I did practice my lines so I got them right, which could be fun. And I got to meet Ray Parker, Jr., who was a producer on the show. He was cool. Michael Ajakwe, Jr., died just as the show was airing. Only fifty-two years old. Pancreatic cancer. He had been diagnosed even before he started the show but worked through it anyway. Damn.

Ken was gone. Jerry was going. I was, finally, getting up onto my own two feet. I moved to the Valley. Arlene and her husband helped me find a house. She took me to shop for furniture. They mounted my gold and platinum records on the wall. They connected me with a place that customized my Dodge Magnum with a new silver wrap and colored neon everywhere: underneath, inside the headlights, around the sound system.

Then came the Four Visits. Fifty years of drugs, plus age, plus stress, made the hospital a regular stop.

The first time I went in, I made sure to get out quick so I could get back home and get back to using. Dealers would still come to the house, weigh out rocks, name their price. We weren't writing checks that said "Drugs" on the memo line. One guy had a catering business and ran his money through there.

The hospital stays kept on, second, third, fourth, and then I kicked. For real, all at once. I spent years not regretting the drugs. They served a purpose when the stresses mounted up from the start: new songs needed, new concerts scheduled, people to pay for, people to smile for. In the years after that, I turned over business to others so I could concentrate on making music, which built up a different kind of stress. The drugs kept me from having to think too hard about the fact that I was—at thirty-five, at forty—living in rented houses, on an allowance, not able to truly be free. But I should have stopped sooner. Much sooner: less dust and powder, fewer rocks and pipes, enough days given back that they might have added up to years.

After that fourth stay and fourth return, when dealers came around, Arlene and Phunne ran them off. They didn't always tell me about it, but I would see them out in front of the house, standing with hands on hips. One guy showed up in his bright red truck—he had something to do with the Bloods. Arlene or Phunne, working as a team, would point back up to the main road. A few times they had to start a call-the-cops countdown. During this time, Arlene tried to convince me that I should write my life story. People had been asking but the terms weren't right. The time wasn't right. "It will be therapeutic," she said. Was she right? I wasn't ready quite yet. But I was getting closer to getting ready.

In 2019, we did a deal with Michael Jackson's publishing company, Mijac. The headlines said that Mijac bought a majority interest in the catalog, but the truth was closer to what Michael had proposed back when he was alive. They gave me some money and let me keep a minority interest in the catalog, free and clear of any other complications from the past, other litigation, other representation, which meant that I could collect on my own music again.

I watched Obama wrap up his second term, wondering if he had been too cute to be president. He was too good-looking in a way. As president, he was all right. I didn't know what to expect and it was just what I expected. Trump was different at first. I expected good and bad both, and it was some of the first for a little while and then lots of the second for a long while. It felt like we were losing sight of what I knew to be true: The point is to care about all living beings. That's the bottom line. There's got to be room for all of us to live, to move, to breathe, to say what we mean, to argue, to not argue.

That goes in all directions. When George Floyd was killed I felt terrible. But police aren't the only problem. When people get pulled over, they don't know how they're going to feel. They are sitting in their car and a cop comes up along the side. That cop is a man or a woman with a gun. And then suddenly the people in the car know how they're going to feel. They're going to feel scared. But they need to manage that feeling so they can do what the situation calls for. Treat a cop like a cop. Otherwise it can get bad or worse fast.

After George Floyd was killed, George Clinton came to L.A. with the civil rights attorney Benjamin Crump to protest. You can say that George Floyd's death was an injustice. You should. But let's be honest. If George Clinton got pulled over, he was going to be good. He'd put his hands on the wheel. Same with Ben Crump. But Goddamn. Just the other day there was another young black guy pulled over and then beaten to death. It's not progress and maybe it's the opposite. A writer asked me about that recently: whether things had gotten better since Rodney King, since the Watts riots, since ever. "Sometimes it's one step up, two steps back," I said. "The country feels divided." Was there hope for bringing it together? "We just have to work on it every day," I said. "Let that sink in."

And then, slowly at first and then more quickly, the past has turned into the present. I'm in the house, TV on much of the time. When people are in the news, I try to learn as much as I can about them. When Bill Cosby had his trial, I watched all the coverage and whatever old shows I could find. When R. Kelly had his, I watched every special and commentary.

Otherwise, I watch basketball if it's on, football if it's play-offs or Super Bowl. Boxing is still my favorite. There's a cop show I like. The star is a good actor but he's an ugly mother-fucker. And every once in a while, I'll sneak a cowboy movie. The other day someone showed me an old video of Lash LaRue on the David Letterman show. It was from the eighties, about a year after I was on. He wasn't dressed all in black anymore. He talked about his movies and did some whip tricks. I was glad I saw it.

Family still comes around. I feel so lucky to have them. My kids drop by. All of them are in the business, in a way, but mind-ing their own business, too. Sylvester Jr. does lighting design for movies and TV. Phunne does some singing and tours with Jerry Martini. Nove was a club manager around L.A. and is a deejay on the morning show at KCRW. I love them all so much, and I love seeing them. If they have to miss a visit, I get upset.

My brothers and sisters visit. Rose and Vet came by recently, and we hung out and talked, good memories, memories that aren't as good. I can see sometimes that there's hurt feelings, maybe about the way the band ended, maybe about what hap-pened after that, maybe just about the way that life twists and turns. All I can hope is that time heals and that people forgive. Blood is still thicker than mud. Freddie was here a little while ago. He's thinking about his legs. "Our dad did not work on his legs," Freddie said. "That's what contributed to him falling. If your legs are not strong, you will be surprised how easy it is to fall." Freddie fell a couple of times. He was so surprised. "Dad and Mom didn't tell us about this," Freddie said, smiling but serious. "They didn't tell us you can get older." I knew exactly what he meant. The ground isn't something you want to be on or in. Muhammad Ali went there in 2016, Dave Kapralik in 2017, Roy Clark in 2018, Little Richard in 2020. Bubba in 2021. Each time someone passes, it's hard to fully understand. I couldn't believe how Little Richard looked at the end, no big hair, no mustache, just an old man with wisps of white on his head.

Friends don't come as often as they once did, but they call to check up, tell me they're thinking about me, catch me up on what's happening with them. I hear from people from childhood, from bandmates, from people I met along the way. Some of them want to see me or talk to me. I feel bad but I just can't do it anymore. My health makes it impossible—I have COPD and reduced lung capacity. I want people to know I am thinking about them and to know that I appreciate that they are thinking about me, remembering me and the music I made. That's where the focus should be. Life has not always been easy. On top of the health issues, there have been other kinds of pressures, some financial, some legal. Time has taken some of them away, lessened them if not completely lifted them. And remember, you are free—at least in your mind if you want to be.

I keep listening to music. My Alexa lets me request any song I want. I want old singers like Jackie Wilson or new gospel artists like Le'Andria Johnson. I'll listen to a player like George Benson or Hank Crawford, both in the years he was with Ray Charles and in the years he was on his own. My kids and grandkids play me Drake or the Weeknd or Nicki Minaj, whoever. If they like it, I try to like it. I also like Ludacris. I rap along to "Get Back" for fun. I watch enough news about entertainment that I probably know more about their lives as celebrities than I do about their music, though I just recently found out that Drake is Larry Graham's nephew. Sometimes I try to listen to new music by people from the old days. I heard a song from a new Bob Dylan album. He sounded drunk. Someone asked me if it was the kind of thing that I would have thought he would have made when I first heard him sixty years ago. I said it sounded like it *was* made sixty years ago. Other names pop up here and there. Gloria Scott, who I worked with all the way back before Bobby Freeman, is still making records today. I mean *today*: I just saw her new album, *So Wonderful*. It has a song called "Running Away" but it's not the Family Stone song.

I keep my ears open for songs that connect back to my music. I feel proud when I hear it echoing in what other people make. I had forgotten that Janet Jackson had used "Thank You (Falettinme Be Mice Elf Agin)" for "Rhythm Nation." I didn't know that Kanye West had used the Mojo Men's "She's My Baby" for "Hell of a Life."

One day a writer played me an album by a singer named Tony LeMans, who was on Prince's label back in the eighties. The first song sounded like one of mine, was titled like it too, "Higher Than High," and my name was even on the back of the record. Had I worked on the song? No: It was just dedicated to me. That was cool. I'm proud when people are inspired by my music. It makes me feel like I did something right.

The writer who played me the Tony LeMans album threw a hell of a question at me: If you wrote a song now, what would it be called?

"Change," I said.

I haven't written "Change" yet. There isn't much. I'm home most of most days. I get itches in places I can't reach. I have a backscratcher for that, and when I want people's attention, I knock it against the table. There are other times when I don't want anyone's attention, and I leave it there and knock against nothing.

The other day was my eightieth birthday. Kids and grandkids came over to the house. People sent video messages. I even played a little harmonica for the family. Babies making eighty. I think of something that Dave Kapralik said all the way back in 1970. "I don't think Sly has ever or will ever live anything vicariously," Kapralik said. "He is a prime force, a prime mover himself and will never sit back reflectively and experience through print, theater, or anything else. He is a penultimate pragmatist. He lives by his sheer own personal experience."

Kapralik spoke from a height. Freddie said something similar but simpler in an interview. He was talking about how the world has lost certain kinds of figures that it needs to see itself clearly. He said there's no one like Bob Dylan anymore. When I heard that, I nodded. He said there's no one like John Lennon anymore. I nodded again. He said there's no one like Sly Stone anymore. I couldn't nod so I just shook my head.

Jim Brown died in May of 2023. Tina Turner passed less than a week later.

More and more I have been watching gospel choirs on YouTube, and the sermons that go with them.

When I came back from the hospital the fourth time, Arlene and I had a little game. I'd be lying down on the couch or bed, thinking on the ceiling, not saying much. There's a quiet goin' on. She would try to break into my silence. "Who loves you?" she'd say, and I'd have to answer. The other day I was thinking on the ceiling again and she started the game. "Who loves you?" she said. I didn't answer but my Alexa did. "Kojak," it said. "Always a pleasure."

That's how I feel: It's always a pleasure. Human beings, we all come and go. Some of us have not gone yet.

*

## Postlude: Right Now!

Are you tired today?

*A little.*

Okay. We can keep it short. If you wanted people to take
one thing from your life, what would it be?

*To take something from me?*

No, I mean take something away from your story. A lesson,
a message.

*They could.*

What would it be?

*Music, just music. It's been that always from the start. I
don't want to get in people's way and I don't want them
to get in my way. I just want to play my songs. I would
do it for nothing.*

If there was a new Sly album coming out right now, what
would it be called?

*Right now . . .*

Yes, right now. What would it be called?

*Right Now!*

# Selected Discography

## I. Sly and the Family Stone

### *A Whole New Thing* (Epic, 1967)
"Underdog"
"If This Room Could Talk"
"Run, Run, Run"
"Turn Me Loose"
"Let Me Hear It from You"
"Advice"
"I Cannot Make It"
"Trip to Your Heart"
"I Hate to Love Her"
"Bad Risk"
"That Kind of Person"
"Dog"

### *Dance to the Music* (Epic, 1968)
"Dance to the Music"
"Higher"

"I Ain't Got Nobody (for Real)"

"Dance to the Medley": (a) "Music Is Alive," (b) "Dance In," (c) "Music Lover"

"Ride the Rhythm"

"Color Me True"

"Are You Ready"

"Don't Burn Baby"

"I'll Never Fall in Love Again"

## *Life* (Epic, 1968)

"Dynamite!"

"Chicken"

"Plastic Jim"

"Fun"

"Into My Own Thing"

"Harmony"

"Life"

"Love City"

"I'm an Animal"

"M'Lady"

"Jane Is a Groupee"

## *Stand!* (Epic, 1969)

"Stand!"

"Don't Call Me Nigger, Whitey"

"I Want to Take You Higher"

"Somebody's Watching You"

"Sing a Simple Song"

"Everyday People"

"Sex Machine"

"You Can Make It If You Try"

## *Greatest Hits* (Epic, 1970)

"I Want to Take You Higher"

"Everybody Is a Star"

"Stand!"

"Life"

"Fun"

"You Can Make It If You Try"

"Dance to the Music"

"Everyday People"

"Hot Fun in the Summertime"

"M'Lady"

"Sing a Simple Song"

"Thank You (Falettinme Be Mice Elf Agin)"

## *There's a Riot Goin' On* (Epic, 1971)

"Luv N' Haight"

"Just Like a Baby"

"Poet"

"Family Affair"

"Africa Talks to You 'The Asphalt Jungle'"

"There's a Riot Goin' On"

"Brave & Strong"

"(You Caught Me) Smilin'"

"Time"

"Spaced Cowboy"

"Runnin' Away"

"Thank You for Talkin' to Me Africa"

## *Fresh* (Epic, 1973)

"In Time"

"If You Want Me to Stay"

"Let Me Have It All"

"Frisky"

"Thankful N' Thoughtful"

"Skin I'm In"

"I Don't Know (Satisfaction)"

"Keep On Dancin'"

"Qué Sera, Sera (Whatever Will Be, Will Be)"

"If It Were Left Up to Me"

"Babies Makin' Babies"

### *Small Talk* (Epic, 1974)

"Small Talk"

"Say You Will"

"Mother Beautiful"

"Time for Livin'"

"Can't Strain My Brain"

"Loose Booty"

"Holdin' On"

"Wishful Thinkin'"

"Better Thee Than Me"

"Livin' While I'm Livin'"

"This Is Love"

### *High on You* (Epic, 1975)

[credited to Sly Stone]

"I Get High on You"

"Crossword Puzzle"

"That's Lovin' You"

"Who Do You Love?"

"Green Eyed Monster Girl"

"Organize"

"Le Lo Li"

"My World"

"So Good to Me"

"Greed"

### *Heard Ya Missed Me, Well I'm Back* (Epic, 1976)

"Heard Ya Missed Me, Well I'm Back"

"What Was I Thinkin' in My Head"

"Nothing Less Than Happiness"

"Sexy Situation"

"Blessing in Disguise"

"Everything in You"

"Mother Is a Hippie"

"Let's Be Together"

"The Thing"

"Family Again"

## *Back on the Right Track* (Warner Brothers, 1979)

"Remember Who You Are"

"Back on the Right Track"

"If It's Not Addin' Up. . . ."

"The Same Thing (Makes You Laugh, Makes You Cry)"

"Shine It On"

"It Takes All Kinds"

"Who's to Say?"

"Sheer Energy"

## *Ain't but the One Way* (Warner Brothers, 1982)

"L.O.V.I.N.U."

"One Way"

"Ha Ha, Hee Hee"

"Hobo Ken"

"Who in the Funk Do You Think You Are"

"You Really Got Me"

"Sylvester"

"We Can Do It"

"High, Y'All"

## *I'm Back! Family & Friends* (Cleopatra, 2011)

"Dance to the Music" (featuring Ray Manzarek)

"Everyday People" (featuring Ann Wilson)

"Family Affair"

"Stand!" (featuring Carmine Appice and Ernie Watts)

"Thank You (Falettinme Be Mice Elf Agin)" (featuring Johnny Winter)

"I Want to Take You Higher" (featuring Jeff Beck)

"Hot Fun in the Summertime" (featuring Bootsy Collins)

"Dance to the Music" (extended mix)

"Plain Jane"

"His Eye Is on the Sparrow" (traditional; arranged by Sly Stone)

"Get Away"

"Dance to the Music" (club mix)

"Family Affair" (dubstep mix)

"Thank You (Falettinme Be Mice Elf Agin)" (electro club mix)

## II. Other Releases

"On the Battlefield" / "Walking in Jesus' Name" (Church of God in Christ, 1952)

"Stop What You Are Doing" / "I Guess I'll Be," with the Viscaynes (Tropo, 1961)

"Yellow Moon" / "Uncle Sam Needs You (My Friend)," with the Viscaynes (VPM, 1961)

"Yellow Moon" / "Heavenly Angel," with the Viscaynes (Tropo, 1961)

"A Long Time Alone" / "I'm Just a Fool," as Danny Stewart (Luke, 1961)

"Help Me with My Broken Heart" / "Long Time Alone," as Sylvester Stewart (G&P, 1962)

"I Just Learned to Swim" / "Scat Swim," as Sly Stewart (Autumn, 1964)

"Buttermilk Part 1" / "Buttermilk Part 2," as Sly (Autumn, 1965)

"Temptation Walk Part 1" / "Temptation Walk Part 2," as Sly (Autumn, 1965)

"Dance to the Music" / "Music Lover" / "I Want to Take You Higher," from *Woodstock: Music from the Original Soundtrack and More* (Cotillion, 1970)

"Eek-a-Bo-Static Automatic"/ "Love & Affection," from *Soul Man* soundtrack (A&M, 1986)

"I'm the Burglar," from *Burglar* soundtrack (MCA, 1987)

### Stone Flower

"You're the One, Part I" / "You're the One, Part II," Little Sister (1970)

"Life and Death in G&A, Part I" / "Life and Death in G&A, Part II," Joe Hicks (1970)

"Stanga" / "Somebody's Watching You," Little Sister (1970)

"I'm Just Like You" / "Dynamite," 6ix (1970)

### Selected Guest Appearances

"Advice," "It's Got to Happen," "Free Funk," from Billy Preston, *Wildest Organ in Town!* (Capitol, 1966)

"Ground Hog," from Elvin Bishop, *Let It Flow* (Capricorn, 1974)

"You Can Fly," from REO Speedwagon, *Lost in a Dream* (Epic, 1974)

"Insane Asylum," from Kathi McDonald, *Insane Asylum* (Capitol, 1974)

"Sweet Gypsy Jane," "Up the Creek (Without a Paddle)," "China Doll,"
  from the Temptations, *Wings of Love* (Gordy, 1976)

"Free Me from My Freedom," "Ah Shoot," from Bonnie Pointer, *Bonnie
  Pointer* (Motown, 1978)

"Jimmy Mack," "Nowhere to Run (Nowhere to Hide)," from Bonnie
  Pointer, *Bonnie Pointer* (Motown, 1979)

"Funk Gets Stronger" from Funkadelic, *Electric Spanking of War Babies*
  (Warner Bros., 1981)

"Be All You Can Be," from Godmoma, *Godmoma Here* (Elektra, 1981)

"Catch a Keeper," "Hydraulic Pump," from P-Funk All-Stars, *Urban
  Dancefloor Guerillas* (Uncle Jam, 1983)

"Crazay," from Jesse Johnson, *Shockadelica* (A&M, 1986)

"When the Weekend Comes," from Bobby Womack, *The Last Soul Man*
  (MCA, 1987)

"Just Like a Teeter-Totter," from Bar-Kays, *Animal* (Mercury, 1989)

"Good Times," from Earth, Wind and Fire, *Heritage* (Columbia, 1990)

"Tell the World," from Maceo Parker, *For All the King's Men* (4th and
  Broadway, 1990)

"Ain't That Peculiar," "Fever," from George Clinton, *George Clinton and
  His Gangsters of Love* (Shanachie, 2008)

"If I Didn't Love You," "Mathematics of Love," "The Nazz," "Yellow
Light," from Funkadelic, *First Ya Gotta Shake the Gate* (The C
  Kunspyruhzy, 2014)

## III. Selected Unreleased Songs

"Coming Back for More"
"Day Ain't Got No Business in the Night"
"Eye to Eye"
"Fight to Break Up"
"I Am Red"
"If I'm Tired It's Because I'm Wired"
"Lady Is a Tramp"
"Miles and Miles"
"Not Hot Fun"

"Ruby Shoes"
"Satisfied"
"The Streets Are My Background"
"Time Out"
"Time to Modulate"

## Sly's Acknowledgments

Every star is a body. This one would like to express my love for my children and their mothers, my parents and their children, the original Family Stone and the versions of the band that followed, and friends and funk brothers and fans.

To George: Can I still star? To Neal: I ain't going on stage until I get some Poligrip. To Willem Alkema and Edwin and Arno Konings: Thank you for letting me see myself again. To Michael Rubenstone, for the search and the find. To BayBay, Buck, and their parents—thanks for saving me a spot in front of the house.

And for this book, and for so much more, thank you to Arlene. One more question—am I done answering questions?

## Ben's Acknowledgments

Working on a book rooted in family reminded me constantly that we are created and sustained by others, so I need to start with my wife, Gail, my sons, Daniel and Jake, my parents, my brothers, and everyone who makes all of them possible.

Many journalists, authors, filmmakers, artists, thinkers, and fans over the years have devoted themselves to untangling Sly's genius. I hope they never stop.

Agents (Nicole and Marc), editor (Sean), Alexis, etc. There's a scene behind the scenes. Arlene was invaluable in helping to make this book happen. Couldn't have happened without her. Wouldn't have. She augmented it.

Finally, I need to thank the people that Sly thanked, and the band, and especially Sly. The music he and the Family Stone willed into existence might mean everything. When I was ten years old, I bought *Greatest Hits* on cassette and wore that thing out on auto-reverse, more than once, until the songs were in my bones, where they remain.

# Index

## T

## A Note About the Authors

Sly Stone was born Sylvester Stewart in Denton, Texas, in 1943 and moved to Vallejo, California, as a child. He had brief careers as a doo-wop singer, a radio DJ, and a record producer before founding and fronting Sly and the Family Stone, a black-and-white, male-and-female, brothers-and-sisters, rock-soul-and-funk band that forever changed the face of pop music. When Sly and the Family Stone appeared at Woodstock, they electrified a generation, and Stone's most famous songs, including the chart-topping "Everyday People," "Thank You (Falettinme Be Mice Elf Agin)," and "Family Affair," are enduring anthems that both defined and reflected the evolution of American culture in the 1960s and 1970s. Beginning at the height of his fame, Stone struggled with addiction and receded from the public eye even as his musical influence grew. Mercurial, idiosyncratic, and inimitably brilliant, Sly Stone is a true American original. Now clean, he lives in Los Angeles. This is his first book.

Ben Greenman was born in Chicago, raised in Miami, and shaped largely in Brooklyn. He is a *New York Times* bestselling author who has written both nonfiction and fiction, including collaborations with Questlove, George Clinton, Brian Wilson, and Stevie Van Zandt. His criticism and journalism have appeared in a number of publications, including *The New Yorker*, where he was an editor for more than a decade, and the *Miami New Times*. He would also like to thank you (falettinhim be hymns elf agin).